RELIGION IN 20 TH CENTURY AMERICA

THE LIBRARY OF CONGRESS SERIES

IN AMERICAN CIVILIZATION

EDITED BY

RALPH HENRY GABRIEL

RELIGION

IN 20 TH

CENTURY

AMERICA

HERBERT WALLACE SCHNEIDER

HARVARD UNIVERSITY PRESS

CAMBRIDGE, MASSACHUSETTS

1952

FOREWORD

There are histories of American religion and there are sociologies, psychologies, anthropologies, philosophies of American religion. This study fits into none of these standard modes of research and knowledge, though it relies on all of them. It is first of all a reminiscence. There is still a rapidly diminishing generation of Americans who can remember what religion was like at the beginning of the century, and who can compare religion then and now, not in terms of the literary remains and records to which historians usually resort, but in terms of events and ideas that are now familiar but were then strange and of events and ideas now strange that formerly were familiar. The familiar is often the most elusive, for we seldom think it worth while to tell what everyone knows; but when the familiar becomes strange, there is something to be explained as well as reported. The past fifty years have so transformed our habits, ideas, and institutions that it is peculiarly appropriate and important for us to recall the changes we have endured and to explain them as best we can. This sketch of our religious revolution cannot go far into the problems of explanation, to which the above-mentioned ologies address themselves, but it can at least report for the benefit of later generations what basic changes have come over American religion during one lifetime. A generation whose faiths and devotions begin about 1950 must necessarily have a different conception of religion from a generation for whom the mid-century represents an achievement or a failure, not a starting-point. To have witnessed and endured transformations of religion gives to religious experience a peculiar gravity and tragic perspective, which no amount of *ex post facto* rationalization can recover.

Accordingly, our primary subject-matter in this reflective survey is religious experience itself — not the American religious traditions, not the churches as social institutions, not the currents

of philosophical theology, but the religious life. Were the religious
life in America monastic, and were religious experience mystic
and solitary, our account of religion might conceivably have little
bearing on what is called in this series of books "American Civilization." The cultural context of religion in America is not something arbitrarily created by a particular point of view or by an
editorial policy; it is intrinsic to American religion. It may be possible to isolate creeds, church governments, dogmas, saints, and
sacraments from a particular civilization or even from civilization
in general; and it may be possible to view life from the point of
view of religion rather than religion as a kind of life, but such an
abstraction does violence to American experience and culture.
Here religion is intrinsic to a civilized life and to the other "humanities." Therefore, a true report of what religion is actually
must present religion as one of man's enduring concerns and must
exhibit its relations to his other concerns. It will not do to construct an arbitrary concept of the man to whom religion "means
everything," nor will it do to assume that religion is a by-product
of a particular stage of human government or production. Neither
the clerical view that religion should be the dominant force in
culture, nor the Marxian and Freudian hypotheses that religion
represents a passing stage of culture can here be taken seriously.
Whatever may be the political or economic role of a particular
church or doctrine, whatever may be the boasts of religious professionals and confessionals, no religion is either above or below
its cultural environment; it is an intrinsic element in that environment, as constitutive as any, and as much in need of civilization as
any. Were I engaged in a theological discussion, I might make this
point more polemically by insisting that God is man's god in
essence, not by accident. But I prefer to make a more empirical
observation and to report what seems a commonplace, namely,
that religion as it exists is not self-contained, but lives in a complex
of human institutions, interests, and ideals, which are an essential
element of its own life even if religion despise or dominate them.
Our task in this portraiture of twentieth-century American religion is to focus our attention on what is essential to the religious
life. There are many incidental consequences of faith, many secular functions of churches, many contributions of religion to the

arts, and these may be important aspects of American culture; but they are nevertheless incidental to our subject. For we are primarily concerned to tell what has happened to religion itself, rather than to estimate its value for other aspects of American life.

There is a theological doctrine, much preached but always betrayed, which asserts that the inner or essential life of religion is eternal, timeless, changeless. Our aim is to get as close to this inner core of religion as possible and to show how it changes from generation to generation. Were the religious life as stable, iconic, and self-contained as preachers often represent it to be, there would be little point in preaching, and no point in trying to understand it culturally. But the facts, the religious facts, so evidently refute this dogma, that it would be idle to argue the point dialectically. Let the facts of religious change now speak for themselves.

ACKNOWLEDGMENTS

In the preparation of this mid-century report on religion in America, I have enjoyed the very extensive and expert assistance of Dr. M. Edith Runyon; in addition to her researches in the relevant literature she has contributed to this analysis many observations from her theological studies and her practical experience with young people's groups, and she labored generously and long over my manuscript. I wish to express my indebtedness and gratitude to her first of all.

The work has been considerably facilitated by several volumes and essays which have attempted something similar, especially by the 1948 issue of the *Annals of the American Academy of Political and Social Science*, which was devoted to a survey of American Organized Religion, by the volume published in 1936 in honor of William Adams Brown, and entitled *The Church Through Half a Century*, edited by Samuel McCrea Cavert and Henry Pitney Van Dusen, by the Chicago volume entitled *Religious Thought in the Last Quarter Century*, edited by Gerald Birney Smith, 1927, and by the volume entitled *Protestant Thought in the Twentieth Century*, edited by Arnold S. Nash, 1951. An invaluable aid has been the *Information Service* of the National Council of Churches of Christ in America, directed by Dr. F. Ernest Johnson, to whose other works I am also deeply indebted. Of all the writers on this subject, Dean Willard L. Sperry of Harvard Divinity School has helped me most by the breadth of his experience and sympathies and by the shrewdness of his judgments; I am glad to have this opportunity of telling my readers that it would have been much better if he had written for this series. Further mention of specific writers and their works may be found immediately preceding the chapter Notes at the back of the book.

Professor Ralph H. Gabriel, in addition to his work as a general editor of this series, has been a thoroughgoing critic of my attempts at generalization and has caught a number of inaccuracies; I hope not many mistakes have escaped his notice and I know that whatever errors remain are due to my negligence, not his. I am grateful to him for his criticism and for his friendly counsel in planning this work.

Several of my colleagues have coöperated in providing the architectural illustrations. In the final revision of the text and notes I have had the help of Mrs. Mary Young Sieg.

Of the publishers who have been generous in giving permission to quote, the first to whom acknowledgment should be made is the Harvard University Press, of whose publications I have made extensive use. Longmans, Green and Company have granted permission to quote extensively from William James's *Varieties of Religious Experience* (New York, 1903). For permission to use material reprinted in the Appendix, I am indebted to Dr. F. Ernest Johnson; and for Exhibit XIV, to Mr. Harlan C. Betts.

H. W. S.

CONTENTS

EXHIBITS

RELIGION IN TWENTIETH-CENTURY AMERICA

I ˒

RELIGION IN A
REVOLUTIONARY AGE

The Transformation of the Sabbath

I can remember, for I am a little older than the present century, when the first automobile rolled down the main street of my native village, which was not very far either geographically or culturally from "Middletown." And I remember when the first motion picture invaded the town. There was then in the town considerable prejudice against the theater, for an "idle show" was obviously more entertaining than a church service, and though not as "ungodly" as the idle waste of dancing, drinking, pool, gambling (or even of nongambling card-games), it was essentially "worldly," that is, vain. The basic moral distinction in the life of this village was between a productive, instructive, con-structive expenditure of energy and the various forms of play and excitement which, precisely because they were tempting, were regarded as temptations, that is, as distractions from the serious business of living. Neither our religious nor our educa-tional institutions were "tempting" or wanted to be so; they were serious business. Education was serious because it was productive. Religion was serious because it cultivated seriousness.

When the motion picture and the automobile came to town, they were very exciting. No one took them seriously at first, but it was useless to condemn them. They were too obviously inno-cent at that time, and though a few men of great imagination foresaw some of their serious consequences for business, morals, education, and religion, the great majority accepted them for no better reason than that they were inevitable.

There were a few groups, such as the religious, communal village of Amana, Iowa, who saw clearly and quickly that the youth of the community would soon take the movies more seriously than the church services, and who therefore refused to admit the motion picture into the community. For twenty to thirty years these religiously devoted people watched their young people move to other towns where there were movies, and thus the older generation fought the good fight to the finish. But the great majority of religious Americans used their unconscious common sense and "accepted" the motion picture and the automobile either innocently or stoically. The same thing is true, more recently, of the manner in which they faced the rapid spread of interest in "Sunday papers," popular fiction, the phonograph, jazz music (and its accompaniments), aviation, radio, and television. There were, of course, sporadic as well as organized expressions among the pious of resistance, fear, and disgust. But on the whole, these inventions of the twentieth century revolutionized American folkways, ideals, and interests before there was any general awareness of what had happened and before their revolutionary consequences for morals and religion made them objects of concern.

A great liberal preacher of the turn of the century said in 1905 in the course of a sermon that became widely publicized and that examined "the changing forms and eternal essence of religion":

> When my father was born, in 1794, no man that lived could travel any faster than Abraham could. All these marvellous changes have come since that day. But why should I ride at the rate of fifty miles an hour instead of four or six or ten? It is a great convenience, but I am not necessarily a better man, and the errands on which I go may not of necessity be any more kindly, just, or humane. It is what we *are*, not what we can do, or how rapidly or how astonishingly we can do it, that makes us civilized.[1]

Though we may smile at the antique "civilization" and complacent morals of Dr. Savage, we are still apt to moralize in the same vein, separating what we are from what we do. What has speed to do with justice or cheap entertainment with kindness? Even to this day there are religious spokesmen who claim to disregard purely "secular" inventions, and who continue to think that fundamentally nothing has changed. It is true that in themselves these inventions are physical and "external" things, mere instruments; but everyone knows, by this time, that in their consequences these instruments have changed not only *how* we express ourselves but *what* we believe and do. The range and focus of our interests has been revolutionized by the new "opportunities" and directions which these inventions have given us.

I need not describe the general revolution in American culture which these inventions have already created, for the facts are too familiar. And I shall not recall what life was like before they existed, for I might indulge in praise of the "simple life" as I seem to remember it nostalgically. I would probably agree with my friend Joseph Haroutunian that the lust for many goods has caused us to lose the love of the good.[2] When we are bombarded continually by new and better opportunities for using our increased purchasing power, it seems anachronistic to ask whether we really want to keep up-to-date, for how can one be civilized if one disregards contemporary civilization? But when this rush for goods distracts us from the pursuit of enduring satisfaction, we look back, idealizing the simplicity and integrity of other days. This is the pathetic theme of most moralizing. We think we might find eternal or true being elsewhere than where we are, and we imagine that our being is less distracted than our doings. But my intention here is not to moralize; I am merely reporting how our religion itself, our love of the eternal, has yielded to the pressures of our times.

I have emphasized, to begin with, the most commonplace, physical innovations of the century, for they alone might have revolutionized religion. But these innovations were products and signs of similar changes in our minds, of new discoveries, new history, new ideals, changed philosophies. These inner movements of the spirit and their effects on religion will concern us in subsequent chapters. Here let us consider the religious implications of the technological and economic revolutions.

I begin with the so-called "externals" of religious interest in church activities, habits of church attendance, and Sabbath observance. In 1900, as in 1800 and 1700, religious Americans walked or drove in carriages short distances to church several times a week. The church building was physically the center of a community and the parish was the central, vital institution of religious activities. Even small villages had at least two or three churches in close proximity; but this sectarianism, or rather this religious pluralism did not destroy the "community center" character of a church or synagogue. Even in New England where the solidarity of a town was supposed to be symbolized by, if not centered in, its single established "meeting house," the other Protestant churches, the Roman Catholic churches, the synagogues which gradually appeared in the larger towns, continued to be meeting places for the members of a community, in addition to being houses for the Divine Glory. The village was thus a neighborhood of communities. Neighbors might go to different churches; but so long as they went to some church or other they observed the same general pattern of conduct and piety. In my village of about four thousand inhabitants there were seven churches, and most of these inhabitants felt a certain community of spirit in spite of their religious differences, which they did not share with the few who went to no church. Such multiparish communities were, whether urban or rural or village, composed of geographical neighbors, who had a genuine interest in knowing each other. When these people went to "meeting" (or to mass, for that matter), they constituted a real public. "Public worship" was more than worship; it was a bringing together of a neighborhood. During the week these neighbors were intent each on his own affairs. On the Sabbath they not only dropped their private affairs but they cultivated what in our business jargon is called "public relations." One meeting a week was usually deemed insufficient: morning and evening services on Sunday were the rule, plus Sunday School and young people's meetings, and during the week there was one general service plus committee meetings, choir rehearsals, and so forth. The church took a very considerable portion of the people's leisure. In addition to appearing in public on Sundays or Sabbaths, there was a general observance of quiet sociability and sobriety. Noisy games or contests were avoided. Strolling, making "calls," reading, chamber music filled up what little time was left after church duties were done. There was no uniformity in all this, but in one way or another, this one day a week was spent either in ecclesiastical or in family sociability. Even among Catholics, who in Europe made less of the Sabbath, this kind of observance soon became customary.

The general formula for what was done on the Sabbath was "things-of-the-spirit." Specifically, religious acts were only a part, though a central part, of freeing oneself from "the world." "Worldly" affairs included politics and play as well as business; Sunday occupations were preferably impractical, unrelated to the "cares," interests and preoccupations of a busy daily life. _Recreation_ and edification were the aims of the Sabbath peace and quiet; and they were pursued with the same earnestness and seriousness that governed worldly affairs. There was no "idle enjoyment" or mere play.

Into such communal habits of religious observances came the above-mentioned innovations, but they came with unequal force. Let us consider first the transformation of those parishes where the basic innovations of the twentieth century have exerted their full force. Such parishes are found throughout the land, in both town and country, though urbanization was itself a revolutionary factor. There are some significant regional differences, to which we shall give attention later, but the basic changes have affected all areas of population. The most significant differences are therefore within any geographical region, but they are not "class" differences.

Extreme Varieties of "Domestic Heathen"

Only the most extreme economic differences are religiously important. People who cannot afford to buy cars, radios, and the rest of what for convenience's sake I shall call by the old-fashioned religious term of "worldly" necessities are conspicuously different from those who can and do afford them. As a rule these various goods "go together": those who think they can afford one of them, believe that all of them are "modern necessities." The really "poor people," who cannot afford civilized necessities become an object of "home missions," "rescue work," or organized religious charity, whether they need secular charity or not. They are pitied; they are "invited" to church, but are made to feel (as they probably do feel in any case) that they do not belong to the religious community in the same sense that the more prosperous citizens belong to it. This religious proletariat has always existed; it is neither urban nor rural nor modern, it is universal. But under American twentieth-century standards of living the cultural differences between prosperous and poor have become exaggerated. Those who are absolute have-nots, who do not enjoy the basic cultural "privileges" of modern inventions, are not hopeful prospects for either conventional religion or revolutionary politics. Except in special cases, such as those Negro communities where an all but nominal slavery prevails, these people seldom form their own churches and have no tangible religious interests. "White trash" are certainly less distinctively religious than are the Negroes and are more an object of missionary concern. These extremely depressed groups, then, may be termed the "domestic heathen," and their heathendom can be defined better in terms of their lack of privileges than in terms of their lack of faith. Though they are not hopeless, they become religiously an alien population. They are equally conspicuous in urban and rural life, and equally unimportant from the point of view of their civilized neighbors. Fortunately, so far during this century they have been a relatively small "class."

At the other extreme of the social scale are the proverbial millionaires. They, too, are outside the pale of organized religion; they are not objects of charity, but all other mortals are such objects to them. They are the "angels" or patrons of religious bodies, but usually feel superior to the bodies they patronize. For them the modern inventions which we are considering are merely incidental comforts; their standards are not seriously transformed by these additional conveniences, since their interests, though "worldly," transcend the commonplace. Such persons show a benevolent interest in churches, as in schools and hospitals, believing them to represent worthy causes. When they occasionally "visit" churches they do so as they would a hospital, either out of benevolence or as patients in extraordinary need. The philanthropists like Andrew Carnegie, who conscientiously regarded libraries as more public and benevolent institutions than churches, are now very rare indeed. A "foundation" may exercise its own discrimination, but a nonprofessional philanthropist is more inclined to accept the general, popular estimates of what is useful and what not. On the whole, the greatest recent invention from his point of view for taking care of some of his burdens is the community chest; for it frees him from so many lesser "drives."

When a very wealthy person devotes himself wholeheartedly (*not* as a patron) to religious pursuits, he is apt to do it in solitary fashion rather than by participating actively in the life of a religious community. Mysticism, quietism, theology, theosophy, and spiritual "amateurship" give varied opportunities for American brahmans to practice the arts of meditation in seclusion or in a choice circle. Such religious individualism among the wealthy is no novelty and need not detain us in our search for twentieth-century traits. There is some evidence that wealthy Americans are less religious in the twentieth century than they were in the nineteenth,[3] but it is difficult to ascribe this trend, if it is a trend, to the direct influence of modern technology. Still less is it due to any distinctive religious beliefs: the religious beliefs of the wealthy are too varied and unpredictable to be worth special analysis. There is a typical philanthropic conscience, expressed in classic form in Andrew Carnegie's *Gospel of Wealth*; but this gospel of wealth, which is still about what it used to be in Carnegie's day, is not the rich man's religion, it is merely his conscience. His religion is apt to be very personal, somewhat unconventional, and thoroughly impractical.

The Modern Urban Churches

Turning now to religious bodies or communities, to the people conventionally designated as the "religious classes," let us look first at the big urban churches. These churches whose members are as a rule individually prosperous, and whose membership is culturally modernized, but whose family "background" or heritage makes them conscious of the difference between their mode of life and their fathers', afford the best illustration of what the twentieth century has created (and destroyed) religiously. These churches are bigger because their members can come to services from greater distances, usually by car. A typical "downtown" church, though it may minister to its immediate geographical neighborhood under the general head of "home missions," draws its members from the outlying residential districts and the suburbs. And a typical village church will embrace not only the more prosperous members of the town, but the more prosperous farmers from miles around. Such churches are "societies" or associations rather than community organizations; they are focal rather than local. The members, who would otherwise be strangers, are drawn together for the work of the church; the church does not belong to a local community, it creates a special organization of persons, who otherwise would not be a group. Such membership is not only scattered geographically but is flexible or unstable and its interest in the church is apt to be less intense. Consequently, it takes a larger membership to support the activities of the church. Under these circumstances there is a natural, financial reason for enlarging the organization and the membership; and the larger such a church becomes, the more it attracts a floating, nonparticipating attendance. Thus small, local congregations or parishes, in the full sense of the term, are encouraged to consolidate both within denominational lines and across them. And it is difficult to tell whether the shortage of clergy, of which most churches complain, is a cause or a consequence of these tendencies. In any case fewer and larger churches under modern conditions do more than the same amount of work that used to be accomplished by the small, local congregations.

At the same time the quality of church service has "improved" — using the ordinary, secular criteria for improvement. There are more professional, trained, better-paid clergymen and workers. Each church has a "staff"-minister or priest, assistant, paid choir, educational staff, social workers, and so on. The church has become "institutional," and its budget is enormously expanded. More members, each less burdened, pay for a more expert type of "service." Though the paid workers continually try to encourage the members to participate in the various activities of the congregation, the "contributions" of the members tend to become increasingly monetary. Participation in the rites of public worship, too, becomes more passive. Gradually people come to "attend" church service much as they would attend a concert or theater. The service is more of a professional performance, less a community expression or folk art. A greater responsibility is put on the minister or priest. More is expected of him, both in the quality of his professional performance and in the range of his leadership. With the spread of critical judgment in literature, theater, music, architecture and the other arts, the church has been compelled to enter the field in æsthetic competition with the other arts. A tawdry, shabby, "spontaneous" service of worship is no longer accepted. Thus the popular secular arts have imposed severer standards of taste upon religious leadership.

The standards set by the wealthier congregations and by the leadership of their clergy affect the standards of the "lower" middle class. Their churches, too, become "standardized" from above. They, too, feel the pressure of competition. For even though the average taste may not be critical, the average citizen is nevertheless exposed by modern inventions to a higher level of performance, and without understanding the new standards he almost subconsciously feels that he is out-of-date or below par, if he does not imitate and support the modern leadership. With increasing standardization there comes the increasing urge to consolidate forces and capitals. Denominational barriers weaken. As a result the trends established among the most literate and critical congregations become the norms for "Middletown" in general.

In these "bigger, better and fewer" churches, a significant change occurs in habits of church attendance. To *drive* to church *once* a week is now considered "regular" attendance. Much less of the average member's leisure time and energy goes into his church activities. During the week the average business man and employee (and even the farmer) is less isolated from public life than he was in 1900. Factories are more sociable, production more institutional, and economic interests closer to public affairs. Secular leisure is spent in more public ways. As a result there is less demand for spending the Sabbath in public; more inclination to stay at home, to go on a picnic, or in other ways to seek privacy on Sunday. And with the growing and intense forms of Saturday afternoon and night leisure, especially in the cities (the effects of jazz, dance, movies, and theater), Sunday morning is apt to be spent literally resting, and the whole Sabbath is apt to be spent in private relaxation or "idleness" rather than in public edification. There is just enough edification in the Sunday papers, the radio, the movies to put the average conscience at ease when it accepts them as entertainment. It is probably still too soon to judge the effects which radio and television will have on habits of public worship, but already the growth of "churches of the air" and the increasing availability of better-than-average services of worship by broadcasting testify to the growing habit of "worshiping at home" and in private, if at all. Thus relentlessly the effects of these inventions are modifying, if not undermining, the traditional habits of worship and church activities.

But more important for religion than this external threat to traditional religious habits and observances are the various ways in which religion has changed internally under these circumstances. Noteworthy are better educated clergymen, more secular content in sermons, very secularized evening "services" (practically entertainments), theatrical effects, reviews of current fiction, discussion of secular public problems, vaguely "religious" education in place of "Bible schools," and a broader religious press. In many and subtle ways, which we must examine in more detail, religion itself has accepted the ways of modern life. That is to say, much of what in 1900 would have been recognized as "worldliness" is now embodied in the conventional forms and habits of "liberal" religion. And I am not now speaking of theological modernism. I mean that even apart from any profound change of doctrine or faith, there has been an accommodation in religious conduct and activities to the forces and inventions of secular life to such a degree that the *practical* meaning and influence of religion has been revolutionized. Religious institutions and customs, willingly or unwillingly, have been compelled to "accept" and even exploit the far-reaching transformations of purely secular and seemingly irrelevant inventions.

Varieties of Stubborn Religion

Turning next to a less modernized form of religion, we come to those groups and regions for which the essentials of religion have been relatively unaffected by the external changes in modern life. The so-called "lower" middle classes in America are not economically low — at least not to a conspicuous extent. They too enjoy the basic secular goods and have a basic education. But they have little more than the basic, and their sense of what is basic is part of their inheritance. They are as complacent as they are comfortable. It is possible to have an elementary and a high school education, or even a high school education given in a college, without knowing that anything revolutionary has taken place in the twentieth century. And it is possible to read many newspapers, magazines, and books without getting much more education than the schools provide. It is possible to think that the import of science is mere technology, and that the import of technology is mere "creature comforts." And it is possible to belong to religious bodies which encourage their members to rest assured on such foundations.

To these persons the spiritual side of life belongs, together with their family savings and investments, to their patrimony of culture. Religion means little more than "the faith of our fathers," and culture means little more than carrying on a tradition. They attend church as they do concerts with gentility and satisfaction, and they go to confession regularly much as they take baths. The more self-conscious of them enjoy religion as they do other antiques — venerable, still useful, elegant objects of pious affection. But the majority are not culturally self-conscious; they participate eagerly in the life of their times as if it were a direct preparation for eternity. They are not necessarily conservative in their "views" but they assume that God is conserving their values. They are peculiarly sensitive to evils and expect to see them pass inevitably because they undermine themselves; the enduring goods are durable, surviving periods of depression, war, and other "storms." Hence their churches are frankly conventional as their faiths are stable. But they are not aware of the changed status which conventionality and stability have acquired recently.

This unimaginative, complacent population, which can accept the changes since 1900 as merely external and superficial comprises the central core of the American people and accounts for more than half of its religious practices and ideas. Statistically it is normative. It illustrates what some sociologists call "the cultural lag," for the basic events which it endures and the comforts which it enjoys have not transformed its sense of values proportionately to the physical transformation which they have already created. Present meanings have not yet become "signs of the times," indicative of a changed future, nor have new facts suggested new ideas. Under these conditions religious conventionality and stability do not mean what they would in times of general cultural stability. Sociologists, fixing their attention too narrowly on this central religious "cake of custom" have ascribed to religion in general the function of providing stability, both personal and cultural. As a general proposition, however, this is no truer of religion than of any other institution. It would be more exact to observe that the cultural lag which affects institutions generally, shows itself in this kind of religion, which, though it be statistically normative, should not be interpreted as embodying religious normalcy.

Lastly we come to a large element of the population which is not religiously complacent, but which expresses its unrest in antiquated terms. This is militant fundamentalism. It is not related closely to the economically restless population; and all attempts to correlate it with political liberalism, or political conservatism, or any other secular trend have proved unsuccessful. Its members suffer from the same intellectual and educational limitations which we have just described, but they are not on the whole either "the disinherited" or the secure. Neither are they merely leftovers from the nineteenth century. Militant fundamentalism is a twentieth-century movement of protest and unrest; it is apocalyptic, prophetic, critical of modern life and apprehensive of the future.

The earlier generations of "Bible Christians" accepted as a generally recognized fact the dualism between soul and body and they grew up in a conventional application of this fact, so that they knew in terms of practical experience how to be *in* the world but not *of* the world. They lived in two worlds, the temporal and the eternal; so that religious seriousness was as separate from secular seriousness as church was from state. There was here no conflict, but simply duality. But when, during the twentieth century, the world encroached upon the spirit and the two were hopelessly confused in fact as well as in theory, it was necessary to be militant and defiant in order to maintain the familiar distinction between the affairs of the body and the salvation of the soul. To recover a faith in their separateness implied a conscious purification of religion itself. The primary object, therefore, against which these reactionary faiths had to fight was modernized or worldly *religion*. They had to make plausible what to Christians who had become reconciled to the world seemed absurd, namely, that the old dualism could be defended as both reasonable and fundamental. Such a gospel would naturally appeal to those classes or groups who, either for worldly or spiritual reasons, had become discontented with the trend of affairs. Before the era of world conflicts and wars such gospels were not very popular. They owed what general appeal they had to their demagogic diatribes against the growing power of "mammon." But when world war appeared beside capitalism as dominant forms of modernity, and when modern knowledge became increasingly technological, the fundamentalist churches grew by leaps and bounds, and they grew precisely in those regions and classes which believed that as a practical program the salvation of their souls could be isolated completely from the affairs of the modern world. This religious isolationism is reactionary, to be sure, but it is also a positive movement of protest. Such a divorce of religious and social concerns was called by Pope Pius XI, ironically, "social modernism," since it implied that secular affairs could manage themselves without benefit of clergy. And in the nineteenth century, it is true, this gospel was a form of liberalism. But in the twentieth century, it became an escape mechanism from a social order and from a "social gospel" which were felt to be damnable. We must therefore look beneath the biblicist surface of contemporary evangelistic and apocalyptic sects, to understand their rebellious character and their prophetic mission.

Of quite a different character is the traditionalist fundamentalism of the Roman and Anglican Catholic churches. In these churches there is a cultivated and sophisticated dualism between fixity of form or creed, and modernity of action. These authoritarian forms of church government are eagerly participating in democratic politics and in economic mediation. They are no longer, at least in America, class-conscious; they are neither conservative nor proletarian in their appeals. Like modernist Protestantism the Catholics are a powerful expression of middle-class ideals as moderating, equilibrating forces in American society. But unlike the Protestant liberals they are what they always have been. Here again we must look beneath the superficial formalism and authoritarianism in order to understand how these churches are really playing their part in the struggles of contemporary society. For example, when Father Leonard Feeney and some of his colleagues in St. Benedict's Center, Cambridge, Massachusetts, tried to go on a fundamentalistic "doctrinal crusade," they were promptly disciplined by the hierarchy for "ideas leading to bigotry." Here authoritarianism made it clear that it wished to be understood with reasonable sophistication.

The Outward Prosperity of Religion

It is clear that, contrary to what many of our leading historians and sociologists asserted early in the century, religion has not declined in America since 1900. In 1800 only about ten per cent of the adult population were church members, and probably not more than thirty per cent were regular church attendants. During the nineteenth century membership in religious institutions increased to about fifty per cent in 1900, and now at least fifty-five per cent are members. There are another twenty-five to thirty-five per cent who regard themselves as belonging to some religious tradition or other, and who may be individualistically religious in a vague way. Not much more than ten per cent of the population acknowledge no religious affiliation whatsoever. These figures, though not exact, indicate statistically a very familiar fact, namely, that though religion never was confined to active participation in religious institutions, it is now more institutionalized in America than it was at the beginning of the nineteenth century. In general, practically all major types of American religion have staged what is vulgarly called a "comeback," and religious leaders are today much less on the defensive than they were a generation ago. But to regard this phenomenon as simply a "revival" or turning back is to miss entirely an understanding of what has happened. Religion has come forward, or at least it has come forth; it has abandoned many of the things which it held dear fifty years ago and has given new meanings to things which it still cherishes. It is sobered by bitter experience, less optimistic but stronger. It has survived a crisis only because it has had enough intelligence and power to reconstruct itself in the context of the general reconstruction which American life has undergone.

The religious leaders are naturally dissatisfied with the amount of reconstruction that has been accomplished and they are themselves among the most incisive critics. For example, a distinguished worker in the field of home missions, Dr. Herman Nelson Morse, writes as follows:

As an institution the Church continues to grow, but at a diminishing rate. Its expanding membership no longer makes substantial inroads upon the unchurched segment of the population. It is institutionally weakest and least well adapted at the two extremes of our national life, in the great cities and in the open country. More even than the school, it retains, in organization, method and point of view, the marks of our nineteenth-century agrarian civilization. Far more than the school, it depends upon an imperfectly trained and poorly supported leadership and remains essentially an amateur enterprise. Every social development of a hundred years has encroached upon its field of pre-eminence and has made its influence more difficult to exercise. In the establishment and maintenance of its separate units, it has resisted and still resists the implications of deep-seated social change.[4]

This criticism is carried into more detail by Dr. R. A. Schermerhorn, as follows:

Emphasis on ritual, denominational politics, and ecclesiastical fence-mending has led to an isolation of the church from the ongoing concerns of our contemporary culture. Modern art, music, and literature are removed as definitely from the average minister's range of appreciation as though they were in another planet. . . . Where is the church which dares to express itself in the bolder forms of the newer architecture, or harness the revolt of modern poetry? It is difficult for the pastor to be a leader unless he gets to the front of the line. Here are the myriad values of our culture lying dormant so far as religion is concerned, and yet the frenzied attacks on secularism continue. Incredible it is, but more — it is tragic.

The secularism of the twentieth century is due partly to the fact that we do not find all our richest values in the church, as the medievalist or Puritan did. He had nowhere else to go. But we have. Science, art, literature, and the drama all give us the sense of significant depth in life — a function performed in the past by religion alone. . . .

The only way to meet the whole issue of secularism and naturalism is *through* it, not *around* it. Once this journey is made, not grudgingly nor of necessity, but with buoyant hope, the old bugbear has lost its terrors. In the words of Professor Lyman, "What we need is not a return of past religion unmodified, nor a totally new religion, coming like Melchizedek without father or mother or descent. What we need is to find certain new things sacred, to gain new objects of reverence, to enter into companionship with God through certain new relations." [5]

Such self-criticism was not a sign of weakness, but, coming as it did during the dark 30's, was a beginning of the offensive which has grown steadily since then.

It is difficult to get a statistical picture of recent trends in the growth of religious bodies.[6] Measures of growth by percentages give too much prominence to the growth of small, mostly Fundamentalist churches. Membership statistics are not comparable, since some groups (for example, the Roman Catholics) reckon membership from birth (or baptism), others adult membership only. The relation of the Jewish population to active participants in synagogue congregations is also impossible to measure accurately. In Exhibit I a rough graph shows the relative strength of the chief types of religious bodies and their rates of growth compared with each other and with population growth. The net effect of this graph is to indicate that there is nothing sensational in the general quantitative changes, or relative strengths of religious bodies, though there are sensational changes within smaller bodies. In general, religious bodies are holding their own and a little more in view of the population increase. A more detailed study of the available figures would show that during the second quarter of the century, there was a notable growth of churches in the Northwest and the Southeast, that is, in the great rural areas. This has some relation to the facts we have been considering in this chapter; it probably proves not that there is a greater interest in religion now in these areas, but that with modern improvements in communication and transportation "frontier" farmers have been enabled to attend and support churches in areas where previously the scattered nature of the population made such organization impractical.

Automobiles, trucks and buses, operating on vastly improved highways, have enlarged the boundaries of rural communities, made the rural village the capital of rural America, enabled schools to consolidate, multiplied manyfold the contacts of the farmer with the outside world, increased greatly the number of group meetings and of organizations and, along with the radio, all but banished the isolation of rural life. The church too felt the effects of these developments. Open-country churches, many of them with less than 50 members and planted close together as befitted the days when the community was measured by a team haul, died by the thousands. The proportion of farmers in village church membership was about 40 per cent of the total by 1940, the highest percentage ever reached.[7]

A recent survey of a fairly typical Eastern city, Wilmington, Delaware, made under the auspices of the Wilmington Council of Churches produced no very startling results: 37 per cent of the population is Roman Catholic, 27 per cent Protestant, 3 per cent Jewish, leaving 33 per cent unaffiliated with any religious body. Among the Protestants (three-fourths of whom are Methodist, Presbyterian, or Episcopalian) only three-eighths of the members attend church on an average Sunday. Sunday School membership is 55 per cent of church membership, and Sunday School attendance slightly better than church attendance. One-third of the membership is suburban. Other studies reveal that there is a slight tendency toward decentralization, the urban churches gaining less rapidly than the suburban and adjacent rural churches.[8]

The Appendix reports a very recent attempt to measure by the techniques of public-opinion polls the differences among religious groups on public issues and general social outlook. This attempt yielded results which are significantly different from results similarly attained in 1940–1945, and which lead even so cautious and expert a student of "religion and the class structure" as Liston Pope to conclude that there may be greater changes during the last decade in the social status of the churches (notably of the Roman Catholic Church) than had been generally supposed.

But many of the most significant changes in religion have not been measured; most of them probably cannot be measured. In any case, the following chapters, in which the various phases of religious reconstruction are described, fall far short of a scientific report. Generalizations must be hazarded, based on inadequate evidence, and values assigned based on personal impressions.

2

INSTITUTIONAL
RECONSTRUCTION

The Diversification of Religious Institutions

The revolutionary consequences for religion of our social revolution are clear to anyone who looks at religion from the inside, but are not conspicuous to anyone who merely observes the façade of religious institutions. They cannot be shown statistically, at least not by the kind of statistics which are available. The most populous churches are the most stable and, as far as membership goes, keep a little ahead of the birth rate. The percentage of the population which belongs to religious bodies has not varied nearly as much during the twentieth century as during the nineteenth. And the percentages of Protestants, Catholics, and Jews have not varied significantly despite the anxieties and boasts which appear repeatedly in the press. On the fringes there are casualties and novelties. During these fifty years two new American religions have achieved memberships well in the hundreds of thousands and have become extraordinarily stable — stable almost to the point of being static — the Church of Jesus Christ of the Latter Day Saints (the Mormons) and the Church of Christ, Scientist (Christian Science). The Mormons are a people, who like the Israelites have been obliged to live among gentiles against their wishes; and their church is a church in the fullest sense — the expression of the spiritual life and heritage of a distinctive culture. The Christian Scientists, on the other hand, are what the German sociologists would call a sect. Their church performs for them a specialized function, giving them a distinctive kind of healing and health, or at least what Willliam James somewhat satirically called "healthy-mindedness." Otherwise they are not a distinct people, and their religion is practically irrelevant to their citizenship. These two religious bodies received their revelation during the nineteenth century and have used the first half of the twentieth century resisting further inspiration. Though there have been minor divergencies, these churches now have well-defined orthodoxies and are perhaps the most rigid of all American ecclesiastical authorities. They have ceased to be "movements."

In the American environment this sociological distinction between "churches" and "sects" is not very useful, since practically all of our churches are sects from the national-church point of view, and even those groups which are based on European nationalities are rapidly losing their original significances. The Mormons, the Orthodox Jews, and a few small religious communities are religiously organized peoples, but almost all other religious bodies of the United States, including the Roman Catholic Church, are neither national churches nor sects; they are commonly known as denominations or "communions," each of which gathers into a religious association members who otherwise belong to diversified groups. These denominations collectively express the spiritual life of the American people, but no one of them can be conceived as representing a distinctive culture or class. More important for American culture is the distinction between religious "bodies" or denominations and religious "movements." A religious body is a stable institution with a heritage which it cherishes, a government which gives organized expression to its faith, and a body of members whose duties and values are generally recognized. Most movements culminate in bodies, as most faiths become creeds. A movement is endangered when it does not create a body, and a body is endangered when it ceases to move.

Applying this distinction we may note those religious groups which, like the two just mentioned, received their chief impetus in previous centuries and are now "coasting" or declining. Spiritualism, for example, was a vigorous movement in the nineteenth century, and even during the first two decades of the present century its camp meetings, seances, and visions of the "summer land" still had life in them. But today the spiritualist "churches" are mere vestiges of the movement, perhaps not moribund but certainly without spiritual power. A general decline seems to prevail also in the Church of the New Jerusalem (Swedenborgian), the Universalists, the Liberal Catholic Church, the Amana Society, the Christadelphia Fraternity, the Shakers, Bahai, Rosicrucians, and Theosophy.

More than a score of religious bodies listed in the 1906 census have disappeared entirely. In the case of Theosophy, the 1936 United States census authorities explained: "Theosophical Society — Because of the nature of these organizations a decision was reached whereby the Theosophical Societies would no longer be classified as religious denominations or be enumerated in the Religious Census." [1] This decision was probably based on statements in theosophic literature such as the following: "Theosophy . . . is not at all a new religion, science, or philosophy. Nor does it conflict with fundamental truths of any world-religion. It is a universal doctrine." (Publisher's announcement by the Theosophical University Press, Covina, California.) But such statements have always been made by theosophists and do not reflect a tendency on the part of the movement "no longer" to be religious. Theosophists are divided among themselves between those who prefer an educational, "Theosophical University" emphasis and those who have religious interests and rites.

However, more than a score of new bodies have appeared. The twentieth century, too, has had its movements — many of them evanescent, but several of them creative of stable bodies. Among the more familiar are the Ecumenical Movement, Fundamentalism, Zionism, Inter-faith fellowships, the Oxford Group Movement, New Thought, the United School of Christianity, Jehovah's Witnesses (successor to a nineteenth-century movement), the Peace Mission of Father Divine, the International Church of the Four Square Gospel, Youth for Christ Movement, and the Inter-Varsity Fellowships. Such movements may or may not be sectarian, but they are significant as contemporary religious movements, whether fleeting or creative of new bodies. They are forms of religious ferment and as such we must give them due attention in the following chapters.

Here we must call attention to another kind of institutional diversification which promises, if it continues, to achieve a revolution in the structure of religious bodies. The kind of bodies which are listed in the United States census are for the most part "denominations," all of them bodies whose primary purpose is defined (both by the Census authorities and the bodies themselves) as worship or divine service. They center in the kind of buildings known for centuries as temples, churches, houses of God, monasteries, synagogues, etc. But our century has created a number of religious societies whose outward appurtenances resemble the office buildings of big business more than they do church buildings. Some of them are popularly known as "storefront churches." They are organizations for work, religious labor. Even within the conventional framework of the Christian churches such terms as "New England meeting-houses" and "Societies of Friends" foreshadowed the nonecclesiastical religious bodies, informal fellowships, mission boards, committees for social action, youth organizations. During the last decades the work of the American religious bodies has become so specialized, organized, and practical, that the very life of religion seems to be shifting from worship to "service" and from altar to office. Even at the dawn of the century a far-sighted theologian had a premonition of this diversification and wrote the prophetic paragraph which we reproduce here. (See Exhibit II.)

Whether all these activities are religious or not is, after all, an academic dispute, for no one can tell precisely where business leaves off and religion begins, or at what point politics becomes "the strategy of the Kingdom." Suffice it here to classify the most important religious institutions that have grown up recently in or about our churches and temples.

1. Institutional churches, as they now function in a complete, up-to-date, city congregation comprise an educational staff, recreation facilities, club rooms, and kitchen; settlement work and professional social services, psychiatric counseling, and employment service.

2. "Store-front" churches and "gospel tabernacles" are the antithesis. These are mission rooms for evangelism, consolation, and impromptu charity. Sometimes they are financed by churches,

but now they are mushrooming in big cities with apparent spontaneity, without much organization, capital, or stability.

3. Community centers are usually supported in Christian communities by community or federated churches, of which there are now three thousand autonomous congregations with a million members, and in Jewish communities by the various branches of Judaism.

4. Church boards and administrative agencies have been consolidated for federated programs of missions, social action, education, evangelism, and relocation of displaced persons. The actual work of these boards is usually done by professionally trained laymen.

5. Youth associations, organized for fellowship, recreation, religious education, and missionary activity, have expanded religious work beyond the activities of the churches. Such organizations as the YMCA, YWCA, YMHA, YWHA, B'nai B'rith, Christian Endeavor Society, and the Student Volunteer Movement were organized on a nondenominational basis. Roman Catholic youth organizations which have had similar functions include the boys' work of the Knights of Columbus, Catholic Boy Scouts,[2] Catholic Girl Scouts, Catholic Youth Organization, and Catholic Students' Mission Crusade. Protestant denominational foundations, the Newman Club, and Hillel organizations have recently become influential on college campuses, and there have also been experiments in inter-faith work.

6. The educational work of religious bodies now includes all phases of education, from elementary schools (including releasetime classes) and Sunday Schools to colleges and universities, theological seminaries and training schools for many kinds of technical service.

7. There are many associations and endowments for religious education, both elementary and higher, and periodic conferences for the discussion and planning of religious programs in schools.

8. Religious presses and publicity are now on a professional basis and compete with all aspects of secular journalism, providing general news and entertainment features as well as religious edification and instruction. Religious publishing houses are expanding the range of their publication program and are also

publishing results of research projects as well as the more conventional religious literature.

9. Religious lobbies have been established by the larger churches, and some inter-faith bodies have paid lobbies which function as powerful pressure groups.

10. Inter-faith and international organizations have been established to defend religions against secularism and to promote their common interests.

The mere listing of such institutions indicates how complicated and "vested" religious interests have become, and how antiquated is the notion that religion is practiced in solitude. Private devotion is, of course, still carried on, but even the most personal piety is now apt to be stimulated by the concerted efforts of skilled and organized religious workers. In the three decades 1920–1950 almost twice as many Catholic Societies of all kinds were founded than during the preceding three decades, and the statistics for Protestant and Jewish organizations tell a similar story. Of "joining" there seems to be only a beginning.

The Public Status of Religious Institutions

During the Enlightenment, when the American principles governing the relations between state and church were formulated, religion was commonly conceived as being private. The Virginia Declaration of Rights of 1776 made a characteristic distinction between religion, which is "the duty we owe to our Creator," and morality, "the mutual duty of all to practice Christian forbearance, love and charity towards each other." Here the adjective "Christian" may have been a mere slip or a careless use of a common expression. In any case the distinction that was then basic in theory was between duties toward God which must be exercised freely by each individual "according to the dictates of conscience" and civil or mutual duties (not necessarily Christian) of tolerance or "forbearance." As late as 1931 Chief Justice Hughes appealed to this distinction in the case of conscientious objectors (*United States* v. *Macintosh*, 283 U.S. 633). He wrote: "The essence of religion is belief in a relation to God involving duties superior to those arising from any human relation." What he had in mind, as the context makes clear, is "duty to a moral power higher than the state," but like the Catholic theorists, he assumes that any duty which transcends political duty is not based on human relations. This individualistic interpretation of religious conscience or transcendent duty has gradually been broken down, so that today there is a wider recognition on the part of both secular and religious leaders of the social responsibility of religion. Whether one agrees with the radicals that this social responsibility is of the very essence of religion, or whether one merely recognizes the power of religion in maintaining public morality, there is a general realization that religion is an important, if not basic element in the structure of our culture. Thomas Jefferson begins the famous passage in which he spoke of the "wall of separation" with the clause, "Believing with you that religion is a matter which lies solely between man and his God; that he owes account to none other for his faith or his worship." And he ends with the clause, "convinced man has no natural right in opposition to his social duties." The contemporary defense of natural rights and natural law would be much more defensible if, like Jefferson's, it were based on the assumption that no natural right can be in opposition to social duty. A church may be free from government control, but it is never free from social obligations. Hence, no matter how strong the "wall of separation between church and state" may be built, responsible citizens and democratic governments have a manifest duty not to be "neutral" toward religion, nor "benevolent" toward any kind of religion whatsoever, nor hostile to all religions, but critically concerned for the humaneness and nobility of the various faiths which exercise public functions even though they are legally "private." There is a National Laymen's Committee headed by Charles E. Wilson called "Religion in American Life" whose objective is: "To emphasize the importance of all religious institutions as the foundation of American life and to urge all Americans to attend and support the church or synagogue of their individual choice." Such an agency might well add to its concerns a careful study of how well various religious bodies actually provide "the foundation of American life."

For purposes of taxation, religious bodies are classed as nonprofit-making and are exempt on that score, but for other purposes they are commonly referred to as among the "benevolent and charitable" organizations. In general, the Federal Amendment prohibiting a religious establishment, though it may be interpreted broadly as implying the "separation" of church and state, does not imply that the state takes no cognizance of the activities and values of organized religion. The difficulties in defining precisely the historical relations between churches and the United States were examined by E. B. Greene in his *Religion and the State in America* (1941); and since then the debate concerning what these relations ought to be has become an acute public issue. Professor Greene showed clearly that the separation has never been complete and that the actual relations depend more on the shifting of sympathies than on precise legal theory. A monumental examination of this whole question has been achieved by Dr. Anson Phelps Stokes in his three volumes of *Church and State in the United States*. These volumes exhibit in great detail the truth of Greene's conclusions.

In 1900 there was comparatively little interest in this question. The issue became of general public concern during the presidential campaign of Alfred E. Smith in 1928, and his much publicized personal "creed" was taken as a formulation of the "liberal" Catholic position. (See Exhibit III.) His statement against "interference" was prompted by Catholic pressure to intervene in behalf of the Mexican churches which were being persecuted.

During the last two decades there have been numerous court decisions which attempt to define the meaning of "separation." Since there has been an increasing need on the part of all institutions, and especially of nonprofit-making institutions, for more or less government support, the churches realize that their radical independence may be in jeopardy. Most churches feel that they can no longer compete with the state in getting the people's money. The church would now be more than content with tithes (10 per cent of member's income), whereas the state would now not dream of getting along on so little. This situation is in itself of considerable historical and moral interest, for time was, even in this country, when the state envied the churches' ability to raise money. Partly as a matter of economic need, partly as a matter of moral principle, the churches (and especially the Roman Catholic Church) have demanded a modification of the traditional idea of separation of church and state.

The most outspoken formulation of a changing policy came from the manifesto on Nov. 20, 1948, of the American Roman Catholic bishops, in which they suggested as a working formula "the cooperation of church and state," as follows:

To one who knows something of history and law, the meaning of the First Amendment is clear enough from its own words: "Congress shall make no laws respecting an establishment of religion or forbidding the free exercise thereof." . . .

Under the First Amendment, the federal government could not extend this type of preferential treatment [establishment] to one religion as against another, nor could it compel or forbid any state to do so. If this practical policy be described by the loose metaphor "a wall of separation between Church and State," that term must be understood in a definite and typically American sense. It would be an utter distortion of American history and law to make that practical policy involve the indifference to religion and the exclusion of cooperation between religion and government implied in the term "separation of Church and State" as it has become the shibboleth of doctrinaire secularism.

Within the past two years secularism has scored unprecedented victories in its opposition to governmental encouragement of religious and moral training, even where no preferential treatment of one religion over another was involved. In two recent cases, the Supreme Court of the United States adopted an entirely novel and ominously extensive interpretation of the "establishment of religion" clause of the First Amendment.

This interpretation would bar any cooperation between government and organized religion which would aid religion, even where no discrimination between religious bodies is in question. . . .

We feel with deep conviction that for the sake of both good citizenship and religion there should be a reaffirmation of our original American tradition of free cooperation between government and religious bodies — cooperation involving no special privilege to any group and no restriction on the religious liberty of any citizen. We solemnly disclaim any intent or desire to alter this prudent and fair American policy of government in dealing with the delicate problems that have their source in the divided religious allegiance of our citizens. . . .

We stand ready to cooperate in fairness and charity with all who believe in God and are devoted to freedom under God to avert the impending danger of a judicial "establishment of secularism" that would ban God from public life. For secularism is threatening the religious foundations of our national life and preparing the way for the advent of the omnipotent State.[3]

Much depends on how this doctrine of "coöperation" will be applied. The intent of the bishops seems to have been to distinguish the American "pluralistic" moral structure from the Spanish concept of "Catholic unity," and to adapt Catholic doctrine to democratic government. However, in their statement on the education of children made public by the Administrative Board of the National Catholic Welfare Conference, Nov. 18, 1950, the bishops applied the theory of coöperation in an ambiguous way. They pay their respects to the doctrine of dual citizenship in "two worlds," but then expound the doctrine that only religion can be an "integrating force" — giving the child a "complete and rational meaning for his existence," that the child must be "either God-centered or self-centered," and that therefore all education, especially sex education, must be kept in a "religious and moral context," so that "the child will see . . . the controlling purpose of his life, which is service to God." The development of the doctrine of coöperation thus seems clearly to involve the subordination of secular to religious morals and the subordination of public schools to the "natural rights" of the parent-church combination in matters spiritual.

The clearest and most democratic Catholic exposition has been made by the distinguished theologian, Father John Courtney Murray, who in a noteworthy essay came to the following conclusions:

History and experience have brought the Church to ever more perfect respect for the autonomy of the state (as a form of respect for an essential element in the "whole man") and consequently to ever more purely spiritual assertions of her power in the temporal order. Moreover, in proportion as these assertions of a power have become more spiritual they have become more universal and searching, reaching all the institutions of human life, to conform them in their idea and operation to the exigencies of the Christian conscience. With seeming paradox, the withdrawal of the Church from a certain identification with the *state* in the medieval *respublica* and (in a different way) with the confessional state has not meant a withdrawal from *society*, but rather a more profound immanence, so to speak, in society, as the spiritual principle of its direction to both the temporal and the eternal ends of the human person. . . . In other words, the question is whether the concept of *libertas ecclesiastica* by intrinsic exigence requires political embodiment in the concept of "the religion of the state", with the "logical and juridical consequences" that have historically followed from that concept. Surely the answer must be no.[4]

To this statement might well be added the observation of a recognized legal scholar:

The mutual obligations of Church and State remain what they always were — cooperation for the improvement of human society. This obligation of the Church to society, however, must be performed in the spirit which informed the words of St. Paul: "Though I speak with the tongues of men and of angels, and have not charity, I am become as sounding brass, or a tinkling cymbal." It is as a divine organization, confident in its mission and proclaiming the gospel of charity to the people of this country and to the people of the world, that the church will perform its obligation to society and thereby to the State.[5]

Such attempts to reconcile a legal separation between state and church with a moral coöperation between religion and society raise old problems in new perspectives. What is peculiar to recent developments is the practical urgency of the issues involved. For behind the theoretical formulations lie several important legal decisions and group conflicts, all of which tended to weaken the position of the few remaining militant atheists or freethinkers and of the many anticlericals, who consistently opposed such tendencies as violating the "free church in a free state" principle. The great majority of presumably religious Americans allowed these encroachments on the strict "neutrality" of the state to accumulate with relatively little concern or with ineffective opposition. There were always minor complaints arising from the introduction of religious materials in the public schools: Jews protested at being taught Christmas carols, Catholics protested against the use of the King James version of the Bible, atheists protested against the use of prayers in legislatures and the presence of sectarian religious workers and teachers on state university campuses. But such problems were of long standing. The new problems were created directly or indirectly by the world wars. Both President Wilson and President Roosevelt did not hesitate to include religious appeals and sentiments in their public utterances and documents during wartime. The use of such phrases as "this nation under God" was intended to give a general religious solemnity to the struggles and to suggest officially that "in God we trust." Though such sentiments were received cordially by most citizens, they served to stir up the wrath of the dwindling band of radical secularists who objected even to chaplains in the military service.

The appointment in 1939 of Myron Taylor to the Vatican as the personal representative of President Roosevelt and later of President Truman was accepted by the general public as a measure of military expediency and for military intelligence. But the leading Protestant organizations launched vigorous protests on the suspicion that this move might be an entering wedge for establishing regular diplomatic relations. The attempt by President Truman in 1951 to make a similar appointment of General Mark Clark supported these suspicions and led to a prompt, vigorous, organized opposition by Protestants and others.

Similarly Catholic pressure toward establishing normal diplomatic relations with Generalissimo Franco's Spain caused widespread resentment among Protestants and secular liberals. But the most serious issues arose over new educational policies. During the 1930's and 1940's there was an increasing concern over the spread of juvenile delinquency and of criminal acts by children in high schools. The National Council of Protestants, Catholics, and Jews, and other interdenominational bodies suggested that one reason for the alarming immorality was the absence of religious education, and on this supposition there was a widespread appeal for the support of religious education in the interest of public morals. The spread of "religious illiteracy" was commonly regarded as a public menace, and various remedies were discussed which might provide the desired religious sanction for public morals without increasing sectarianism. Thus there arose a belief in the public need for religion in general, which particular faiths were prompt to exploit. Added to this circumstance was the fact that indirectly, by Federal Government scholarships to veterans, many struggling church colleges had been helped through the financial crisis of the war years; and several states had passed legislation permitting the use of public funds to aid religious schools.

It is difficult to generalize with confidence while the debate on these issues is still raging (1952), but it seems to be generally recognized today that the problem of religious freedom has shifted its focus considerably since 1900. There seems to be relatively less agitation for freedom *from* religion on the part of atheists, freethinkers and radical secularists; at least, this hostile attitude toward organized religion as such gets less of a hearing today than a century ago, or even a half-century ago. But if religious bodies continue to misrepresent "secularism" not only as immoral but as itself an "established religion," they will undoubtedly arouse again the organized enmity of those nonreligious citizens who had imagined that organized religion would become enlightened enough to tolerate unorganized irreligion. Otherwise there seems to be a general acceptance of the principle of freedom *for* religion, with the exception of a minority of American Catholic theorists, who still defend persecution of "false" religions in principle, though they do not advocate it in practice. But there is a genuine concern for freedom *in* religion; that is, for cultivating a spirit of mutual respect and coöperation among the two hundred independent religious bodies that exist in the United States, whose traditions make them divisive, if not hostile forces. In other words, the church-state problem is not solved by a negative public policy of "hands off religion," but by building the kind of intellectual and moral environment in which the free exercise of religion is of constructive and positive value for public life. The reconciliation of the spirit of freedom with the spirit of religious devotion or commitment has become a serious problem of public morality. Neither state nor church can now be indifferent to each other's moral structure.[6]

Institutions of Religious Education

Various programs for promoting religious education have raised, in addition to educational problems, the basic issues of church-state relations both morally and legally. One was the bid for federal funds to extend to parochial schools school-bus service, lunches, and other provisions which federal legislation had given to public schools on the ground that such measures were more closely related to public health and child welfare than to religious instruction. The Taft bill in the Senate and the McGowan bill in the House before the 80th Congress definitely raised the constitutional question. Many educational leaders were urging the need of federal spending for public education, but the Catholic lobby obstructed all moves in this direction so long as such public aid to parochial schools was blocked. This apparently has created a deadlock. What caused more serious alarm among Protestants, Jews, and secularists was the frank statements of Catholic leaders that they felt justified in asking for even more: "just enough tax funds to make the Catholic schools an integral part of American education."

At the opening of the century the opinion of American Catholic leaders was divided on the subject of parochial schools. In 1870 Father McGlynn of St. Stephen's Church, New York, had attacked the parochial schools system, and there had consequently been much bitter debate among the bishops. This attack was interpreted by Pope Leo XIII as an illustration of the growth of "Americanism" within the Roman Catholic Church, for which he finally censured in effect both Archbishop John Ireland and Cardinal Gibbons in his letter *Testem benevolentiae* (1899). A compromise plan was worked out in 1892 between the Papal legate, Monsignor Satolli, and the American bishops, but after six months the Pope condemned these concessions to the public school system. As a result parochial schools grew rapidly during the twentieth century, until now about one half of Catholic children attend parochial schools. This meant a general repudiation of the compromise of 1892 that "there is no repugnance to Catholic children learning the first elements and the higher branches of art and the natural sciences in public schools controlled by the state," and in its place a policy that there must not only be parochial religious education but that even the teaching of reading, writing, and arithmetic must be under religious auspices.

Meanwhile among the Jews there grew an urgent demand for Hebrew schools. Jewish educational leaders during the early decades of the century emphasized the universal elements in Jewish religion and went even further than did the Christian liberals in assimilating their religious education to American secular education, with the inevitable result that the learning of Hebrew, the observance of the Jewish "sacra," and the study of the Torah lost some of the religious urgency which they possess for the Orthodox, and became mere historical elements in Jewish "civilization." This they were frankly called by the leaders of the "Reconstructionist" Movement, in which the problems of religious education were treated with exceptional and radical insight. But with the growth of secular Jewish nationalism and Zionism, and with the disillusionment over the general program of assimilation, there grew rapidly during the last two decades a demand, even on the part of secularized Jews, for a revival of the knowledge of Hebrew, of the Torah, and of the peculiar institutions of Judaism. The cultivation of these institutions now seemed *educationally* important, whether they were *religiously* essential or not.

These schools [7] did not raise the church-state issue since they were willing to accept the "wall of separation," but they raised the question of their relevance to American culture. The usual Jewish justification has been well formulated by Joseph H. Lookstein in terms which are relevant to all religious bodies. (See Exhibit IV.) And a philosopher, Horace M. Kallen, also speaking in behalf of the American Association for Jewish Education, added a word of timely warning to this view: "This task can be accomplished only in the degree that it becomes clear to the parents of American Jewish children, and to the children themselves, that the Jewish values of their inheritance are, like all values which liberal education undertakes to transmit, essential dynamics in the liberation of their own powers of growth in freedom." [8]

These same issues were again raised practically and legally by the spread of "released time" (usually one hour a week) from public school instruction for purposes of religious instruction, administered by religious bodies. The Supreme Court (in the McCollum case, 1948) ruled that public school buildings could not be used for this purpose. But the program in general is not stopped by this decision, and the Supreme Court by a 6–3 decision upheld the New York State system. Opinion is sharply divided not only on the question of the religious value of this program, but on the question of whether or not it violates the principle of religious freedom. Parents who have no religious affiliation or interest complain that their children are robbed of an hour's instruction. A majority of Jews object to any segregation of school children on a religious basis, both because it promotes sectarianism and because religious differences are irrelevant to public education. Some Protestants object because the Catholics are making the most effective use of the program, and because no significant contribution is made to religious education by this meager allotment of time. The program is still highly experimental, varying greatly from community to community. But it has raised a basic question in a practical way, namely, can the public interest in religion as a general civilizing agency be promoted, without aggravating religious differences and conflicts? The problem is complicated by the growth of two evils: religious illiteracy and illiterate religion.

In the realm of higher education American Protestants had acted throughout the nineteenth century on the assumption that the churches must take the lead, and hence during the twentieth century they were only reluctantly yielding to the growth of municipal colleges and state universities. The original aim of providing a well-balanced education in a religious environment and of providing religious education along with general education is becoming increasingly difficult to realize. Many colleges that were founded under definitely religious auspices are now frankly secular or "liberal arts" colleges and are financially independent of their original church sponsors. But even among those colleges that are known as church colleges the religious "atmosphere" and curriculum have declined drastically. Compulsory chapel attendance is as a rule resented as compulsion. Bible courses and other specifically religious courses are now as a rule "electives" and are frequently not elected. And in ways that are more readily felt than described the general moral and religious tone among church-sponsored schools is often not noticeably different from that of similar secular institutions, and occasionally this fact gives rise to serious criticism among pious parents and to scandal in church circles. Thus churches are faced with the negative problem, whether it is worth trying to maintain the original aims, and with the positive problem of finding some new method of providing more effective religious education.

At last several influential Protestant educators, viewing the situation in higher education as desperate, have publicly advocated, following the example of the Catholics and Jews, building Protestant elementary schools. In 1949 the International Council of Religious Education reported that since 1937 there had been an even greater proportionate growth of religious schools among Lutheran, Reformed, Seventh Day Adventist, and Mennonite churches than among Roman Catholics. But the International Council reasserted its faith in the public schools as "the schools of all people" and recommended a program of coöperation with public school boards to prevent a "lofty neutrality between religion and non-religion alike as if there were nothing to choose between the two philosophies of life." On the other hand, secular educators blamed the churches, charging that they were asking for public school time because they had failed to draw young people to their Sunday Schools and church programs, and had failed to integrate religious institutions into contemporary American life.

One reason why the released-time experiment has received serious support from educational leaders is their relization that Sunday Schools (or Sabbath Schools) have failed to cope with the public need for religious education, in spite of the drastic modernization which they have undergone. At the opening of the century these institutions were little more than "Bible schools," as in fact, they were often called. The curriculum was practically limited to the Bible stories and commentary, and the Sunday School "hymns" were about as "low" as one can get in both music and religion. During the first quarter of the century, through the concerted, interdenominational efforts of a devoted group of genuine educators, beginning with the organization in 1903 of the Religious Education Association and culminating in the formation (1922) of the International Council of Religious Education, the Sunday School was transformed (in theory and, among the better churches, in practice as well) into a "graded," comprehensive organ of religious education. Standard texts and lessons were provided; the curriculum was expanded to include discussion of general religious and moral issues at various levels of growth, from nursery to adulthood, and also elements of church history, church discipline ("catechism"), and social problems. The music was somewhat improved, though on the whole the æsthetic side of the Sunday School was neglected. These modernized "church schools" attempted to apply the methods and standards of professional secular education to religious subjects and to the psychology of religious growth. There was even a highly organized, well-planned system for providing teachers with some professional training. In some churches, especially the Episcopal, the emphasis was put upon training for church membership (the Church being substituted for the Bible as the focus of the educational program), but in the majority of churches, the aim was to promote the religious "nurture" or normal growth of children through adolescence, and thus to provide an effective, intelligent substitute for the nineteenth-century emphasis on conversion and emotional appeal. This whole program of religious education still operates, but during the second quarter of the century it declined somewhat. The extent of the decline is a moot question, and its causes are difficult to determine; since 1947 there seems to be an upward trend, especially among non-Protestant schools. It is probable that the religious education program was "over-sold" and that the initial, intense enthusiasm for it naturally produced eventually a relaxation, if not reaction. The results hardly seemed to justify the elaborate institutions and the semi-professional effort. The financial depression of the 1930's compelled retrenchment, and later inflation impoverished its endowments. The "lay leadership" which was supposed to grow out of this type of education is as yet not conspicuous. Then, too, attendance at Sunday School suffered with the recent general decline in the regularity of church attendance, of which we spoke in the first chapter. But underlying all these external factors were certain religious tendencies inherent in the movement. The broader conceptions of religious experience which guided the reform of the curriculum,

instead of remedying the "Biblical illiteracy" of the younger
generations, about which generations familiar with the content
of the Bible complained, merely spread a more sophisticated
attitude toward the Bible, and made the "knowledge" of the
Bible seem less important than it had been. A smattering of
Biblical criticism and a more reasonable theory of Biblical
authority, precisely because they tended to relate religious education to education in general, made the Sunday School of less vital
concern to a generation reared in modernized Sunday Schools.
The more religion was related to "life," the less vitality remained
in the distinctive institutions of religion, and the problem of
religious education was transferred from the Sunday Schools to
schools in general. Religion was to be "studied" as a normal element in the subject-matter of general education. Thus knowledge
about religion threatened to displace religious training, and the
ecclesiastical incentives for liberalized religious instruction on
which the Sunday School movement depended, were secularized
by the very progress made in religious liberalism.

Admitting this diagnosis of the inadequacy of Sunday Schools
to cope with the growing need for professional religious education, the solution of the problem is still not clear. Three general
lines of reform have been suggested.

(1) The most ecclesiastically minded churches are putting the
burden on the family. How can schools provide what belongs by
its nature in the home? The Sunday School can function merely
as "the agency for high lighting and underscoring through-the-
week religious instruction rendered by the family. . . . The
Sunday School cannot underscore what the modern home has
failed to write into the record." [9]

And from the Catholic bishops come the following concrete
suggestions:

Parents should make early provision for their child's growth in God.
This is not something to be postponed for nurture by school authorities. It must begin in the home through simple and prayerful practices.
Morning and evening prayers, grace before and after meals, the family
rosary, the saying of a short prayer each time the striking clock marks
the passage of another hour nearer eternity, the reverential making
of the Sign of the Cross, the inculcation of respect for the Crucifix
and other religious objects, all these are practices which should be en-

couraged in the religious formation of the child. . . Let parents make use of the strong supernatural motivation which can be drawn from the life of Christ. Let them encourage the imitation of Him, particularly in His obedience, patience and thoughtfulness of others; and let them foster the emulation of that spirit of unselfish giving so characteristic of Christ. This can be done in many practical ways, particularly through providing the child with frequent opportunities for making acts of self-denial in the home. . . . "If you love Me, keep My commandments." That is Christ's test and it must be applied to the child. He should be brought to see God's commandments and precepts as guideposts which give an unerring direction to his steps."[10]

Such suggestions not only make modern parents smile, and modern educators writhe, but strengthen the prevalent impression that the clergy assume too complacently and officiously that they are by "natural law" appointed to give advice on moral and religious education. The attempt to subordinate the life of the home to the commandments of ecclesiastical authority is one of the causes of the willingness of parents to put the responsibilities of religious education on the shoulders of professional educators. In any case, it would seem improbable on the face of it, that under present-day conditions the domestic rites of earlier generations can be restored by ecclesiastical pressure. A more natural atmosphere for worship must be culturally created in the home before the supernaturalist motives to which bishops appeal can take effect. However, whether the attempt to revive domestic worship is practical or not, the truth remains that the problem of religious education has been revolutionized by the secularization of family life. It makes a big difference whether education is *within* a religious tradition and community or whether it is the religious education of what some writers call "natural pagans." There are prejudices to be overcome in either case, but they are opposite prejudices; they are in the latter case religious illiteracy, in the former case, illiterate or juvenile religion. In either case, there comes a real crisis, or there is no education.

(2) A second line of reform is to expand the educational facilities and programs of the churches. The efforts to provide more time for educational work within the present Sunday School organization have not been encouraging. It is difficult to get children for more than one hour on Sunday and still more

difficult to extend Sunday schooling into the week. The most practical successes seem to have come from Daily Vacation Bible Schools, which curiously enough seem to be popular with both parents and children. Religious educators who turned to the released-time scheme as an alternative have hopes that the present one-hour-a-week allotment may lead to a one-afternoon-a-week allotment, and thus to the building up of adequate centers of religious instruction, either denominational or interdenominational, as local circumstances may dictate.

(3) A third line of reform assumes that it is hopeless to expect results from elementary schools or Sunday Schools or homes and that the problem must be met primarily in the colleges. At this level the problem is almost insoluble, partly by the very nature of the situation, partly because of the competition of rival professions for control. Not only the public colleges and universities, which are prohibited by law from engaging in religious instruction, but the leading private liberal arts colleges and universities distinguish between instruction *about* religion, which inevitably enters into many courses in many departments, and which is granted recognition toward academic degrees, and education *in* religion, which is not so recognized (except in very limited amounts), and which is therefore set up on the fringe of the campus and the curriculum in the form of church foundations, "Bible chairs," religious institutes, and so forth. The situation has been described in classic style by Howard Mumford Jones:

Practical compromises are worked out, often under the convenient ambiguity of the word "religion." For if the state university be prohibited from maintaining a faculty of theology, courses in "comparative religion" compromise nobody, commit nobody, and perhaps make for general good will — albeit instruction in "comparative religion" has here and there stirred up the very difficulty it was supposed to alleviate. Such courses may be given by a discreet professor of ethics or a philosopher; they may appear in the offerings of the department of history or of anthropology; sometimes they even appear, disguised, in the English department as "The Bible as Literature," "The Great Bibles of Mankind," or something similar. Similarly, courses not so named, in ethics, sociology, social problems, or literature, may be quietly understood to deal with the problem of "religion." In an unobtrusive way these courses often do an immense amount of good in two directions: they help puzzled undergraduates and they reassure the churches that the university is not a hotbed of "atheism." But of course "religion" taught comparatively is religion on an objective or impersonal basis and does not necessarily lead to that direct influence upon conduct and thought which many denominations desire to exercise.

A second device is the maintenance of a "religious counsellor" at the expense of the state, wholly or in part: such an official, presumably kindly and impartial, serves as a liaison officer between the university and the denominations. . . .

But on the whole it cannot be said that undergraduates characteristically take their troubles to the religious counsellor. To begin with, the counsellor has to be all things to all men — to be, in other words, strictly impartial among Catholics, Protestants, Jews, agnostics, and all the rest. This is in itself an impossible assignment. In the next place, even if he is impartial, the best he can do is to canalize the problem with all of its emotional overtones in the direction of the student's church, and yet it is sometimes this very minister that the student is trying to get away from. And finally it must be gently said that in a faculty of experts the religious counsellor fares badly because the philosophic and scientific competition is very great, and up to now his job has attracted few persons of outstanding genius. The puzzled undergraduate, if he goes to an adult at all, is therefore far more likely to confide in a sympathetic member of the faculty.

These are two principal ways in which the university has tried to solve the problem. The denominations have also made friendly approaches. Characteristic is the assignment to the nearest local church or synagogue of a "student pastor". . . . Adjoining the campuses of many state universities, particularly in the South, one will find one or more buildings housing a so-called Bible chair or chairs. This means that the denomination in question supports a teacher of its own faith who offers in a building owned or rented by his denomination instruction in the Bible, in theology, or in "religion," sufficiently mature in character as to challenge the interests of undergraduates and to compete on an intellectual level with the courses offered in the university. These courses are mostly extra-curricular in nature, and it is a tribute to the earnestness with which they are taught and to a quality of soul-searching among undergraduates that they continue to survive, even where no college credit is given for them. . . .

On the other hand, the university trains its students to higher intellectual expectations than the average church, the average minister, can satisfy. After being lectured to by expert men, however dull these men may be, the student is likely to find the ordinary sermon, Catholic, Protestant, or Jewish, singularly unsatisfactory. After training by professional thinkers, the vague good will of the Sunday-school superintendent is less than the dust. It is not the university, but the churches that must become intellectually alive if they are to retain the allegiance of graduates from state-supported institutions of higher learning in the United States. Single ministers and single churches see this; it must be confessed that the majority of churches do not.[11]

Whether the churches and the politicians see the whole problem or not, there are many theologians, who being professional educators, are aware of the fact that they must remove this conventional antithesis between knowledge *about* religion and religious knowledge. The present trends in theology and toward theology are favorable to progress in the solution of this problem. One professor, for example, writes as follows, and there are many who would agree:

Most instructors in religion in the colleges are men trained in the seminaries and graduate schools before theological winds blew toward doctrine. A "cultural lag" therefore exists between their teaching and current spearheads of Christian thought. . . . Moreover, the prevailing opinion of other academic departments is that the teaching of religion must always display the aloofness from personal involvement required by the scientific ideal of impartial objectivity. Thus, even when the staffs of departments of religion would themselves elect to do otherwise, accommodation to the opinion of their colleagues often compels the adoption of a primarily historical or comparative approach, and this in a day when a new supply of competent college teachers of religion interested in comparative religion is almost unavailable.[12]

The problem of reconciling religious education with the scientific study of religion is clearly not so much a problem of institutional reconstruction as of intellectual reconstruction. There is no reason why religion should not be intelligently, devotedly, and critically cultivated in educational institutions as well as in institutions of worship and service; religion can be educationally significant in so far as it is recognized for what it certainly has been, namely, one of the basic "humanities." If it loses its basic role in human civilization, no amount of education can save it. Religious illiteracy is a *public* evil only so long as religion is a public service. This humane status and educative function of religion is endangered not only by the ignorance bred of anticlericalism but also by the transcendent arrogance of fanatics who fail to interpret their faith in a way compatible with civilization. The other-worldliness of the church will be respected only so long as its criticism of the world actually has redemptive power. In other words school, church, and state must be genuinely coöperative, and not seek a monopoly either of power or of moral authority.

Missions

It would be impossible and irrelevant here to discuss the institutional changes in the foreign mission fields. What concerns us here, besides the changes in home missions, are the changes in the missionary spirit and organization within the United States. The American colonies were all originally mission fields, and for the Roman Catholic Church the United States was officially a "mission territory" until 1908.

It is inevitable that home missions and foreign missions should compete, despite the efforts of the Missionary Education Movement since 1921 to coördinate them. Among Protestants for more than a century the foreign fields have enjoyed the greater popularity, expansion, and support. The enthusiasm for work and investment in these fields, notably in India, China, and Japan, antedated and greatly transcended the growth of American economic and political interests. Of course, when secular interests and imperialistic policies "opened up" new fields for American missions, the churches were prompt to exploit their opportunities. But it is significant of the general spirit of missions that in the twentieth century, as well as in the nineteenth, the most popular mission fields were still those areas in which "heathenism" was most spectacular — India, China, and "darkest Africa." In general, however, it is safe to say that this popular appeal, through dramatizing the horrors of heathenism, though it continues to be used for missionary campaign purposes, was gradually subordinated to the more intelligently planned work of the mission boards. The increasing centralization of the Protestant Missions, culminating in the Foreign Missions Conference of North America (1893), the Edinburgh Conference (1910), and the International Missionary Council (1921), together with the increasing support by American Catholics of the world-wide Catholic Missions, have succeeded in making missionary activities more orderly, constructive, and intelligent, without diminishing the traditional sentimental interest among laymen, on which the support of the foreign fields ultimately rests. But both the highly institutionalized work of the mission boards and the sentimental religious enthusiasm for missions have undergone several serious crises during the last two decades.

The first crisis came in 1920. The missionary enthusiasm and the centralized planning based upon it reached a dramatic climax in the Interchurch World Movement (1919–1920). American religious leaders who had helped to promote World War I and who had become familiar with the techniques of floating war loans met late in 1918 in order to harness the moral and financial resources of the country toward more constructive goals. Under Methodist leadership a large number of denominational "world movements" were consolidated and in 1919 an ambitious campaign was launched in behalf of the Interchurch World Movement as a "cooperative effort of the missionary, educational, and other benevolent agencies of the evangelical churches of the United States and of Canada to survey unitedly their present common tasks and simultaneously and together to secure the necessary resources of men and money and power required for these tasks." [13]

The purposes of the Interchurch World Movement were announced in the form of an ambitious and expensive plan.[14] (See Exhibit V.) Elaborate offices were set up and the work of the Protestant churches was organized as a big business. Hardly was the campaign launched when the reaction against wartime drives hit it, and bankrupted it. Another factor in its sudden collapse was that one of its committees, under the chairmanship of Bishop Francis J. McConnell, published a much publicized report on the steel strike of 1919, which was definitely pro-labor; such "world" work had not been anticipated by some of the heaviest subscribers to the campaign!

However, the normal programs of the mission boards continued to expand under the joint stimulus of liberalism and social service. Serious financial difficulties arose even before the Depression, when financial support failed to keep pace with missionary zeal. The basic issues were discussed at the Jerusalem Congress of 1928, when several important policy decisions were made. In view of the common enemy of "secularism," Christians were asked to appeal to members of other religions as to allies in a common cause, without denying the "uniqueness" and truth of Christianity. Missions to Jews were to be discontinued entirely in favor of inter-faith organizations which were seeking to promote friendly relations. In general, "civilizing" missions were to take the place of "evangelizing" missions. This typically liberalist attitude toward the mission field led to an expansion of educational, medical, rural, and industrial services in the Orient. But the Conservatives feared the abandonment of evangelical Christianity completely and made energetic protests. In 1930 a group of laymen, under the instigation and with the help of John D. Rockefeller, organized a Laymen's Foreign Missionary Inquiry, which sent several commissions of experts into the major mission fields to find out what was really worth supporting in foreign missions. The fact finders' reports were submitted to a Commission of Appraisal, under the chairmanship of Professor William Ernest Hocking of Harvard, and its report, published in 1932 and entitled *Rethinking Missions*, was a thoroughgoing vindication of the liberal point of view. (See Exhibit VI.)

There has been a vigorous debate about this policy, especially since a neo-evangelism has been championed by European Barthians who are convinced that America is hopelessly "activistic." More effective in practice in reconstructing missionary methods were the attempts on the part of American leaders in the field to adapt Oriental religious practices (like the Hindu *ashram* and meditation generally) to Christian evangelism. A mediating position is suggested by John C. Bennett:

Social teachings alone will not usually convert people to the Christian gospel. But the impression that Christianity is socially irrelevant can keep them away. In the next period Christianity may win many souls because it is both this worldly and other-worldly, because it meets the deepest inner needs at the same time that it stimulates people to change social conditions, because it provides a radical diagnosis of life that cuts through the illusions of both economic individualism and Communism. My chief reason for stressing evangelism is my conviction that within the past twenty years there has developed in the Churches which have a background of theological liberalism a surer grasp of the uniqueness of the Christian gospel. Much of the contemporary missionary work was originally inspired by a type of theology that had lost to some degree this sense of the uniqueness and irreplaceable character of Christianity.[15]

Professor Bennett seems here to be hoping that Christianity will be more "unique" than it has been in providing a "radical diagnosis" of "economic individualism and Communism."

World War II produced the most serious crisis for missionary institutions, and it might have been even more disastrous had not the above-mentioned developments prepared the ground for a new attitude toward oriental religions and cultures. The War gave to the general public some elementary information about the Orient, which undermined much of its sentimental feeling toward the "heathen" in general and which may change radically the fundamental incentives for missionary work. The rude, un-expected "meeting" of East and West in the form of hand-to-hand conflict or other brutal business, pushed the religious aspects of the missionary enterprise into the background and exaggerated the tendencies already noted before the War to give more atten-tion to secular relief, land reform, health, and education. Where all this will lead, whether to more missions or to no missions, one can scarcely even guess. But the important fact to note as already a present reality is that the whole concept of missions has under-gone radical changes, despite the continuity and integration of missionary institutions.

The most conspicuous case in point is the current reorienta-tion of Catholic missions in which American Catholics are bound to play an important role. Until recently American Catholics were preoccupied with home missions and had neither the re-sources nor the interest to support foreign missions actively. But since 1911, when the Maryknoll Fathers were founded, Catholic missionary activities have grown steadily and have grown along the general lines of Protestant missions. In 1921 the St. Columban's Foreign Mission Society opened its Seminary, and in 1943 the Academia for Mission Study provided a program of mission instruction in all Catholic Seminaries. The chief Catholic mission fields of American interest are Japan, China, the Philippines, and

South America. The relations between the Catholic and the
Protestant mission boards and missionaries are notoriously
friendly! On the whole, Catholics have continued to place more
emphasis on conversion to Christianity, as the Protestants did
before the advent of liberalism. Catholic methods are somewhat
different — less reliance on preaching and education, more on
works of charity such as orphanages and famine relief. But the
circumstances created by the War have induced Catholics to con-
centrate their efforts not on other religions but on the forces of
"irreligion" and atheism, that is, on Communism, regarding the
saving of the world from such godlessness as its primary present
task. Protestants are not apt to follow this lead wholeheartedly;
and yet they, too, are forced to revise their missionary programs
radically in order to adapt them to the new political situation, and
to the spread of the "secularist" spirit in the Orient.

The immediate effect of the need for rethinking foreign
missions has been to draw attention to home missions. But in this
field, too, though less dramatically, a complete reorientation has
taken place during the half century. Whereas the missions among
"foreigners at home" (work among Indians, immigrants, isolated
mountain areas, churchless communities) used to be regarded as
primary, such activities are now coördinated with, if not subordinated to, a broader program of "social-welfare" or what is
known professionally as "social work." The conception of social
work itself has expanded to include much more than elementary
charities and health services. As a result a complete urban parish
is not only itself an "institutionalized church" (having trained,
salaried social workers) but it coöperates with secular local
welfare work and with large-scale national agencies. These
agencies have been compelled by circumstances to subordinate
traditional philanthropies to the study and solving of problems
of labor, legislation, international relations, and other matters
which a half-century ago were generally regarded as at most
incidental to the work of religious bodies.

All these developments suggest, though they may not prove,
that along with the thorough institutionalization of missions
the very nature of the missionary enterprise has been transformed.
Christian missionaries have not brought the world to Christ, but

they have brought Christianity to the world; they have served humanity in many ways and have contributed more than their share of the world's work. A typical missionary today has, as he always has had, the spirit of religious devotion to the salvation of mankind, but he shows this devotion by being of genuine service as a worker. He may be a teacher, physician, nurse, agricultural expert, or labor leader; even as a clergyman (and clergymen now constitute a minority among missionaries) he is much more engaged in "ministering" than in preaching; that is, he serves men in ways which even non-Christians must admit to be useful. Thus institutional religion has justified itself even to a hostile world in practice far beyond its *propaganda fidei* in doctrine, for there are few institutions today that cultivate practical fidelity to mankind as a whole.

The most ironical and spectacular development has overtaken American Judaism. For Judaism, which never believed in missions, and whose social work has traditionally been local and secular, now finds itself with the most sensational of all mission fields, the homeland of Israel, and with a strong urge toward investing in it as the Jewish nation's most basic and common cause. The effort on the part of extreme Zionists to "Israelize all Judaism" is visionary, to say the least, for the majority of American Jews will certainly maintain their double loyalty and not regard themselves as in exile, except for technical theological purposes. But for some time to come American and Israeli leaders will probably regard each other as reciprocal mission fields.

Ecumenical Trends

It is a commonplace observation among European religious leaders that Americans are more eager to promote unity in work and service than unity in "faith and order." The general program which more than anything else has fired the imaginations and efforts of Protestant leaders during the twentieth century has been to coördinate and federate the work of all churches, while preserving their independence and diversity in faith and worship. During the early years of the century there was a concerted attack against "denominationalism" as such, in the interest of church unity. In fact several important denominations united, but they united into *stronger denominations*. The separate churches, though they have consolidated here and there, have maintained their historic identities fairly well even when their character ceases to be what it was traditionally. There remain about 250 independent religious bodies in the United States, but only 54 churches report more than a 50,000 membership, and only 14 a membership of more than 1,000,000. These bodies in order are: Roman Catholic; Methodist; Southern Baptist; National Baptist Convention, USA; National Baptist Convention of America; Presbyterian Church in the USA; Protestant Episcopal; United Lutheran Church in America; Disciples of Christ; Northern Baptist Convention; Evangelical Lutheran Synod of Ohio and other states; Congregational Christian; African Methodist Episcopal; Church of Jesus Christ of Latter Day Saints. The Jewish congregations in the United States number about four and a half million, though this figure probably includes many Jews who are not Judaists.

The attempt to unite all Christian groups organically has been practically abandoned. Especially the lines between Catholicism, Protestantism, and Judaism are now fairly well established and the three groups have settled down to programs of coöperation without attempting conversion. The chief object of coöperation now is the attempt to end hostilities, but more positive areas of common interest are beginning to take shape, as they combat the growth of "secularism."

Within each of these three major religious groups there have been notable gains in institutional consolidation. Among Jews the traditional lines between Orthodox, Conservative, and Reform are beginning to weaken, chiefly because of the common problems created for all Jews by the Nazi persecutions and by the creation of the Homeland of Israel. These circumstances have led to the rapid growth of a double nationalism in American Judaism: emphasis on the religion of Israel as the nation's historic faith; and emphasis on the American leadership of Jews who are American born. Though this has played into the hands of the Conservative group, it has at the same time compelled them to seek a conciliatory position which might serve as a practical unifying basis for the whole American community of religious

Jews. The recent attempt to unite all groups of rabbis into the Synagogue Council of America has met with little success, however. Perhaps even more significant is the fact that the rabbis and their three national organizations have been coöperating with various nation-wide organizations of Jewish laymen across the traditional lines in the meeting of their common needs (such as the American Jewish Congress and the American Jewish Committee).

The Roman Catholic Church is, of course, an organic unity, and yet American Catholics have greatly integrated on a national scale the work of the church, which formerly was conducted either locally or internationally. The National Catholic Welfare Conference (created in 1919) through its several departments is one of the most powerful and active of such agencies. But there are many others, usually for fairly specific purposes, such as the Catholic Interracial Council, the Catholic Association for International Peace, the Federation of Catholic College Students, the Catholic Rural Life Conferences, and the Association of Catholic Trade Unionists. Such bodies testify both to the increased scope of Catholic action, and to the increased professionalization of its workers.

Attempts on the part of Roman Catholics to promote an informal (nonecclesiastical) type of fellowship beyond the borders of Catholic unity have been halfhearted or else discouraging. Intellectual contacts between Thomists and secular philosophers have increased notably (though less than in Europe), and on the whole it is easier for Catholics to enter into friendly exchanges with secular groups or with Judaism, than with Protestants or Eastern Orthodox groups. For with fellow Christians there is always the temptation to seek the kind of fellowship which implies communion or membership in the mystical body of Christ, and there is no obstacle in Catholic doctrine against entering into such communion despite the variety of rites among the churches, provided the diversity does not affect "the substance of the worship instituted by Christ." But the question of the "substance" of the faith immediately raises the whole question of sacramental legitimacy and apostolic authority, which prevents anything that might reasonably be called "unity."

The Protestant churches present the greatest problem and have made the most determined effort to promote unification of work. There are many nondenominational Protestant bodies, such as the YMCA, the YWCA, the Student Volunteer Movement, the Sunday School Union, the Christian Endeavor Movement, and the WCTU, which antedate the century, and which helped greatly to pave the way for interdenominational official federations. The mission boards and religious education councils, mentioned above, were the leaders in promoting federated work. Two types of local union also were very influential: (1) urban or state-wide federations of churches; and (2) community churches, either nondenominational or interdenominational.

The nation-wide movement for coöperation took shape in 1908 with the formation of the Federal Council of the Churches of Christ in America, which grew steadily in size, scope, and power. It represented about 75 per cent of the Protestant church membership, and after its extension in 1950 into the National Council of Churches it now embraces practically the whole of Protestantism.

The period of the First World War and the first attempts at dealing with industrial relations proved to be stormy and highly experimental. But in 1932, on the basis of its first two decades of experience, the Federal Council reorganized and revised its constitutions for the purpose of better integrating its activities and better defining its responsibilities. It cut loose from all local federations, it protected the independent action of member denominations by no longer professing to "represent" officially the views and policies of the denominations. At the same time it gave greater stability and definiteness to its Commissions and increased its staff of experts. Apart from the carrying on of all kinds of investigations, social work, and missions, one great achievement of these organs of coöperation has been the working out in detail of principles of comity among the churches.

By 1938 the Federal Council had an annual budget of over $250,000, only one-fourth of which came from the membership directly; the remainder was raised for specific projects from various sources. Its most active committees or commissions, as they were called, were: on Councils of the Churches, on Evangelism and Life Service, on Social Service, on International Justice and

Goodwill, on Race Relations, on Temperance, and on Christian Education. Especially active was the Department of Research and Education under the leadership of F. Ernest Johnson. The work of the Federal Council was enormously increased in 1941 when it federated loosely with the Home Missions Council, the Foreign Missions Conference, the Missionary Education Movement, the National Council of Church Women, the United Stewardship Council, and the International Council of Religious Education. After ten years of intensive coöperation among the eight inter-denominational agencies, this union led to the establishment in Cleveland, on November 28, 1950, of the National Council of Churches of Christ. (See Exhibit A.) The work of the Council is organized into four Divisions: Life and Work (the former Federal Council), Foreign Missions, Home Missions, Christian Education.

The growth of the Ecumenical Movement among Protestants and the series of international conferences designed to bring about a "reunion of Christendom," should not be interpreted as having undermined the diversified religious bodies of America. Though there have been a few mergers, the general denomina-tional structure is stronger than ever. The attacks on sectarianism may have created more friendly relations, but the denominations remain basic among American religious institutions, so much so, that even those churches which most insist on the necessity of unity really serve to add one more complication in our religious pluralism. Dean Sperry states the situation admirably:

Our American denominations are denied either the complacent voice of authority or the strident note of dissent. . . . Without forfeit-ing the truth of his own native insight every churchman ought to be willing to concede the possible validity of the position of the party of the other part. The practical difficulty is that few persons seem able to do so without feeling that they have turned state's evidence against their own convictions. . . . Nothing will be gained by genial indifferentism. By virtue of our denominationalism, as against a church-sect pattern for our corporate religious life, America has given the fullest and freeest opportunity for the statement of the problem.[16]

But it still remains to be seen whether the major religious bodies will agree to live and let live on the basis of what Dean Sperry calls "American denominationalism." It is no secret that

Protestant Ecumenicalism is a challenge to Catholicism and that the tension between both wings of Christianity is growing as each feels strength in unity. So long as all religious bodies can join in attacking Communistic atheism and liberalistic secularism they may subordinate their religious differences and seem to represent the forces of righteousness. But it is possible (scarcely probable) that in the United States the religious wars may be renewed and that there will again come an appeal, as it came during the days of the Founding Fathers, for a secular form of reasonable liberty, equality, and fraternity.

Meanwhile, ecumenical Protestants and Roman Catholics are inclined to accept religious differences without cultivating either sectarianism or conformity. Protestantism is now more than Protestant or anti-Catholic in spirit and in doctrine. It has realized the need for united action on public issues; in this respect it is both following and fighting the Roman Catholic model of ecclesiastical power. The Protestant churches have a double incentive to federation: they are jealous of their majority status as a religious tradition in American life and cannot afford to let a well unified minority exercise an authoritative role in matters of "public decency," sexual morality, international relations, labor movements, and politics generally. If they were secure, they might prefer *not* to present a common front, but with the rising opposition, both secular and ecclesiastical, they sense the practical need of drawing together. Thus, like all other institutions, the federation of churches is a compound of fear, courage, and work. The program of work dominated its early life, but the program of conflict seems to be inevitable and increasing.

We should note that a kind of federal spirit has come over even those sectarian and fundamentalist churches which have refused to enter into the ecumenical fellowship. Prominent among such interdenominational agencies is the American Council of Christian Churches which was founded in 1941 to "offset the modernist, socialistic influence" of the Federal Council of Churches, and the Inter-Varsity Fellowship, a Fundamentalist organization among college students.

The Religious Press

No more striking index to the change that has come over religion can be found than the contrast between "religious literature" (especially periodical literature) as it existed in 1900 and as it exists today. Though the circulation of religious magazines has increased steadily, it has decreased relatively, compared with the growth of secular magazines.[17] One investigator, Professor A. McClung Lee, estimates that "rather than reaching three-fourths of America's reading public as it did a century ago, the church presses' impact — in terms of copies published — is now probably somewhere near one-tenth that of the secular daily press." [18] But more significant than the relative quantitative decrease of religious literature, is the extent to which the content of religious publications has been revolutionized. The Methodist *Christian Advocate* (the largest Protestant weekly, with a circulation of over 340,000) and the *Christian Herald* (approximately the same size) contain at least three times as much secular journalism now as they did in 1900; and *Extension*, a leading Catholic periodical (434,000 monthly), in the words of Professor Lee, "resembles the secular *Saturday Evening Post* in both make-up and content." [19] Even more spectacular are such publications as *Commonweal*, *America*, *The Christian Century*, *Christianity and Society*, which are widely read in religious circles for their political and social news and comment. And most conspicuous of all is the *Christian Science Monitor*, which has set a high standard for all journalism. In short, the churches have journals and journalists competing actively with secular periodicals by discussing the world's affairs — religiously, perhaps — but the interest to which they appeal is radically different from the kind of interest in "elevating," devotional, homiletical, and exegetical literature which dominated the religious press fifty years ago. And this shift of interest is not a shift from clergy to laymen, for the clergy themselves have taken the lead in making this shift.

Religious Lobbies

It goes without saying that the American people's vested interest in religion would be ineffective in democratic politics if it were not organized as a pressure group for political influence.

Public hearings imply public expression, which in turn implies agencies competent to compete with other interests. The progress of religious bodies as national pressure groups has been notable during the last thirty years. Religious organizations for particular objectives are more than a century old; among the early ecclesiastical attempts to sponsor legislation were the antislavery crusades, temperance leagues, and peace organizations. But recently there have developed standing lobbies with two major functions: to guard and promote the legal interests of religious bodies, and to add a religious sanction to those legislative efforts which affect the consciences and ideals of church members. Of the first kind are offices which limit their business to protecting the interests of particular groups, such as the service boards for conscientious objectors, the Christian Science Committee on Publication, several Jewish councils, foreign missions committees, Protestants and Other Americans United for Separation of Church and State, and so on. Of the second kind are the more general agencies for influencing legislation on a large variety of social problems; these are here of special interest as twentieth-century creations.

The first major lobby was formed by the National Catholic Welfare Conference and began to work in the early 1920's, following the work of the National Catholic War Council (1917–1919) whose purposes were restricted to activities incidental to the First World War, and coöperating with the older National Conference of Catholic Charities. Not only the Legal Department but all of the departments of the National Catholic Welfare Conference are organized for political action and, with their Washington staff of about two hundred and fifty persons, make it possible for the bishops, under whose direct control the Conference operates, to bring legislative pressure wherever desired promptly and systematically.

At about the same time that the Catholics were organizing for social action, the Methodists were expanding the activities of the Washington office of their Board of Temperance, which led the campaign for the Eighteenth Amendment, into a general effort to "crystallize opposition to all public violations of the moral law." It now has a staff of about twenty-five members which coöperates with the staff of the Washington office of the Methodist Foreign Missions Board. Together they seek actively to suppress "salacious and corrupting literature and degrading amusements, lotteries, and other forms of gambling," to promote the Christianizing of international relations, and to improve public morals generally.

The chief interdenominational Protestant agency is the Washington office, established in 1945, by the Federal Council of Churches, which now reports to the National Council pending legislation and "proper channels for contacts in Washington." According to Professor Ebersole's summary,

More than sixty resolutions and statements were passed between March 1944 and March 1948 by the Council or by the executive committee. These statements cover a wide variety of topics including trade agreements, separation of church and state, emergency overseas relief, commendation for the investigation of charges against Senator Bilbo, prisoners of war, payment of claims to Japanese Americans, income tax, displaced persons, aid to Greece and Turkey, full employment, Federal aid to education, civil rights, census of religious bodies, Bretton Woods and food and agriculture, United Nations, etc.[20]

Rival spokesmen for Protestants are the National Church League of America, The National Association of Evangelicals, and the American Council of Christian Churches, a fundamentalist organization.

Religious lobbies, of course, frequently coöperate and join with secular lobbies in promoting common causes. And they use practically all the methods used by lobbies generally to influence legislation.

Summary

Perhaps more than enough has now been said to indicate the extent to which religious life and work has been organized or institutionalized during the first half of our century, and we might now summarize the chief generalizations which this survey suggests.

(1) Religion, whatever else it may be, is one of America's biggest businesses. Technically it is nonprofit business — philanthropic. But it represents an enormous investment of capital and

labor for services which are generally recognized as useful, which parallel many secular organizations, and which are conducted by technically trained professionals, of whom a majority are laymen. It owns extensive properties and tries increasingly to administer them in a businesslike way.

(2) Though competition among religious bodies is by no means a thing of the past, the primary objectives of this religious activity are now not so much directed against the religions but against secular evils and social problems. That is, the churches are much more than agencies of public worship; they are at work, and at work in the secular sense. Such work or "ministry" is regarded by the churches as essentially religious. In other words, institutional religion of this type is the opposite of monasticism; it compels persons who wish to lead a religious, consecrated life to live it in the thick of the world's work. Such religion can hardly be interpreted as a retreat from the world, as an escape mechanism, as infantilism, or as an opiate. It keeps millions of persons busy; and whereas there is always in such busy-ness a certain amount of busy-body-ness, waste motion, and specula-tion, there seems to be little more of such idle activity in religion than in other forms of business.

(3) Religion is a pervasive institution. It gets mixed up with education, medicine, politics, business, art — there is nothing free from its grasp and grasping. All efforts to fence off certain areas of life from which the churches must "keep out" have been as futile as similar efforts to curtail government or science. Anything can be done religiously, and nothing is safe from ecclesiastical concern. Gone are the days when the salvation of the soul was a distinct and separate business. The separation of church and state does not separate religion and politics, any more than the separation of school and theater separates educa-tion and art. There are certain institutions, among them those of religion, government, education, and art, which place any con-ceivable action or idea in a special context or discipline. Such pervasive institutions form the basic patterns of a culture and give what is called "civilized" shape to life. Religion claims, often, to take life "whole," whereas other institutions are "partial." This may well be doubted. But certainly religion like government,

now, more than in our recent past, affects or seeks to affect the whole of life. It is true that religion is not as central to our civilization as its professional devotees would like to have it be, but it is pervasive, reaching all classes and affecting all our interests and arts.

3.

MORAL RECONSTRUCTION

The Religious Conscience at Work

Before examining the basic changes in America's religious conscience, let us consider the changes which have come over the methods by which religious bodies exercise their moral power. The traditional methods, which in 1900 were still prevalent, depended on a close coöperation between home and clergy and were focused on the elementary educational problem of giving definite form to a child's "knowledge of good and evil," giving emotional appeal to religious sanctions, and instilling the *fear* of God into the young until divine grace converted the will from its natural corruption to its regenerate *love* of God. This process of creating a childlike trust and love of God and of divine law in the individual soul implied a system of habitual religious observances in the home, a system of catechetical instruction by a priest, minister, or rabbi, an initiation rite into a religious communion, and a periodical evangelical appeal to the member's integrity by rites of confession, conversion, penitence, and assurance of divine grace. This general pattern of shaping a religious conscience has been followed by peoples in all ages and places.

If there was anything distinctive in the American pattern early in the century, it was the concentration of religious educators on the period of adolescence. The domestic rites were already being widely neglected, the clerical instruction of children was becoming increasingly perfunctory and abbreviated; but from first communion, confirmation, or bar mizvath up to adulthood, the youth of the land were subjected to intense, emotional appeals. Youth organizations are easy to foster, since adolescents will band together for anything or nothing; once banded together,

they can readily be won for a cause, especially if they are appealed
to by the motives of devotion, self-sacrifice, loyalty, and love.
The forces of organized religion, feeling their controls over
childhood slipping somewhat, exploited to the full their opportunities to control youth. All sorts of young people's religious
societies (some of which have been mentioned in the previous
chapter) flourished, and in addition to the general societies
there were special groups, where religious appeals were most
intense, such as Student Volunteer Bands for foreign missions.

As this traditional and orthodox discipline was gradually transformed among the liberal or modern religious bodies into "religious education" and put on a basis of normal growth or
"nurture," religious morality was gradually shifted from conversion to the adult religious life after conversion. Thus there arose
during the twentieth century among religious bodies special
organizations of adults to meet special moral and social problems,
and these organizations, though they approached problems from
the point of view of a religious conscience, coöperated increasingly in methods and contents with secular philanthropic organizations. This involved a shift of emphasis from the religious
problem of cultivating a sense of right and wrong, to the practical
discussion of particular moral issues on which there were serious
differences not only of opinion but even of conviction. And this
shift of content carried with it a shift from catechism to discussion, from ten commandments to critical debate, and from evangelistic appeals to social propaganda, from revivals to lobbies.
Theoretically, of course, the churches can be both traditional
and modern, and in practice, too, the traditional religious disciplin-
ing of children and youth goes on, and conversions are not un-
heard of; but the characteristic efforts and current aims of
organized religion are now closer to secular education and
mundane affairs. It is by no means as easy today to discern and
preach "the will of God" in concrete moral issues as it was fifty
years ago. Morality itself is now problematic, and the easy reliance
on the Ten Commandments and the Golden Rule is gone for both
religion and morals. Whether it be rational or not, religious
ethics is now more reasoning. Thus both in method and content
religious conscience has undergone a radical reconstruction, which

has brought it closer to the issues of social morality and has entangled the salvation of the soul in the affairs of the world. Let us now examine the chief phases of this reconstruction, beginning with those which are most closely related to the individualistic charity and philanthropy of the preceding centuries.

Religious Social Agencies

The Salvation Army, both in name and appearance, came to us from the nineteenth century. It arrived in the United States from England two decades before the twentieth century and was first known popularly as an adjunct of "Bowery Missions," feeding and housing the bodies of derelicts as a prelude to winning their souls; its street-corner meetings are a quaint vestige of the revivalistic methods. It professes to be "an evangelical organization."

Its spiritual purpose is paramount. Founded originally for the religious enlightenment of the masses, its primary and persistent aim still is to proclaim and exemplify, through song, word and deed, the regenerating revitalizing message of the Scriptures. The Social Service Work is supplementary." [1]

But it has become a big philanthropic corporation, making itself useful and respected in a score of different ways, and getting much public support with or without a community chest. During the wars it was a major service institution for both soldiers and civilians. It now runs secondhand stores, hotels, employment bureaus, farm colonies, homes for workers and children, day nurseries, boys' clubs, women's "home leagues," programs of restoration of prisoners to civilian life, slum resettlements, etc. Thus it supplements in helpful and constructive fashion the social work conducted by public authorities and private social agencies. Hence, what is more significant than its "evangelical" motivation, is its practical principle, namely:

Christianity is considered synonymous with service. A person may attend meetings on Sundays, but if he is not willing to demonstrate his faith in the form of tangible helpfulness to others, or to the organization as a whole, he is not regarded as a good soldier . . . Therefore, it [the Salvation Army] wants its welfare service recognized, not merely as the doling of alms, in response to a sentimental impulse, but as Love in Motion, Christianity in Action. . . . The Salvation Army aims at the permanent regeneration of the "whole man." [2]

In theory, its concept of salvation is evangelical; in practice, it is thoroughly social, and operates on the general principle of "good-will industry." In many American cities, the churches, imitating the practical sense of the Salvation Army, have established branches of Good-will Industries, an organization which combines rummage sales and secondhand stores with home missions.

The YMCA and the YWCA have grown during the twentieth century from being religious clubs for youth to general community organizations, serving the needs of all ages and classes. They provide hotels, gymnasia, courses of instruction, lectures, concerts, forums, and summer camps. They have strong organizations in the foreign mission fields, on college campuses, and at army posts. Wherever they operate they carry on specifically religious services, but in practically all instances these are much less conspicuous than their secular services. And, what is perhaps even more significant, they resent any sharp distinction between the two kinds of service. A similar story could be told of the growth of YMHA's and YWHA's as Jewish community centers. The Catholic youth organizations carry on a great variety of activities and services which are religious only indirectly insofar as they broaden the appeal and work of the church.

A Series of Crusades

Everyone knows the recent dramatic career of our religious "temperance" drives. For at least half a century the National Temperance Society, the WCTU, the Anti-Saloon League, and the Prohibition Party, all of them begun and sponsored by religious groups, kept up a steady campaign which has aimed at the abolition of saloons, and which owed its chief successes to local prohibition or "local option" at town and county elections. These victories at the polls were made possible by a continual temperance propaganda carried on within the churches and by occasional public demonstrations against saloons. In practice, the antidrunkenness crusade, which was of long standing, became identified during the twentieth century with "dry" legislation and the attempt to abolish all alcoholic beverages. Between 1907 and 1917 the growth of "dry" sentiment and voting power made it possible to proceed to Prohibition by states, so that almost three-fourths

of the states became "dry" during this decade, the movement
being strongest in the West and South. Taking advantage of this
fact, and of the War Emergency, the Prohibition forces, operating as lobbies, pushed through the Eighteenth Amendment to the
Federal Constitution in 1917, which was not repealed until 1933.
It is the period since the Prohibition victory of 1917 and especially since its defeat of 1933 that has produced the most profound changes in the religious approach to all moral problems,
including temperance. In the first place, those religious bodies and
communities which were wholeheartedly behind the Prohibition
drive are now divided on this issue. In the second place, the experience has produced a general disillusionment in the efficacy of
moralistic legislation and in the moral value of compulsory prohibitions. In the third place, it has related the problem of temperance, which had been isolated, to other moral ideals, especially
those of freedom, education, responsibility, integrity, respect for
law. As a result, not only temperance, but the virtues in general
are given a more realistic and relativistic consideration than the
previous religious absolutism in morals had permitted. The former
attitude of absolutism, which is now popularly labeled "idealism,"
and which was the practical implication of the belief that morals
is the warfare between good and evil powers, is giving way gradually to a greater willingness to deal practically rather than militantly with particular moral problems. Not that most religious
persons would be willing, as a matter of theory, to give up their
belief in the "warfare'" theory of morals nor admit the ethics of
compromise; but in practice they are more concerned with problems of "strategy" than with attitudes of condemnation. Thus
many religious persons were as susceptible as secular moralists
were to the arguments of the "wets" that drinking could be reformed by changing saloons into liquor-selling restaurants or
"taverns," and that taxation might discourage those whom Prohibition did not deter. They were thus reconciled to accepting
"Repeal" not as temporary defeat, but as a new beginning of an
entirely different kind of campaign for temperance. A larger
minority of religious laymen and clergymen are now willing to
consider temperance in the Aristotelian fashion of eating-and-
drinking-well, that is, of civilizing our habits, but the majority

still hope to destroy not only alcoholism but alcohol, as the only tenable moral ideal. Meanwhile many religious leaders are study-ing the semireligious techniques of such groups as Alcoholics Anonymous and the possibilities of making religious fellowship more attractive than convivial fellowship. In any case, the dis-couragement and righteous indignation produced among religious leaders by the failure of national Prohibition have already given way to a more sober study of how to promote sobriety.

The career of the various efforts to promote world peace points a similar moral, though it is more complicated. Two religious antiwar efforts are of long standing and have continued to play significant roles during this century as well: one is conscientious objection to acts of violence; and the other is interchurch societies for promoting pacific international relations. The conscientious objectors were, until the last two decades, confined largely to those religious bodies who make it a part of their corporate re-ligious duty to refuse to bear arms. Chief among these in the United States are The Society of Friends (Quakers), the Mo-ravians, the Mennonites, the Dunkers and Schwenkfelders, Je-hovah's Witnesses (Russellite Millennialists). Probably the Fellowship of Reconciliation should be included here, for, though it is an interdenominational body, it is specifically devoted to absolute pacifism or nonviolence ("non-violent non-cooperation with the enemy"). The Vedanta Missions, together with the per-sonal influence of Mahatma Gandhi, also strengthened the faith in "harmlessness" and "soul-force" as remedies for violence, though not (curiously enough) among theosophists.

During World War I these conscientious objectors were given some legal protection and consideration; but the unfortunate cir-cumstance that several of these bodies were mostly German mili-tated against them. "Conscientious" objectors who were not mem-bers of such bodies but who as individuals had religious scruples against bearing arms received no consideration whatsoever; on the contrary, they were vilified. But after the War and its after-math, and especially after the forceful publicity given to the workings of the international armament ring or cartel, religious pacifism became widespread. As a result, conscientious objectors were numerous in all churches, and many leading church bodies officially condemned war in general as a sin and adopted other pacifist and "conscientious isolationist" policies. When the United States entered World War II, the government was obliged to extend much more generous treatment to, and give a broader definition of, conscientious objectors. The requirement of church membership was dropped in the Selective Service Act of 1940, and conscientious objectors were respected as such if they opposed "participation in war in any form" and if such opposition was based on "religious training and belief." Of the seven thousand pacifists in the Civilian Public Service Camps and Units, only two-thirds came from the historic "peace churches." In fact, one reason for the decline of the Quakers in the Middle West was the spread of pacifism among the Methodists and other Protestant churches which had never taken a corporate pacifist stand. About 8 per cent in the Civilian Camps were Methodists, 3 per cent Jehovah's Witnesses, and 6 per cent had no church affiliation whatsoever. It is significant that the Friends were relatively ready to coöperate with the War effort, mostly in civilian services, but some were even willing to bear arms. Most important was a group of influential ministers, who had agreed never again to "bless" a war, and who stood by their position throughout the conflict.

In general, then, the question of the "sinfulness" of war became a vital and personal moral problem for a whole generation of American Protestants. For Catholics and Jews it involved no such moral struggle, since only a negligible per cent were pacifists. American Catholic leaders, even during the Spanish-American War, have been eagerly patriotic ("for God and country") and have supported war efforts conscientiously, even when their political convictions were isolationist. American Jews during the First War fought as American citizens for whom democracy was a religious tradition, and during the Second War both as Americans and as Jews who had a special interest and obligation in helping to end the Hitler terror. An intense moral struggle has become increasingly evident in those Protestant consciences which have made the most determined effort to reconcile a Christian pacifist absolutism with democratic civic morality. After so many Christian ministers during the First War had followed their Presbyterian President, Woodrow Wilson, in regarding the fight for "making the world safe for democracy" a holy cause and a moral crusade, and after their bitter disappointment and disillusionment at the failure of their fight, a wave of humiliation, repentance, and dedication swept the Protestant ranks. This resentment against the "war machine" reached its height about 1930, when the exposure of an international munitions cartel led directly to the legislation for American neutrality. Never again would they regard war as holy! And yet the Second World War was eventually (after a struggle) accepted by the majority of Protestants as a sacred duty. Very few indeed in the summer of 1941 were willing to agree with the Anglo-Catholic Bishop Manning of New York when he said solemnly: "Speaking as an American, as a Christian, and as a bishop of the Christian church, I say that it is our duty as a Nation to take full part in this struggle." [3] Even among Episcopalians such a statement was shocking, and most Protestants thought it blasphemous; and yet a year or two later the majority were in substantial agreement with him. Only a few kept up the inner struggle as did the pacifist editor of the *Christian Century*, Clayton W. Morrison, who wrote after Pearl Harbor: "Our country is at war. Its life is at stake. . . . It is our necessity, an unnecessary necessity, therefore a guilty necessity. . . . Our fighting, though necessary, is not righteous. God does not command us to fight. His condemnation, written with our own hands, is that we must slay our human brothers and be slain by them. This condemnation, we now affirm, is hell." [4] The majority more complacently prayed with the editor of the *Living Church*: "May we seek always, not that God may be on our side, but that we may be on His side, so that the victory may in the end be His." [5] This is a prayer which is traditional among Christians, but which secular moralists must receive with a smile and a sigh.

As for the organized planning to *make* peace, the initiative toward such efforts during the nineteenth century came less from organized religious bodies than it did from the secular humanitarians, with whom individual Protestants, mostly left-wing, cooperated. But during the twentieth century the churches took an increasing interest in peace societies and in plans for building international agreements on a "just and durable" basis. During the first years of the century they organized the Lake Mohonk Conferences, the Conference of Friends, the American Association of Ministers, and other associations whose chief aim was to promote peace and arbitration. They supported enthusiastically the League of Nations, and in 1942, at Delaware, Ohio, they drafted an influential statement on "The Basis of a Just and Durable Peace," which was one of the steps leading toward the founding of the United Nations. Catholics and Protestants have joined Jewish leaders in formulating and promoting the *Declaration of the Rights of Man*. In general, the religious forces of the land have taken an increasingly practical and political interest in the problems of peace and war, coöperating with secular agencies in a spirit of realistic planning for peace, even by means of war, whether or not they can reconcile themselves theologically to pragmatic tactics.

While Protestants have been preoccupied with the moral problems of temperance and peace, the Catholics have concentrated their attention on problems of sexual morality, on "public decency," and on "saving the family." The public-decency campaign, which in 1934 created the National Legion of Decency, centers on the theater and the motion pictures. By local political pressure and by a standing censorship in Hollywood, the Catholic Church (usually with the "benevolent neutrality" of other religious bodies) prevents not only gross obscenity on stage and screen, but obstructs as far as it can prudently the presentation of anticlerical plays or anything that may offend the religious sensibilities. Blasphemy, for example, is regarded as immoral not only on stage and screen, but even in literature and journalism. Even philosophical atheism and political atheism are persecuted on the grounds that religion as such deserves public protection, and therefore radical "secularism" is supposed to be immoral as well as antireligious. Though other religious groups, especially some Jews and all Humanists, have openly repudiated such attacks on antitheistic thought and action, the great majority of Christians and Jews are willing to make common cause against their chief enemy, on the general supposition that morality needs religious support. On such grounds Catholic authorities justify their attempts to exclude certain anti-Catholic books from public libraries and schools, and, in theory at least, they would regard the censorship of "false" religion as a public service, much as some Protestants believe that the Catholic Church is a *public* "menace." Jews, on the other hand, censor even secular or public anti-Semitism on the grounds that it is *religious* persecution. But on the whole the lesser faiths, when they attack each other, do so on religious grounds, not on grounds of public decency. The Publication Committees of the Christian Science Church, for example, which exercise constant vigilance and make frequent attempts at private censorship, do so frankly to prevent what they regard as misrepresentations of Christian Science. But the more powerful a faith becomes, the more ready it is to identify its cause with the public welfare. The great Christian churches are, therefore, in a most serious and difficult moral situation. They evidently perform many public services and enjoy a general support, and hence they naturally come to believe in their indispensability. And, since no one can prove them to be merely private interests, they are naturally tempted to identify their own welfare with public decency and order. This all too human foible, which can be overcome only by supernatural grace, makes it necessary in contemporary morality to seek a clearer understanding and observance of the relation of religious faiths to public decency. Neither dogmatic identification nor dogmatic separation is as convincing as it used to be.

Similarly, the conflict on questions of sexual morality, birth-control, and divorce have raised in a serious way the general question of the relations between medical problems of physical and mental health, and the moral problems which are conventionally associated with religion. The Catholic position is dogmatic and clear: any moral issue needs the guidance of religious authority. Since the Church has officially recognized all problems of passion (especially "lust"), of marriage, of reproduction as moral problems, since it tries to regulate them by its system of confessions and penances, it makes authoritative pronouncements from time to time for the guidance of "cases of conscience." The Papal pronouncement of 1951 on the morals governing certain medical decisions, especially in difficult cases of childbirth, caused widespread discussion and criticism in the United States.

In 1943 the Catholics introduced from France the Cana Conference Movement, which organizes meetings for newly married couples to discuss problems of marriage and parenthood. The substance of its advice to couples is stated officially as follows: "Mindful of the words of its patron, the Blessed Mary, at the Marriage of Cana, 'Do whatever He tells you,' this movement presents to married people the Mind of the Creator when He made man and woman and commanded them to increase and multiply." In Orthodox Judaism and Fundamentalist Christianity, the concept of moral "authority" is less precise. The liberal Protestants and Jews have had the advantages and disadvantages of flexibility. Intending to be prudent, they are conservative; and intending to lead laymen wisely, the clergy have followed other professional counselors cautiously. Accordingly they have blessed as "valid and moral" what medical men are ready to sanction as prudent. There has been relatively less conflict between medical moral advice and religious moral prescription among these Protestant and liberal religious circles; whereas in the Ethical Culture Societies, among Humanists, and among Reform Jews there has been a positive effort to keep up-to-date with the medical profession.

The net result of these developments has been to bring the medical profession, especially the psychiatrists, and the pastoral and priestly professions together either in explicit recognition of their common problems or in clandestine consultation. The medical men are more willing to discuss morals and to recognize the therapeutic value of certain religious disciplines, however amateurish or mythical the traditional diagnoses may have been. And the clergy are more eager to learn the elements of secular psychiatry and to use this knowledge either openly or covertly in counseling their parishioners or confessants. There is a gradual, if grudging, *rapprochement* between these two approaches to moral problems, and a gradual, if vague, recognition that most, if not all, problems of sin and salvation are also problems of health. "Salvation" has become as vague a concept as are "mental health" and "social health"; and all these concepts are more intimately related to morals and ethics than either the clerical or the psychiatric professions have been willing to admit in the past. This gradual assimilation of religious casuistry, scientific psychiatry, and secular ethics to each other, their willingness to meet each other in saving human lives and spirits in spite of their theoretical incompatibilities, is one of the major moral creations of the twentieth century.[7]

Most recent of the major moral problems to be taken seriously by religious groups is the problem of interracial relations,[8] and more particularly the problem of Negro churches and of Negroes in the churches. In 1920 the Federal Council proposed a program for "legal justice" and "applied brotherhood" toward Negroes; it condemned ideas of racial superiority, and gradually included in its program legislation against lynching and racial discrimination. For the large Protestant denominations, which were seeking closer union between Northern and Southern branches (especially Methodists and Baptists) the race problem was embarrassing, and the Roman Catholics, too, were slow in coming to grips with the problem. But sooner or later all religious bodies were obliged to face it. In 1934 the Catholic Interracial Council and Center of New York was founded to deal with the situation in New York City. Through its publication, *The Interracial Review*, it has had a wide influence. Protestants have organized several "interracial religious fellowships" as experiments in breaking down the color line. In the case of the Negroes the religious problem is different, more complicated than the general problem of racial prejudices and barriers, for the Negro churches in the course of a century have developed their own types of worship and spirituality to such a degree that not only do they themselves take pride and satisfaction in their religious services, but their contribution to the spiritual life of the world and to American culture in particular is now generally recognized. It is important, therefore, not to undermine this genuine construction by using too hasty methods of breaking down segregation. Both artificial segregation and artificial unions must be avoided. It is possible, however, as recent experiments and trends show, to abolish social interracial barriers without disturbing the religious values of the Negro churches. A notable fact is the leadership that has been given by the youth of this generation in both North and South in overcoming discrimination. The change in attitude is almost revolutionary, but how much of it is due to religious motivation is difficult to tell. It is certain, however, that religious youth organizations have done intensive work. The religious aspect of relations with oriental races is different and not much progress has been made in interreligious fellowship with the Orient. However, a significant achievement of social engineering and home missions is to be credited to the churches for their care of displaced Japanese during and after World War II.

The Social Gospel

The most far-reaching and apparently permanent moral reconstruction in American religion has been the spread of the so-called "Social Gospel." It has a strong hold on Catholicism, Judaism, and the dominant groups and churches of Protestantism, and it represents the culmination of the process of reconstructing religion on the basis of social ethics, which we have been sketching, and it may appropriately be called the "religious revolution of today." The central idea is that the redemption or salvation of mankind collectively, the regeneration of the social order, is the ultimate goal of religion. This gospel, which is at least as old as utopian socialism, had several radical versions preached in America during the nineteenth century. Perhaps the most radical, theologically, was the theology of Henry James, the Elder, who, taking his doctrine from Calvinism, Fourierism, and Swedenborgianism, taught that as in Adam all men fell from God individually, so in Divine Mankind all men would be redeemed collectively. More influential among American Christians were the Writings of Elisha Mulford and the sermons of Washington Gladden. After Henry George and Edward Bellamy and the Populist Movement had created a practical interest in "social nationalism," a number of "Christian Socialists," both clergymen and laymen (including distinguished economists) gave the movement an academic foothold and a practical impetus among American Protestants before 1900. Among the most radical of the religious socialists was Henry Cheronny who in the 1880's tried to organize a "National Council of Toilers." [9]

During the first quarter of the century the Social Gospel was taught and preached by a minority in the churches and seminaries, the clergy showing much more enthusiasm for it than the laity.

And though one church vied with another in establishing central boards for social service during the first decade of the century, the activities and pronouncements of these boards found relatively little response among the local churches and the majority of the clergy. Though Pope Leo's encyclical embodying a social gospel had long been a basis for social action among European Catholics, the American clergy paid little heed to it until the bishops urged it upon them in 1919, and even then there was no general response until almost ten years later.

The first inroads on the individualistic and other-worldly conceptions of salvation were made by appealing to individual benevolence, and by representing exclusive concern with one's own salvation as spiritual selfishness. It was typical of the temper of the early twentieth century to worry more about others than about oneself. "Doing good" accordingly became the commonly recognized way of "loving God." This doctrine was notoriously the central appeal of the YMCA's, YWCA's, and other youth organizations. Even among Princeton Presbyterians, the stronghold of individualism, the change of moral atmosphere became noticeable, for example Woodrow Wilson in 1909, speaking as an influential layman to theological students, said:

> For my part, I do not see any promise of vitality either in the church or in society except upon the true basis of individualism. . . . He [the minister] must preach Christianity to men, not to society. He must preach salvation to the individual, for it is only one by one that we can love, and love is the law of life.[10]

But in 1914 he cautiously approached a social gospel to accompany his political "new freedom." Speaking to the YMCA on "Militant Christianity," he said:

> For one, I am not fond of thinking of Christianity as the means of saving *individual* souls. . . . Christ came into the world to save others, not to save himself, and no man is a true Christian who does not think constantly of how he can lift his brother, how he can enlighten mankind, how he can make virtue the rule of conduct in the circle in which he lives.[11]

But the Christian Social Gospel soon went much further than Wilson ever dreamed of going. In 1907 Professor Walter Rauschenbusch, then at the Baptist Seminary of Rochester, New York, formerly engaged in practical social work in New York City, published his *Christianity and the Social Crisis*, which kindled the religious imagination and sentiments for the social version of the gospel among the rank and file of Protestantism. By translating programs of social reform into the language of crisis and of "bringing in the Kingdom of God on earth," he succeeded in giving a new, practical content to the traditional themes of evangelism and millennialism. This gospel soon generated an apocalyptic fervor for reform. Among the twentieth-century pioneer Protestant workers, who developed the social services of the churches into something much more radical than the conventional philanthropies, should be mentioned: (1) Charles Stelzle, who as early as 1903 established the Department of Church and Labor of the Presbyterian Board of Home Missions and who waged an uphill campaign against the conservative majority in his denomination; (2) Harry F. Ward, who performed a similar service among Methodists, and who has tried to swing the churches into the politics and tactics of the Socialist Party and the Civil Liberties Union; (3) Shailer Mathews and Graham Taylor, who led the movement in Chicago both in academic circles and in practical social work; (4) F. Ernest Johnson, who guided much of the work of the Federal Council of Churches, and who helped to modernize during the thirties the now antiquated "Social Creed" published by the Federal Council in 1908; (5) Reinhold Niebuhr and his brother, H. Richard Niebuhr, who have given a more realistic and radical sociological orientation to the social gospel and have tried to free it of the taint of bourgeois liberalism. By the work of these, and a score of other leaders, not only the central administrative boards and agencies of the big churches, but the rank and file of the clergy have been enlisted in the cause of "Christianizing the social order."

In their Pittsburgh Platform of 1885 the Reform Rabbis asserted somewhat timidly their "duty to participate in the great task of modern times, to solve, on the basis of justice and righteousness, the problems presented by the contrasts and evils of the present organization of society." [12] But since then all three branches of American Judaism have made vigorous pronouncements on social justice.

The Catholics went into "social action" after the Pastoral Letter of the American Hierarchy in 1919, which formulated a program of social reconstruction. Among the Catholics the chief protagonists of the Social Gospel have been John A. Ryan of the Department of Social Action, National Catholic Welfare Conference, and R. A. McGowan, who has served in various capacities. Among the most successful religious agencies in reaching the workers is the Association of Catholic Trade Unionists (1937). During the early 1920's the National Catholic Welfare Conference was organized, which is now one of the most powerful and centrally organized agencies of religious social action in the country. It operates through eight departments: Executive (which includes Service to Immigrants, Doctrine, Information and Publications), Education, Press, Social Action (which includes Industrial Relations, Family Life, Rural Life, Peace and Post-War Problems, Credit, and Health), Legal (which operates lobbies at legislatures), Catholic Action Study, Youth (including the National Catholic Youth Council, Federation of Newman Clubs, etc.), and Lay Organizations. In addition to these standing departments it organizes special services as needed, such as the War-relief and Refugee Service (1936), the National Legion of Decency (1934), the Catholic Interracial Council of New York (1934), the Association of Catholic Trade Unionists (1937), the Commission on American Citizenship (1939), and the National Catholic Community Service (1940). In the field of industrial relations, where Catholics have been especially strong, the Catholic Worker Movement has operated since 1933, and publishes a monthly magazine, *The Catholic Worker*, which has a circulation of 65,000.

By 1946 Protestants, Jews and Catholics were able to unite in a "Declaration on Economic Justice," which went far beyond anything that any one of these groups had attempted in the nineteenth century. Meanwhile, in New York (under the inspiration of Dr. Felix Adler) and in other cities, Ethical Culture Societies arose, which brought together persons from many faiths and no faiths who could unite in promoting religiously and practically a social ethic. These societies gave radical expression to the tendency which was increasingly noticeable among liberal American faiths generally, the tendency to subordinate theological differences to a practical program of social reconstruction. They also emphasized, as did the Christian socialists, the doctrine that a social order must be judged by the kind of human beings it produces, and not by impersonal criteria.

It is not easy to describe the general course which religious thought and action has taken on economic issues, for it is as varied as secular thought and action. On the whole, it is safe to say that the churches have *reflected* the secular conscience; they have neither led nor followed as a rule. The churches tend to think of themselves as the moral leaders of men in matters of social justice; and the anticlericals tend to think of the churches as hopelessly conservative. Neither extreme generalization is true. Though there have always been members of the clergy and religiously motivated laymen among the *leaders* of social reform, the chief function of the churches is to be only a mouthpiece of the unreformed. More than secular journalism and theater, more than professors of social science, more than political party campaigns, the pulpits and presses of the religious bodies have given popular form and emotional power to the average Americans' sense of right and wrong. They may have relatively little to do with *producing* reforms (see Chapter I), but they certainly "register" the need for reform very effectively.

During the early days of the social gospel the emphasis was clearly a reflection of the populist movement — a denunciation of "capitalism" (by which was meant the banking system, rather than the factory system — "mammon" in religious parlance) and a denunciation of the profit motive. The aim was to *humanize* the economic order by appealing to the sense of interpersonal coöperation, to a respect for human dignity and fraternity, and to the mutual "service" motive. Greed was the great evil to be conquered, and greed was twofold — an institution and a motive. The realization of human brotherhood (both as an institution and as a motive) was the basic message of this gospel. There was little appeal to class consciousness; on the contrary, the very idea of classes (as of "masses") was repugnant to the religious ideology, and even the secular forces of American socialism had to take into account this unpopularity of class appeal and the foreignness of Marxian analysis. The ideal of social justice among Christians, and even more strongly among Jews, was conceived not in impersonal terms of law, but in terms of a lively sense of personal rights and needs. Hence the program of action was directed less at government (except for antimonopoly and anti-trust legislation) than at cultivating among employers and employees a concern for the workers' welfare. Similarly, the trade and labor unions were supported not as agencies of collective bargaining and class conflict, but as "protective and benevolent" organizations. Even Rauschenbusch, whose intellectual background was the German sociology of Ritschl and Troeltsch and who was less optimistic than the utopian reformers of the nineteenth century, conceived his "kingdom of God" in terms of a revolution in human motivation. He wrote in 1907:

If it were proposed to invent some social system in which covetousness would be deliberately fostered and intensified in human nature, what system could be devised which would excel our own for this purpose? Competitive commerce exalts selfishness to the dignity of a moral principle . . . . It makes men who are the gentlest and kindliest friends and neighbors, relentless taskmasters in their shops and stores.[13]

The Church should help public opinion to understand clearly the difference between the moral qualities of the competitive and the communistic principle, and enlist religious enthusiasm on behalf of that which is essentially Christian.[14]

Later, in 1912, Rauschenbusch wrote: "To set things above men is the really dangerous practical materialism. To set mammon before God is the only idolatry against which Jesus has warned us." [15]

And as late as 1933 the Federal Council of Churches issued a statement saying: "The Christian conscience can be satisfied with nothing less than the complete substitution of motives of mutual helpfulness and good will for the motive of private gain." [16]

The American Catholics, taking their clues from Leo XIII's Encyclical, *Rerum Novarum* (1891), made the same basic plea, that the social order must be humanized, but put less stress on motivation, more on regulation. Basic to a just and charitable social order are the living wage and the just price; to secure these, both competition and "economic domination" must be "kept within just and definite limits." The Catholics also, more than the Protestants, emphasized equality, that is, the democratic distribution of ownership through coöperative and copartnership arrangements.

But in general, all the religious groups united in urging "economic democracy," and they meant by this a coöperative economy in which conflict (or extreme competition) is supplanted by a harmony of interests or voluntary coöperation within the framework of democracy. This did not imply a general program of nationalization or "state capitalism," which had been the chief object of enthusiasm among late nineteenth century socialists. In fact, it implied no very specific program at all; its aim was not political. It was intended to be broad enough to bring laborers into churches, without being so specific as to commit the churches to a partisan program of reform. The churches, especially the Protestant, had been accused, and the accusation was widely believed, of being bourgeois, of not only being indifferent to the cause of labor but being positively an instrument of the dominating class. The Social Gospel was to prove to the proletariat that organized religion was actively concerned in its welfare, and to invite labor to work with and through religious agencies. Thus when the Congregationalist leaders organized their Council for Social Action in 1934, they talked about sacrificing the church itself to the world: "Believing that the church will find itself as it loses itself in the struggle to achieve a warless, just and brotherly world, we launch this venture, dedicating ourselves to unremitting work for a day in which all men find peace, security and abundant life."

Along with the Congregationalists the other Protestant churches whose laymen were relatively more conservative politically (Presbyterians and Episcopalians) joined with the Federal Council during the Depression in sponsoring a wave of "national repentance," which, though it did not commit them to the New Deal, at least indicated that their consciences were not easy and that they were receptive to some kind of planning and social security schemes. But this broad and vague appeal to labor began to lose most of its power, and in order to make a serious contribution to the cause, the churches were forced to descend into the political arena. This they did and took the consequences: the movement lost its moral unity, but it got down to economic business. Within each congregation the practical issues of economic planning and labor organization were debated and evaluated in terms of the ideals that had been formulated. Sharp divisions of belief and interest began to agitate the churches locally as well as nationally.

When the federal church boards and national lobbies as well as the clergy generally came nearer to "socialism" than many of the influential laity, the Church League of America was formed in 1937 which worked against the spread of "the new social gospel in the field of religion" and tried "to present to the clergy throughout the Nation the viewpoint of laymen, the members who really support the churches and who have a great stake in the private enterprise system in this country." Accordingly they counteracted those "clergymen and teachers and other social leaders [who] were accepting, in a large measure, the idea that . . . there might be something evil in the idea of profit, or profit-motive." [17] And in general there were many signs of impatience among pious business men who thought the clergy were venturing into realms in which they lacked "experience." They compelled the Federal Council and the clergy in general to refrain from representing their views as the official platforms of the respective churches and welcomed the idea that the churches should be content to "be the church," preaching repentance and reformation without specifying details of business or politics.

Nevertheless the commissions and boards for social action, though they find it impossible to get general support for the particular policies which they recommended, have gone ahead carrying the diverse issues of secular life into their religious communities and forcing the concrete moral issues into the foreground. Thus the pulpits, Sunday Schools, and YMCAs became important forums for clarifying American consciences. The leaders of the Social Gospel, meanwhile, assembled for personal conference, and instead of seeking like politicians to concoct inoffensive platforms, they tried like true moralists to arrive at policies which they themselves could endorse. A result was the reformulation by the Federal Council in 1932 of "The Social Ideals of the Churches." (See Exhibit VII.)

In addition to this more specific reformulation of principles, the National Council is sponsoring numerous research projects and investigations. Among them is a study (sponsored also by the Rockefeller Foundation) of "the application of Christian principles to economic life." The chief kind of problem to be studied, according to the director, Mr. Charles P. Taft, is the way in which moral responsibility and decisions are affected by the growth of corporate economic organization and power.

Though without official endorsement, the National Catholic Welfare Council, the Federal Council of the Churches of Christ, and the Synagogue Council of America made joint pronouncements in 1946, which indicate that clarification of America's religious conscience has made considerable progress since 1932 in the direction of expressing common principles of social reform. And there is substantial evidence that the stand taken by central, authoritative ecclesiastical bodies has had a considerable influence upon the consciences of laymen and legislators.

In addition to this common moral ground, the various religious presses and lobbies have urged particular economic or political reforms. Thus the Catholics have sponsored coöperatives of many kinds, and recently, influenced by the papal "corporatism" and the syndicalist experiments in Italy and Portugal, have urged the establishment of "economic councils" which will coördinate collectively the chief interests and functions of the nation, giving each as much democracy and autonomy as possible, and giving all an agency of centralized planning. Thus the American Bishops in their manifesto of November 20, 1948 (see Exhibit VIII), favored "the free organization of capital and labor in permanent agencies of cooperation for the common good" and "freely organized cooperation between the accredited representatives of capital and labor in each industry and in the economy as a whole, under the supervision, but not the control of government. The agencies of this freely organized coöperation have been called by various names: Occupational Groups, Vocational Groups, or more recently, Industry Councils." This "distributism" or syndicalistic pluralism (similar to the British guild socialism) is intended to avoid the bureaucracy of state capitalism and of party dictator-ship. The organizations of Rabbis have emphasized economic planning for a balanced economy, economic equality and security for all, abolition of private monopolies, public ownership of banks, transportation and communication systems, and power resources. The Protestants have endorsed the "social welfare state" in principle, but have not committed themselves to any very definite program. However, they have sponsored protective legislation for women and children in industry, which the Catholics have been unwilling to do.

Rethinking the Social Gospel

This descent of the religious bodies into the arena of politics was so successful that it became embarrassing. The more thoughtful and responsible leaders of the movement began to fear revolutionary consequences for organized religion. The fears became all the more real when it became known that some of the leaders positively welcomed revolutionary changes. Would a Christianized social order be a substitute for Christian churches? If not, what distinctive role would the churches play in such a "kingdom"? Would religious socialism be different from secular socialism? To these more or less speculative questions the recent course of events has suggested unexpected answers. Depression, dictatorships, and world war have made political reform so complicated, even in America, that the reformers themselves were thrown into confusion. Especially the liberals were dismayed when they felt the growing demand for authority. Laymen began to complain to the clergy, "Don't complicate matters politically, but simplify moral authority!" And youth began to expect teachers to tell them "what's what." The popular bewilderment was playing into the hands of authoritarians to such an extent that the most immediate and pressing problem for the American leaders of socialized religion was: How can we provide authority without becoming authoritarian?

Gradually it became clear to the preachers of the Kingdom of God on earth that within that Kingdom there must be room for a peculiarly divine or holy society, a community within the larger community of associations whose primary function it is to be the guardian and spokesman of the divine revelation. And they now gave willing ear to the refrain which came drifting from across the ocean: "Let the church be the Church!"

To the Catholics this situation posed no problem, for they were prepared both in theory and in practice to speak with authority on any moral matter. But to the Protestant promoters of the social gospel the situation was disconcerting. How could the many American churches be the Holy Church? To them the theory of the church now became an essential aspect of the Social Gospel, and this theoretical problem reduced itself to the practical problem of reconciling democracy with religious authority. A "radical exploratory approach" toward revelation itself was needed. This was provided by a group of theologians who explained, to use the words of H. Richard Niebuhr, that "revelation is not a development of our religious ideas but their continuous conversion." Whether it was this Protestant view of continuous conversion through continuous revelation that was accepted, or the liberal Catholic view of Cardinal Newman that there is a development in revelation, in either case a flexible concept of absolute authority was provided, which enabled the churches to cling to their divine task and at the same time share in the moral experimentation of democratic society. Thus the voice of God might be heard even in antiauthoritarian churches.

Despite their enthusiasm for the ecumenical movement and for centralized religious authority, many of the American churchmen retained the Congregational conception of a church. Certainly a typical American church is a *local* community, whose members join it as they do any other voluntary organization. Thus it takes its place among secular institutions as a particular kind of sociability, and makes no pretense to anything but a technical "holiness." And especially the leaders of the Social Gospel were eager to conceive the Christian church thus as an integral element in a Christian society or culture, rather than as a supernatural voice crying in the wilderness of the world. But they were being criticized by the more churchly theologians of Europe for being mere sectarians. F. Ernest Johnson, who had to bear the brunt of much of this criticism, states it well.

You join your church as you do your club. The Church cannot be so regarded. Membership in it is rather of the nature of membership in a family. You may, to be sure, desert your family, but you cannot resign from it at will . . . . The communal church here confronts the 'gathered' church — the voluntary society of believers. The latter conception is predominant in America.[18]

Dr. Johnson faced this issue squarely and in his reëxamination of the Social Gospel formulated an American solution to the problem of ecclesiastical authority as follows:

The distinctive thing about the Church is that it is the community in which men share the process of total evaluation of every aspect of life, arrive at what they conceive to be a spiritual judgment on their own lives in the light of an absolute imperative, formulate corporate ethical standards for their governance, and unify the entire experience in corporate worship. In all these communities the principle of authority is recognized, for that principle is precisely the superiority of group thinking, group aspiration, and group testing of values, in a shared experience of personal discipleship carried on against a background of a rich tradition — the superiority of this group life over anything the individual can achieve in isolation. And the fact which attests the authority of the religious community is the stimulus given to what I have called the self-transcending process — the religious experience *par excellence* — by fellowship of inquiry and of striving. What else can be the significance of that great character of Christian community, "Where two or three are gathered together in my name, there am I"? Community is not an *additive* concept. It is not a sum-total. It is a distinctive *somewhat* in the nature of human association.[19]

"True prophecy is representative," he says. In other words, a church is authoritative in a democratic society only insofar as it embodies more completely than do other institutions the process of living-in-community. A church must do more than proclaim symbols of holy communion; it must give a corporate example of how thoroughgoing community of experience can bear witness to divine revelation.

Parallel to this reinterpretation of the prophetic function of the church came a reinterpretation of its priestly function. The democratization of the priestly office, proclaimed by Luther, had in effect served to minimize the need of a priesthood among Protestants, except among certain radical "lay" churches such as the Disciples, the Mormons, and the Christian Scientists. But with the recent world-agony came the idea that a religious body is a community of suffering, as other institutions are communities of interest. The church is socialized atonement. Speaking to an English audience in the midst of World War II, Dean Sperry confessed:

> Perhaps we shall be condemned to moral mediocrity in the history of the next half-century because we shall not have won a place for ourselves in the "aristocracy of suffering" in our time. One feels that this may be particularly true of our churches. Their untested platitudes will hereafter mean little to those who have been tried by the fires of persecution.[20]

The Jewish communities obviously felt the relevance of this doctrine of collective atonement and redemptive suffering. And the Catholic sacraments and symbols had always made the cross central in the life of the church. Now the Protestant liberals were willing to join them in reasserting the sacrificial ideal as essential to religious ethics. And in general there has grown recently in America a new appreciation of the peculiar opportunity of the church to foster the sense of historical continuity — the communion of saints, the society of the living with the dead, especially with the martyrs. Thus the churches are injecting into society what Tillich calls a "theonomous" quality and are creating a collectivist kind of mystic sense of the presence, sovereignty, and holiness of God.

In these various ways the Social Gospel has been reconstructed to adapt it to recent events, and in general its early utopian socialism has given place to a more realistic understanding of what religion can contribute to the general task of social reconstruction.

It has become conventional among Protestant theologians to mark this recent shift from a program of secular social reform to an emphasis on the continuing redemptive function of the church in society by pretending that "the Social Gospel" ended in the thirties and that the growth of neo-orthodox theology represents a new kind of social gospel. Hence we read of the "post-social gospel" and of the "end of the social gospel." Such phrases are misleading, for though it is true that theologically and ideologically there has been a radical reorientation of Christian social ethics, there has been a general continuity in the practical social work of the churches. "Rethinking the social gospel" is a more accurate phrase, for the basic aims and efforts of Christianizing society are more deeply rooted than ever, and Christian politics is more realistic than ever. Hence the lay reader must be on his guard against inferring that the theological reaction against liberalism involves a reaction in practical politics; on the contrary, the programs of the churches today are more radical and complicated than was their "bourgeois socialism."

Perhaps we have now given enough historical detail to substantiate the generalization made at the opening of this chapter concerning the nature of the moral reconstruction which religion in America has undergone during this century. The focus of concern has been shifted from saving souls to saving society, from reliance on supernatural grace and mercy to working for social "redemption" by economic and political measures, from religious revivals to social reconstruction, from moral platitudes to moral criticism.

Supernatural Supersocial Gospels

This secularization and socialization of religious liberalism was bound to incur the opposition of two kinds of consciences: those who had little or no faith in "recreating the world" and those who had regarded the whole social gospel as bourgeois sentimentality or optimism. When these two types of opposition were united, as is often the case, the result was the organization of movements of religious protest which were socially reactionary and religiously "apocalyptic" or supernaturalist. In opposition to the social gospel there arose the churches of the "Full Gospel" and of the millennial hope. These churches are usually represented by sociologists as the "churches of the under-privileged," but we must be careful not to misrepresent them. From the point of view of social science and academic political education, the members of these new evangelistic churches are relatively illiterate and educationally "under-privileged," but they come from rich and poor alike and most of them from the "lower middle" class where most Americans are anyway. Wealthy business men have endowed such movements, their presses, schools, and campaigns. They might fairly be accused by Marxians of feeding "opium" to the people, were it not for the fact that they, too, feed on the same "opiate" and act in religious faith rather than out of economic strategy. They are usually "hard-boiled" characters, who share with the rank and file of the American proletariat the belief that the world is essentially wicked and evil and that it will remain so until God Himself finally destroys it. The world is not intended to be saved. Man's religious business is to flee the world and all its abominations. This attitude of protest and escape is not an attitude of resignation. It is fed by bitter, realistic experience and appeals to common sense. When the American poor turn to religion, as most of them do, they turn not to a faith in revolution, but to a more radical revolt against faith in their fellow man. "In God we trust" has always had its seamy side. Salvation will come from "on High," but not from higher-ups! Though the social gospel has captured the consciences of the comfortable, it has made relatively little progress among the proletariat, which, at least in America, has been generally pessimistic about economics and disgusted with politics.

Moral fundamentalism is today more than ever a movement of condemnation: man and society are both immoral, from its point of view, and religion is a faith in more than human resources and more than worldly happiness. Among the educated Christian fundamentalists, of whom there are more abroad than at home, the popular prophets are disillusioned individualists like Kierkegaard and Unamuno who ridicule the whole idea of "Christendom" and Christianizing the Social Order. A Christian is not supposed to be at home in the world! And among the fundamentalist Jews, if I may apply this epithet to them, the Christianizing of society was received with a sardonic grin, and they now listen to those who in despair cry "back to your ghettos" rather than to the messianic Zionists. But, in general, the "churches of the underprivileged" are built not on despair, but on the hope that God, before he finally destroys the earth, will in His own way and time produce a "crisis" which will bring a reign of peace to this world as a prelude to a new and better world. This might be called the supernaturalist version of "New Deal" faith, which is a deep-seated element in American morality.

During the "New Deal" decade the extreme evangelistic

churches and sects in Protestantism, which had begun to take on new life during World War I, grew by leaps and bounds. The Church of the Nazarene, for example, which is typical of at least a dozen similar religious bodies, in 1906 had 100 churches in 19 states with 6,600 members. In 1926 it had 1,400 churches in 47 states with 63,000 members. And in 1949 it had about 3,000 churches in 48 states with 220,000 members.

The Zion's Watch Tower Tract Society, the followers of the millennialist preacher, Charles T. Russell, who in the nineteenth century prophesied the imminent (1914) Second Coming of Christ, were a small, devoted, but isolated band, who distributed the "Russellite booklets" and a few thousand copies of their magazine, the *Watchtower* (begun in 1879). But during the years 1900–1910 this society distributed millions of copies of its *Studies in the Scriptures* and now distributes 600,000 copies of the *Watchtower* semimonthly.

In 1914 an eight-hour motion picture or "Photo-Drama of Creation" was shown. In 1919 eight thousand "ministers" or "witnesses" in convention agreed to "advertise, advertise, advertise the King and the Kingdom." In 1931 they took on the name, *Jehovah's Witnesses*. In 1946, eighty thousand Witnesses in convention at Cleveland launched another magazine, *Awake!* Meanwhile increasing radio broadcasts led to the establishment of Radio Station WBBR, Brooklyn. By these thoroughly modern techniques Jehovah's Witnesses have proclaimed their own version of how God is bringing in his Kingdom. (See Exhibit IX.) A summary of this gospel, in the words of the President of the Society, will reveal the interesting relations which such a gospel has on the one hand to secular events and concerns, and on the other to the liberalist versions of "The Kingdom."

Since 1880 Jehovah's witnesses had publicized the year 1914 as the end of the "times of the Gentiles", according to Bible prophecy. That year 'nation rose against nation!" . . . The witnesses as a whole understood that this second coming and end did not mean a fiery end of the literal earth, but meant the end of Satan's uninterrupted rule over "this present evil world" and the time for Christ's enthronement in heaven as King . . . . The Kingdom is not an earthly one, is not to be and never will be found in any political government or combine of governments on this earth. "My kingdom is not of this world," said Jesus. (John 18:36) However, the righteous rule of that heavenly kingdom will descend earthward and effect the answer to the Lord's prayer, "Thy will be done in earth, as it is in heaven."

Most striking is the belief of Jehovah's witnesses that the Kingdom is established, is at hand and is operating. This sounds strange to many, in view of continued woes and distress. However, the Scriptures foretell a transition period from old world rule to Kingdom rule, a time in which Christ would "rule in the midst of his enemies" while Satan the Devil increased earth's woes.[21]

Not only is "man's wisdom foolish in God's sight," but man's institutions are destined steadily to pursue "the broad, downward way. . . . Nothing can stop 'the downward path' of this age. The refinement of this century is viewed by the Witnesses as 'a very thin veneer, easily peeled off.' . . . The Witnesses reason that although several movements in the course of history have been started by outstandingly moral individuals, these movements have been consistently 'overreached' by Satan until they have come to express the opposite of their original *raison d'être*. This is especially true of religions." [22] The Witnesses practice adult baptism and observe the "Memorial Supper" as being biblical institutions. All other rites and ceremonies are "superstitiousness."

One of the most extreme and instructive of these very "modern" revivals of a naïve faith in Providence is the Father Divine Peace Mission, which, though only thirty years old, has brought thousands of Negroes and many whites into a fellowship of faith and peace which is as unconventional as it is pious. The members live new lives, have a new security and peace, new names — they are "angels" living in "heavens." Their communion meals are genuine feasts and their life with Father and Mother Divine is a sharing in a genuine providence. (See Exhibit X.) From the literature of the Movement which is published under the title of *The New Day*, we quote the following excerpt to illustrate the fact that this kind of revolutionary religious society is consciously opposed to the social program of the conventional churches.

It is understood, the believers of Father Divine voluntarily give their services to the Cause gratis, without compensation.

It is further understood that the co-workers and Representatives of the Peace Missions are willing to TRUST GOD wholeheartedly according to our conscious conviction.

Therefore — in summary, we will not remain on public welfare, neither seek further aid. We will not take out insurance and will resign what we now have for the purpose of giving our whole hearts, souls and minds to that to which we are converted — nor will we take out compensation or liability or other insurance. We will also refuse to receive old age pensions, insurances, veterans' pensions and other compensations. All this is done through their conscious conviction of such being a violation to their religious belief and not according to their religious discipline.[23]

Many other illustrations might be given of the recent growth of gospels which are in sharp contrast to the social gospel of liberalism but which nevertheless reveal clearly that they are responses to present social conditions. It will not do to dismiss them as reactionary, or as mere vestiges or as escape mechanisms. These, too, like their more learned neighbors, are new, modern faiths, reflecting sensitivity to contemporary moral problems, whatever other traits they may have to make them ridiculous as theologies or philosophies.

EXHIBITS

(Pictorial Exhibits A and B follow page 164.)

EXHIBIT I

Growth of Religious Bodies in the United States, 1900–1949, Compared with Growth of Population

These estimates are only roughly reliable but indicate the adult membership (over 13 years of age) in the major religious groups. Figures are in millions. The official census statistics and the estimates made by various religious bodies have been adjusted to make them roughly comparable. The areas used for the key represent average relative strength.

Evangelical Protestant Churches

Roman Catholic Church

Liturgical Churches (Lutheran, Episcopal, Eastern Orthodox)

Fundamentalist Churches (includes all militant fundamentalist organizations, but not the conservative branches of the major evangelical denominations)

Judaism (based not on Jewish population but on synagogue membership)

Others (Christian Science, New Thought, Mormon, Oriental Groups, local cults, etc.)

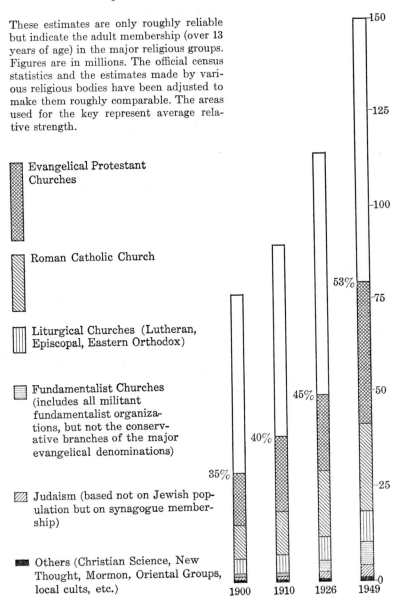

EXHIBIT II

Signs of New Life Reported in 1904
From Theodore T. Munger, *Essays for The Day* (1904), p. 30.

The people have outrun the preacher and the church. Strong
spiritual movements lay hold of the masses sooner than upon those
who live and think among established theories. The Spirit is a wind
and blows freest in the open. Consequently there are to-day
movements going on in the churches of which they are only half
aware or treat but slightingly. One must think twice before one
speaks lightly of such lay bodies as the Young Men's Christian
Association, the Christian Union, the Christian Endeavor Society,
the Brotherhood of St. Andrew, the Epworth League, the Baptist
Union, the Student Volunteer Movement, the Brotherhood of
Andrew and Philip, the Girl's Friendly Society, the King's
Daughters, and others of like nature. These societies stand for an
idea and a movement. No matter how crude or trifling they may
appear, nor what mistakes they make, they cannot make more or
worse than the churches from which they spring yet do not
desert. If they are too enthusiastic, and too gregarious, they are
still unconscious protests against the frequent meagreness and
dullness of the churches. With the instinct of young life, they
look to life for a field of action.

EXHIBIT III

Alfred E. Smith's "Creed" as a Catholic American Citizen (1927)
Widely publicized during 1927 and 1928. Published, for example, in the
Atlantic Monthly, CXXXIX (May 1927), p. 728.

I summarize my creed as an American Catholic. I believe in the
worship of God according to the faith and practice of the Roman
Catholic Church. I recognize no power in the institutions of my
Church to interfere with the operations of the Constitution of the
United States or the enforcement of the law of the land. I believe
in the absolute freedom of conscience for all men and in equality

of all churches, all sects, and all beliefs before the law as a matter of right and not as a matter of favor. I believe in the absolute separation of Church and State and in the strict enforcement of the provisions of the Constitution that Congress shall make no law respecting an establishment of religion or prohibiting the free exercise thereof. I believe that no tribunal of any church has any power to make any decree of any force in the law of the land, other than to establish the status of its own communicants within its own church. I believe in the support of the public school as one of the cornerstones of American liberty. I believe in the right of every parent to choose whether his child shall be educated in a public school or in a religious school supported by those of his own faith. I believe in the principle of non-interference by this country in the internal affairs of other nations, and that one should stand steadfastly against such interference by whomsoever it may be urged. And I believe in the common brotherhood of man under the common fatherhood of God.

EXHIBIT IV

A Rabbi's Plea For Religious Schools and Cultural Pluralism
From Joseph H. Lookstein, "Religion and the Public Schools" in *Jewish Education*, XXI (1949), pp. 40–43.

When we have disposed of the religious zealot and his attitude with respect to religion and the public schools, we are not yet done with the problem. There is another type of zealot whose position is equally untenable. The former seeks to force religion into public educational institutions. The latter would force upon every American child a common form of secular education exclusively . . . .

There is only one reaction possible to that point of view: It is democratic in its intention but totalitarian in its effects. The slogan of "Every Child in a Public School" is as unsound as the parallel slogan, "Every Catholic Child in a Catholic School." Cultural pluralism is a peculiar facet of American democracy. The monolithic concept of culture has long been discarded by us and with it went the old "melting pot" idea. God forbid that the teeming millions of America be poured into a common mold. It is fantastic to assume that Jew, Catholic, Protestant, white, yellow, black, immigrant and native will be thrown into a huge cauldron and permitted to stew for a generation or two in the hope that the result will be a delectable dish known as the hundred percent American. This is a recipe for totalitarian hash not for cultural pluralism in an all-encompassing American democracy . . . . As for the parochial school of Christian and Jew, let us regard it as an element of American democracy and as an expression and index of the freedom of American culture. It is a means of preserving the diversity of cultures within our land and a promise that such diversity will contribute richness and beauty to the totality of American culture.

EXHIBIT V

The High-Water Mark of Pre-Depression Mission Planning (1919)

he Interchurch World Movement proposes:

1. To make a thorough analysis of the total world task of the church, locality by locality and item by item, to the end that neglected fields might be discovered; important existing work strengthened; unjustifiable work eliminated; and helpful relationships between all agencies and workers established.

2. To conduct a continuous campaign of education, making use of ascertained facts, projected upon broad and varied lines and carried out upon a scale adequate to secure the attention of the nation at large, and, if possible, to convince the judgment and awake the interest of millions of people now wholly or largely untouched by Christ's call to world service.

3. To give co-operative leadership to the Church in the fields of industrial relations, philanthropy, evangelism, and education, to the end that the Church may more wisely and amply meet her obligations in these areas of service.

4. To conduct a campaign for recruits to the ministry and mission service.

5. To make simultaneous and united appeal for funds, sufficient in amount to support the sort of effort at home and abroad demanded by the conditions of the hour.

EXHIBIT VI

Christian Laymen Rethink Missions (*1932*)

From the report of the Commission of Appraisal of the Laymen's Foreign Missionary Inquiry, William Ernest Hocking, Chairman; published in 1932 under the title *Rethinking Missions*.

We believe, then, that the time has come to set the educational and other philanthropic aspects of mission work free from organized responsibility to the work of conscious and direct evangelization. We must be willing to give largely without any preaching; to cooperate with non-Christian agencies for social improvement; and to foster the initiative of the Orient in defining the ways in which we shall be invited to help. This means that we must work with *greater faith* in invisible successes. We must count it a gain when without addition to our institutional strength the societies of the East are slowly permeated with the spirit of Christian service. . . .

In our own effort to present the message of Christianity, we desire to use the privilege of laymen in avoiding as far as possible the language of the unexplained symbol. We believe it to be one of the necessities of the present hour that Christianity should be able to make more immediate connection with common experience and thought. Especially in addressing the Orient it is imperative that we present our faith in terms which those wholly unfamiliar with the history of Christian doctrine can understand. . . .

Missionaries who are to go out in the future ought to leave all their sectarian baggage behind and go out to work for a unified Christianity and a universal Church. But much more than that is needed. We must discover some way by which the existing denominations at home can rise above their separate entities and cooperate in a world-wide expansion of Christianity as urgent and essential at home as it is abroad. The tasks which now challenge Christianity will call for the corporate wisdom of the united Church and for all its spiritual resources. It concerns America as much as it does mission lands. Any plan which can be devised for carrying forward toward completion the work which missionaries have begun abroad will almost certainly fail unless the churches in America can draw together for a united spiritual task. . . .

We recommend that the number of theological seminaries in China, Japan and India be greatly reduced and that the type of training be profoundly transformed, so that the emphasis may be put upon preparation for the practical, social and human tasks which confront a spiritual leader in the actual world of the present time, both in the city and in the rural community. More effort should be made to develop and deepen the inner life of those who are to be the spiritual leaders in these countries. The aim of the seminary in training its workers should be to discover and present the universal and essential features of Christian life and thought and service, and the denominational aspect of the training should take a subordinate place.

EXHIBIT VII

The Social Ideals of the Churches (*1932*)

Published by the Federal Council of Churches as a revision of its declaration of 1912.

1. Practical application of the Christian principle of social well-being to the acquisition and use of wealth, subordination of speculation and the profit motive to the creative and cooperative spirit.

2. Social planning and control of the credit and monetary systems and the economic processes for the common good.

3. The right of all to the opportunity for self-maintenance; a wider and fairer distribution of wealth; a living wage, as a minimum, and above this a just share for the worker in the product of industry and agriculture.

4. Safeguarding of all workers, urban and rural, against harmful conditions of labor and occupational injury and disease.

5. Social insurance against sickness, accident, want in old age and unemployment.

6. Reduction of hours of labor as the general productivity of

industry increases; release from employment at least one day in seven, with shorter working week in prospect.

7. Such special regulation of the conditions of work of women as shall safeguard their welfare and that of the family and the community.

8. The right of employees and employers alike to organize for collective bargaining and social action; protection of both in the exercise of this right; the obligation of both to work for the public good; encouragement of cooperatives and other organizations among farmers and other groups.

9. Abolition of child labor; adequate provision for the protection, education, spiritual nurture and wholesome recreation of every child.

10. Protection of the family by the single standard of purity; educational preparation for marriage, home-making and parenthood.

11. Economic justice for the farmer in legislation, financing, transportation and the price of farm products as compared with the cost of machinery and other commodities which he must buy.

12. Extension of the primary cultural opportunities and social services now enjoyed by urban populations to the farm family.

13. Protection of the individual and society from the social, economic and moral waste of any traffic in intoxicants and habit-forming drugs.

14. Application of the Christian principle of redemption to the treatment of offenders; reform of penal and correctional methods and institutions, and of criminal court procedure.

15. Justice, opportunity and equal rights for all; mutual good-will and cooperation among racial, economic and religious groups.

16. Repudiation of war, drastic reduction of armaments, participation in international agencies for the peaceable settlement of all controversies; the building of a cooperative world order.

17. Recognition and maintenance of the rights and responsibilities of free speech, free assembly, and a free press; the encouragement of free communication of mind with mind as essential to the discovery of truth.

EXHIBIT VIII

Principles of Catholic Social Action

This declaration of social principles forms part of a statement made on November 20, 1948, by the American bishops of the Roman Catholic Church on "The Christian in Action."

Human life centers in God. The failure to center life in God is secularism — which, as we pointed out last year, is the most deadly menace to our Christian and American way of living. We shall not successfully combat this evil merely by defining and condemning it. Constructive effort is called for to counteract this corrosive influence in every phase of life where individual attitudes are a determining factor — in the home, in the school, at work, and in civil polity. For as man is, so ultimately are all the institutions of human society. . . .

Christian social principles, rooted in the moral law, call insistently for cooperation not conflict, for freedom not repression, in the development of economic activity. Cooperation must be organized — organized for the common good; freedom must be ordered — ordered for the common good.

Today we have labor partly organized, but chiefly for its own interests. We have capital or management organized, possibly on a larger scale, but again chiefly for its own interests. What we urgently need, in the Christian view of social order, is the free organization of capital and labor in permanent agencies of cooperation for the common good. To insure that this organization does not lose sight of the common good, government as the responsible custodian of the public interest should have a part in it. But its part should be to stimulate, to guide, to restrain, not to dominate. This is perfectly in line with our Federal Constitution, which empowers government not only "to establish justice" but also "to promote the general welfare."

Catholic social philosophy has a constructive program for this organic development of economic life. Pope Pius XI, rounding out the social principles formulated by Leo XIII, laid down the broad outlines of this program 17 years ago. In line with that constructive program we advocate freely organized cooperation between the accredited representatives of capital and labor in each industry and in the economy as a whole, under the supervision, but not the control, of government.

The agencies of this freely organized cooperation have been called by various names: Occupational Groups, Vocational Groups, or more recently, Industry Councils. American Catholic students of the social encyclicals have expressed their preference for the name "Industry Councils" to designate the basic organs of a Christian and American type of economic democracy into which they would like to see our economic system progressively evolve. This evolution can come only as the fruit of painstaking study and effort to safeguard, in justice and charity, the rightful interests of property and the rightful interests of labor, in the pursuit of the dominant interest of all, which is the common good.

EXHIBIT IX

The Prophetic Judgment of "Jehovah's Witnesses"

Taken from the statement of the leader, N. H. Knorr, entitled "Jehovah's Witnesses of Modern Times," in *Religion in the Twentieth Century*, edited by Vergilius Ferm (1948), p. 389.

Armageddon is not a clash between earthly armies or ideologies, but is to be a battle fought by the invisible hosts of heaven. It will end in victory for Jehovah God and his King Christ Jesus, in the destruction of Satan the Devil and his demons, in the cleansing of this earth of all wickedness and evil-doers, and in the complete vindication of Jehovah's name. (Zechariah 14:3,12; Revelation 19:11–21, 20:1–3) Jehovah God is now warning men and nations of this coming battle, through his witnesses on earth, that men of good-will toward God may heed and be preserved alive within the safety of God's organization. . . . The foregoing shows the wide breach existing between the beliefs of Jehovah's witnesses and organized religion in general. . . . The only solution is Christ's kingdom, and this Jehovah's witnesses declare, and will continue to declare in a sincere desire to show the way to lasting peace. This remedy seems foolish to world leaders, and the apostle Paul said it would appear as "foolishness of preaching." But man's wisdom is foolish in God's sight.

EXHIBIT X

A Revelation from "Father Divine"

Taken from the periodical publication of the Father Divine Peace Mission,
The New Day, October 14, 1944; cited by Charles S. Braden, *These Also Believe* (1949), p. 43.

Listen, World, we want you to know
That Father Divine is the God We adore.
He is the One that created the heaven and earth,
He is the One that brought this spiritual birth,
So why stand by and criticize
The One who can open your blinded eyes?
Listen! Stop and realize
That your God is here and not in the skies!
Now, Mr. Preacher, we know it hurts
But you know, God's tired of you playing church,
He is here to show you in the actuated words
And that is why your jealousy is stirred
But Father is merciful, if you'll confess
How you've robbed the poor, barring their success
For hunger will cause a man to steal
But your time is out, for God is revealed.

EXHIBIT XI

The Modernist Gospel According to Lyman Abbott

Taken *passim* from his *The Theology of an Evolutionist* (1897).

Religion — that is, the life of God in the soul of man — is
better comprehended, and will better be promoted, by the philosophy which regards all life as divine, and God's way of doing things
as the way of a continuous, progressive change, according to certain laws and by means of one resident force, than by the philosophy which supposes that some things are done by natural forces
and according to natural laws, and others by special interventions
of a Divine Will, acting from without, for the purpose of correct-
ing errors or filling gaps. . . .

The old orthodoxy is right in regarding the new criticism as
revolutionary. It is revolutionary in its treatment of the Bible, as

the Protestant reformation was revolutionary in its treatment of the Church. . . . Infallible authority is undesirable. God has not given it to His children. He has given them something far better, — life. That life can come only through struggle. There is as little a short and easy way to truth as to virtue. . . . It is given to us, not to save us from struggle, and growth by struggle, but to inspire us to struggle that we may grow. . . .

We are saved by the blood of Christ when we are saved by the life of Christ, — by Christ's own life imparted to us, by Christ's life transmitted; and by Christ's life transmitted, as life alone can be transmitted, through the gateway of pain and suffering. The suffering of Jesus Christ was not a single episode, — one short hour, one short three years: the suffering of Jesus Christ was the revelation of the eternal fact that God is from eternity the Life-giver, and that giving life costs God something, as it costs us something. Evolution, then, certainly does teach that to give life costs something; that the secret of growth is the impartation of life; and this is what the Bible means by what we call vicarious sacrifice. . . . And, assuming this, Christian faith believes in the manifestation of Christ to His disciples after His death as a demonstration of that resurrection which accompanies every dying. . . .

I believe, then, that the great laws of life which natural science has elucidated from a study of natural phenomena are analogous to, if not identical with, the laws of the spiritual life, and that the latter are to be interpreted by the former.

EXHIBIT XII

Modernism According to Reform Judaism
Articles II and VI from the Pittsburgh Platform of 1885.

We recognize in every religion an attempt to grasp the Infinite One, and in every mode, source or book of revelation held sacred in any religious system the consciousness of the indwelling God in man. We hold that Judaism presents the highest conception of the God-idea as taught in our holy Scriptures and developed and spiritualized by the Jewish teachers in accordance with the moral and philosophical progress of their respective ages. We maintain that Judaism preserved and defended amid continuous struggles and trials and under enforced isolation this God-idea as the central religious truth for the human race. . . .

We recognize in Judaism a progressive religion, ever striving to be in accord with the postulates of reason. We are convinced of the utmost necessity of preserving the historical identity with our great past. Christianity and Islam being daughter-religions of Judaism, we appreciate their mission to aid in the spreading of monotheistic and moral truth. We acknowledge that the spirit of broad humanity of our age is our ally in the fulfillment of our mission, and therefore we extend the hand of fellowship to all who co-operate with us in the establishment of the reign of truth and righteousness among men.

EXHIBIT XIII

The Essence of Christian Liberalism

Taken *passim* from Charles E. Jefferson's *Things Fundamental* (1903).

What is the faith which the church demands? What is the faith for which the New Testament pleads? Fortunately for us we have a definition of it in the first verse of the eleventh chapter of the letter to the Hebrews: "Now faith is the substance of things hoped for." Or, as you will see by consulting the margin of your Revised Bible, it is the "giving substance to things hoped for." Christian faith is belief in Jesus Christ. To believe in him is to hope that he is able to do what he says he can do. He says he can save men from their sins. He says that men can follow him and become like him.

And now the question is, Can a man hope to become like him? Can a man hope to have the mind that was also in him? Can a man hope to have his spirit, his disposition, his temper? Can a man hope to live a reverent, filial, godly life? Of course he can thus hope! If he does not hope it, it is because he is morally rotten and has lost the power of aspiration. If he does not hope it, it is because he loves darkness rather than light, and the reason he does that is because his works are evil. A man who will not hope to be a good man is a man who is self-condemned. And if it is possible for every man to hope to become like Christ, it is also possible for every man in less or fuller measure to give substance to the thing that he hopes for. He can begin at once to act in such a way as to realize his hopes. He can by energetic action build into his life the pattern shown. Faith, then, contains two elements: first, the element of hope, and secondly, the element of energetic action — and both these elements are under the control of the human will. We can hope, and we can, with greater or less success, give substance to our hopes. And every man who hopes and gives substance to his hope is a man of faith.

EXHIBIT XIV

Comparison of Theological Beliefs of Ministers and Theological Students During the 1920's

These questions are a selection from the fifty-six questions put to ministers and theological students by George Herbert Betts. The results were tabulated and published in two tables in the book *The Beliefs of 700 Ministers* (Abingdon Press, 1929), Tables I and IV, pp. 26–30 and 52–56.

This explanation is given on p. 25: "In the first group of 500 ministers the distribution of numbers among the denominations was as follows: Baptist, 50; Congregational, 50; Episcopalian, 30; Evangelical, 49; Lutheran, 105; Methodist, 111; Presbyterian, 63; all others (13 denominations), 43. To save any possible embarrassment to denominations or institutions, the names of the theological schools and their denominations are withheld."

These tables are reprinted with the generous permission of Mr. Harlan C. Betts, who owns the copyright.

Do you believe —

	500 Ministers Percentages			500 Students Percentages		
	Yes	?	No	Yes	?	No
2. That God is three distinct persons in one?	80	7	13	44	21	35
7. That the creation of the world occurred in the manner and time recorded in Genesis?	47	5	48	5	6	89

	500 Ministers Percentages			500 Students Percentages		
	Yes	?	No	Yes	?	No
10. That God occasionally sets aside law, thus performing a miracle?	68	8	24	24	16	60
12. That the Devil exists as an actual being?	60	7	33	9	9	82
20. That the inspiration that resulted in the writing of the Bible is different from that of other great religious literature?	70	5	25	26	6	68
22. That the Bible is wholly free from legend or myth?	38	7	55	4	1	95
23. That the principles of criticism and evaluation applied to other literature and history should be applied to the Bible?	67	5	28	88	5	7
24. That the New Testament is the absolute and infallible standard by which all religious creeds or beliefs among men should be judged as to their truth and validity?	77	3	20	33	12	55
26. That Jesus was born of a virgin without a human father?	71	10	19	25	24	51
32. That while upon earth Jesus possessed and used the power to restore the dead to life?	82	9	9	45	28	27
34. That after Jesus was dead and buried he actually rose from the dead, leaving the tomb empty?	84	4	12	42	27	31
37. That heaven exists as an actual place or location?	57	15	28	11	20	69
38. That hell exists as an actual place or location?	53	13	34	11	13	76
39. That there is a continuance of life after death?	97	2	1	89	7	4
40. In the resurrection of the body?	62	5	33	18	13	69

	500 Ministers Percentages			500 Students Percentages		
	Yes	?	No	Yes	?	No
44. That there will be one final day of judgment for all who have lived upon earth?	60	8	32	17	16	77
49. That all men, being sons of Adam, are born with natures wholly perverse, sinful and depraved?	53	4	43	13	7	80
50. That prayer has the power to change conditions in nature — such as drought?	64	11	25	21	22	57
51. That prayer for others directly affects their lives whether or not they know that such prayer is being offered?	83	9	8	58	25	17
52. That God now acts upon, or operates in, human lives through the agency and person of the Holy Spirit?	94	1	5	82	11	7
56. That, regardless of creed or personal belief, persons who love God and do justly with their fellow men are worthy of acceptance into the Christian Church?	56	5	39	85	4	11

EXHIBIT XV

President Eliot Attacks Authoritarianism

From Charles W. Eliot, "Progressive Liberalism in the Closing and the Opening Century," in *Theology at the Dawn of the Twentieth Century*, edited by J. Vyrnwy Morgan (1901), pp. 510–514.

It is not the authority of the Bible only which has declined during the closing century; all authority has lost force — authority political, ecclesiastical, educational, and domestic. . . . What authority is taking in some measure the place of these declining authorities? I say in some measure, because the world has had too much of authority and not enough of love and freedom. There is an authority which during the closing century had been increas-

ing in influence, it is the developing social sense, or sense of kin.
. . .

Sociology rejects also a motive which systematic theology has
made much of for centuries, — the motive of personal salvation,
which is essentially a selfish motive whether it relates to this world
or to the next. Certainly it is no better a motive for eternity than
it is for these short earthly lives of ours. . . . Sociology perceives
that the multitude can no longer be reconciled to a state of misery
in this world by the deceptive promise of comforts and rewards
in the next. It sympathizes with them in loudly demanding joys in
this world. The promise of Abraham's bosom after death should
not reconcile Lazarus to lying at the gate full of sores now. The
multitudes themselves perceive that wretchedness in this world
may easily unfit them for worthy enjoyments either now or here-
after; since it may dwarf the mental and moral faculties through
which high enjoyments come. Sociology is of the mind of the
angel who bore a torch in one hand and a vase of water in the
other, with the one to burn Heaven, and with the other to quench
Hell, that men might be influenced neither by the hope of the one
nor the fear of the other.

EXHIBIT XVI

Fosdick Goes Beyond Modernism

In a widely publicized confessional sermon delivered at his Riverside
Church and published in the *Christian Century*, December 4, 1935, Harry
Emerson Fosdick, the recognized leader of the Liberals, acknowledged
that a modernist theology was inadequate for the world crisis. Without
retracting his liberalism, he joined the ranks of those who felt the need
for a more definite and distinctively Christian gospel.

Because I have been and am a modernist it is proper that I
should confess that often the modernistic movement, adjusting
itself to a man-centered culture, has encouraged this mood,
watered down the thought of the Divine and, may we be forgiven
for this, left souls standing like the ancient Athenians, before an
altar to an Unknown God! On that point the church must go beyond modernism. We have been all things to all men long enough.
We have adapted and adjusted and accommodated and conceded
long enough. We have at times gotten so low down that we

talked as though the highest compliment that could be paid to
Almighty God was that a few scientists believed in him. Yet all
the time, by right, we had an independent standing-ground and a
message of our own in which alone is there hope for humankind.

EXHIBIT XVII

A Hymn for Young American Saints
Taken from the Hymnal of the Protestant Episcopal Church

I sing a song of the saints of God
Patient and brave and true,
Who toiled and fought and lived and died
For the Lord they loved and knew.
And one was a doctor, and one was a queen,
And one was a shepherdess on the green:
They were all of them saints of God — and I mean,
God helping, to be one too.

.   .   .   .   .   .

They lived not only in ages past,
There are hundreds of thousands still,
The world is bright with the joyous saints
Who love to do Jesus' will.
You can meet them in school, or in lanes, or at sea,
In church, or in trains, or in shops, or at tea,
For the saints of God are just folk like me,
And I mean to be one too.

EXHIBIT XVIII

A Methodist Minister Announces a "Copernican Revolution" in Worship
From Floyd S. Kenney, *The Religion of Human Progress*, mimeographed
book published by the author (1940), pp. iv-vi.

Religion is by nature an art. It, too, belongs to the creative.
But like all art, its creative life takes structure; and its true value
becomes attached to institutions and functions. To view religion as
a phase of man's creative mind and spirit requires a consideration

for structure as well as function, and to bring the religious institution into the range of culture makes religion in every sense of the word subject to the principles of cultural change.

There is a sense, therefore, in which the study of religion should be approached as we would examine, critically, a work of art; it must be understood and valued in relation to the culture which produced it. And in so far as religion relates to the motivating ideals and social objectives of living, the value of any religion must be judged by the success of the culture of which it is a vital part. . . .

From now on, religion becomes a conscious and purposeful direction of the spiritual life of man toward the fuller realization of the human values potential in a scientific and democratic culture. . . . That such a perspective involves a Copernican revolution in institutional religion is fully granted. However, that this outlook and the religious reconstruction which it involves is a "break" with the deeper life of religion is rejected. . . . To awaken man's spiritual nature in such a quest is both revelation and inspiration.

EXHIBIT XIX

William James Recommends Modernized Asceticism

Taken from his *Varieties of Religious Experience*, pp. 364–369. This passage belongs to his reflections on imperialistic war.

The folly of the cross, so inexplicable by the intellect, has yet its indestructible vital meaning. Representatively, then, and symbolically, and apart from the vagaries into which the unenlightened intellect of former times may have let it wander, asceticism must, I believe, be acknowledged to go with the profounder way of handling the gift of existence. Naturalistic optimism is mere syllabub and flattery and sponge-cake in comparison. The practical course of action for us, as religious men, would therefore, it seems to me, not be simply to turn our backs upon the ascetic impulse, as most of us to-day turn them, but rather to discover some outlet for it of which the fruits in the way of privation and hardship might be objectively useful. . . . Does not, for example, the worship of material luxury and wealth, which con-

stitutes so large a portion of the "spirit" of our age, make somewhat for effeminacy and unmanliness? Is not the exclusively sympathetic and facetious way in which most children are brought up
to-day — so different from the education of hundred years ago,
especially in evangelical circles — in danger, in spite of its many
advantages, of developing a certain trashiness of fibre? Are there
not hereabouts some points of application for a renovated and
revised ascetic discipline? Many of you would recognize such
dangers, but would point to athletics, militarism, and individual
and national enterprise and adventure as the remedies. . . .

One hears of the mechanical equivalent of heat. What we now
need to discover in the social realm is the moral equivalent of
war: something heroic that will speak to men as universally as war
does, and yet will be as compatible with their spiritual selves as
war has proved itself to be incompatible. I have often thought that
in the old monkish poverty-worship, in spite of the pedantry
which infested it, there might be something like that moral
equivalent of war which we are seeking. May not voluntarily
accepted poverty be "the strenuous life," without the need of
crushing weaker peoples?

Poverty indeed *is* the strenuous life, — without brass bands or
uniforms or hysteric popular applause or lies or circumlocutions,
and when one sees the way in which wealth-getting enters as an
ideal into the very bone and marrow of our generation, one
wonders whether a revival of the belief that poverty is a worthy
religious vocation may not be "the transformation of military
courage," and the spiritual reform which our time stands most in
need of. . . .

Think of the strength which personal indifference to poverty
would give us if we were devoted to unpopular causes. We need
no longer hold our tongues or fear to vote the revolutionary or
reformatory ticket. Our stocks might fall, our hopes of promotion
vanish, our salaries stop, our club doors close in our faces; yet,
while we lived, we would imperturbably bear witness to the spirit,
and our example would help to set free our generation. The cause
would need its funds, but we its servants would be potent in proportion as we personally were contented with our poverty.

I recommend this matter to your serious pondering, for it is certain that the prevalent fear of poverty among the educated classes is the worst moral disease from which our civilization suffers.

EXHIBIT XX

Spiritual Power and Esoteric Knowledge

Selected *passim* from *The Temple Artisan*, 1949 and 1951. Published at Halcyon, California.

"God is in His Holy Temple. Let all the earth keep silence before Him."

For many centuries these words have opened the services of countless churches given up to the Christian religion, and among all the priests by whom they were uttered how many, think you, ever interpreted them correctly?. . . . The Temple is the manifested universe, *a priori*, but its lesser differentiations include every atom of matter, force and consciousness, and every living thing or creature is a lesser Temple for the indwelling Spirit of God.

It is only in the silence, in the innermost depths of each holy Temple, that it is possible for God to manifest Its Self; and it is only in the secret, holy silences of the Temple, as an organization, that any member of the same may hope to gain the least concept of its majesty, power and glory. . . .

In the year 1898 another great Avataric Manifestation, a cosmic seed-time, began for all life on this earth. Because of cyclic necessity the Master Hilarion, Regent of the Red Ray, which Ray rules as the dominant or central activity of the incoming age, in conjunction with the aid of six other great Initiates, called seven chosen people together to form the nucleus of The Temple of the People. This organic center of the Fourth Degree (the connective degree) is destined for several essential cyclic reasons to continuously act as the basic transmitting Heart Center which makes possible the planting and germination of the seeds of regeneration in larger organized bodies. . . .

America is the cradle of a new race, California is the first land of the new race — the remnant in part of a continent now submerged but due to reappear, and Halcyon — Mecca of the coming race — is a Lodge Center, chosen and rededicated because of its prehistoric character as well as for other accompanying occult reasons.

Into the welter and hodgepodge of confused, confusing, and conflicting forces comes the Avataric Force of the New Dispensation — a force that is cosmical and humanitarian, healing and illumining, impersonal and unifying. . . . The forces belaboring humanity in the present cycle have many aspects, which in their last analysis and totality relate to Karma and Kali Yuga — the Iron Age. The present transitional era — an intermediate period — is at once the Avataric Dawn and the age of the anti-Christ, and therefore a time of sifting — the dividing of the sheep and the goats. It is a battle between the Light of the World and the forces of the age — between the God within and the Dwellers within — a religious war truly! . . . Hence the ideological ferment going on throughout the world, America, and the West in particular.

The essential point of difference between the social scientists of the academic world and those under the Lodge is this: in the one case the learning process is horizontal; in the other case it is vertical. In the one case it spreads wider in the field of mental *knowledge about*; in the other it extends higher and deeper into other kinds of awareness and into other ways of being aware. The latter is the way of discipleship, whatever other names may be given to it as it becomes more common among human beings. It is a hard way. But some time, for each individual, it will be the only way left open. To the average man faith is mere belief; but to the advanced occultist it is a universally diffused force like electricity moving from the center of every manifest creature, each of which must develop by the process of germination, growth, extension, expression, and final dissolution. . . .

The faith which removes mountains is a power tapped by every Initiate — ultimately by every aspirant. . . .

There is one great factor in life which all people, all nations will sooner or later feel in this great new Avataric Cycle, that is Justice rules the Universe. . . . This is a cycle of full manifestation of light when everything will be brought out in the open in full view of the great Son of Light, the Christ, the First-born Son of Man. For it is part of His mission to bring Justice to the world . . . . And unless we can bear the light from above, and tame to higher use the elementals of animal man from below, we cannot help the "little ones". . . . The key can never fit the hand that is closed upon material possessions or upon emotional possessions or upon mental possessions. It fits only the hand that is empty of possessions. But in such a hand it unlocks the door to a place in consciousness where there are no persons, as such, and where Unity, Brotherhood and *spiritual* Centralization have their home. In that place each one knows that what his brother or his sister is and does he himself is and does, for we are One and there is no separation . . . It seems necessary to build a bridge, as it were, of Universal Love between mental and spiritual energy.

4

INTELLECTUAL
RECONSTRUCTION

It is difficult to make the faith of the first decade of the century plausible to a youth of today; the religious confusion of 1800 seems more intelligible than the complacency of 1900. Complacency took two forms, one radical, the other conservative, one modernist, the other biblical, but both were expressions of religious confidence. "Life in our time is founded upon optimism," [1] wrote George A. Gordon, one of the chief spokesmen of that age, and he took for granted that religious thought must reflect the spirit of the time. This confidence or "faith" of our fathers had two sides and only one substance, like the real dollars which then still circulated. On the one side was faith in a beneficent providence — "In God We Trust"; and on the other was self-confidence or assurance of progress, of free exchange, of being on the right road, and of possessing the essential body of truth.

Complacent Reliance on the Bible

Biblical complacency need not be expounded at length since it still survives and is relatively familiar. By 1900 a little historical criticism of the Old Testament had been widely accepted among Protestants, Catholics, and Reform Jews. Insofar as it undermined the belief in literal inspiration, it was not unwelcome to the clergy and educated laymen, for the belief in the literal inspiration of the Scriptures had always raised more problems than it had solved. If the religious authoritativeness of the Scriptures could be distinguished from the literal or verbal truth of all sentences in the Bible, so much the better. The Bible remained for the vast majority of religious Americans substantially the Word of God, being a reliable guide to both happiness and salvation. There was no reason assignable why God should have intended the Bible as a textbook in science; science is human inquiry and invention, clearly within human powers. But the Torah and the Gospel, as the ways of life or revealed laws, remained a revelation from on high. The Bible was cherished as authoritative doctrine not in the sense of being infallible knowledge, but in the sense of being an unerring guide in matters which require decision. "We distinguish the revelation from its record," said Lewis F. Stearns.[2] By separating biblical truth (or, as some called it, "Christian science") from experimental science, both secular and sacred wisdom were protected against reciprocal encroachment, and freedom of thought could be accompanied by authoritative counsel or command in matters of practical discipline. A conservative criticism of the Bible could thus be complacently interpreted as making the fundamentals all the more secure and as putting an end to the warfare between science and religion which had raged during the nineteenth century. The more radical higher criticism of the New Testament, which abroad had already eaten away at the fundamentals of Christian faith, was not yet taken seriously by many in the United States. It was regarded as learned speculation for specialists, and as certainly very speculative. Such complacency with respect to biblical authority was different from biblical orthodoxy of earlier centuries or dogmatic theology, for this vague kind of reliance on the Bible was employed to put an end to sectarian controversies and to the overemphasis on creeds. The Bible was supposed to bring together on common ground not only many Christian denominations which had been gradually growing closer together in spite of theological differences, but also Christians and Reform Jews, who cherished what came to be called vaguely the Judaeo-Christian tradition. "The Bible has ceased to be an authority and has become a source book."[3] For these reasons the Bible remained central both for the pulpit and for religious education. Even in the colleges, the elementary (and often the only) course on religion in the curriculum was a course in the Bible. A glance at typical "Introductions to the Bible" during the early years of the century will readily convey to the reader the complacent and "constructive" spirit in which the Bible was being studied. In fact, the line between classroom study and sermonic exegesis was not conspicuous. But this use of the Bible as religiously fundamental, though not historically or scientifically infallible, was small comfort to those whose intellectual security demanded reliance on some sort of infallible authority. And for many such timid souls the easiest refuge was into an infallible church. If disillusionment is uncomfortable, as it should not be, to a healthy mind, the only remedy is an opiate. Professor Walter M. Horton, who has taken the more difficult road of seeking "authority without infallibility," comments wisely on this predicament:

If it be asked how one who has left the "Eden of infallibility" behind him can get back to it again, the answer is that he must take a circuitous route. Disillusioned Protestants, who cannot recover their faith in the infallible Bible, find the infallible Church's voice quite seductive, because strange and unfamiliar. The one possibility that no disillusioned person considers, is the faith of his fathers; and yet secretly, by a devious path, he is trying to return to it.[4]

Complacent Modernism

The complacent radicalism or modernism of the early twentieth century was an entirely different faith and was confined to a small percentage of American Christians, though it was quite prevalent in Reform Judaism. Its chief American sources were New England transcendentalism and absolute idealism, to which had been added a sentimental version of evolutionist enthusiasm. Such religion was not really either Jewish or Christian, but thinly disguised secular philosophy. John Fiske had taken the worst sting out of Darwinism by calling evolution "God's way of doing things," and theologians rushed in to clothe the philosophy of cosmic evolution in clerical garb and to make it "available" for pulpit use.

Among the liberal theologians of New England there had grown up late in the nineteenth century a so-called "New Theology" whose primary purpose was to make a clean break

with Calvinism and Puritanism. Andover Seminary was its headquarters and the *Andover Review* its chief mouthpiece. But it
had able exponents scattered in seminaries and universities of the
Northeast and Midwest. On the Hegelian wing were Elisha Mulford of the Episcopal Theological School at Cambridge, Massachusetts, a disciple of Frederick Maurice and an ardent nation-
alist; Samuel Harris of Andover Seminary, author of *God, the
Creator and Lord of All* (1896); Augustus H. Strong of Rochester
Theological Seminary, author of *Christ in Creation and Ethical
Monism* (1899); and George A. Gordon, whose *Ultimate Conceptions of Faith* (1903) would be a good statement to select for
anyone who wanted a central starting point for twentieth-
century philosophical theology. On the evolutionary wing were
those who tried to follow John Fiske "from nature to God."
Among them notably were George Harris, President of Amherst
College, author of a very popular work, *Moral Evolution* (1896);
Newman Smyth of New Haven, one of the most militant
champions of the biological approach to theology; and Lyman
Abbott, whose *Theology of an Evolutionist* (1897) marked the
culmination of the enthusiasm.

Less extreme than either of these two groups was the school
which descended from Horace Bushnell and whose leader was
Theodore T. Munger. His exposition of "The New Theology"
in 1883 [5] is probably the most careful and balanced statement
of the evolutionary interpretation of Christian theology as it
was preached toward the end of the nineteenth century. Note
how orthodox this new doctrine appears to be:

The New Theology does not part with the historic faith of the
church, but rather seeks to put itself in its line while recognizing a
process of development. It does not propose to commit "retrospective
suicide" at every fresh stage of advance. It holds to progress by slow
and cosmic growth rather than by cataclysmal leaps. It allies itself
even with the older rather than the later theologies, and finds in the
early Greek theology conceptions more harmonious with itself than
those in the theology shaped by Augustine.

It does not reject the specific doctrines of the church of the past.
It holds to the Trinity, though indifferent to the use of the word,
but not to a formal and psychologically impossible Trinity; to the
divine sovereignty, but it does not make it the corner-stone of its

system, preferring for that place the divine righteousness, *i.e.*, a moral rather than a dynamic basis; to the Incarnation, not as a mere physical event, for that has entered into many religions, but as the entrance into the world through a person of a moulding and redeeming force in humanity, — the central and broadest fact of theology; to the Atonement as a divine act and process of ethical and practical import — not as a mystery of the distant heavens and isolated from the struggle of the world, but a comprehensible force in the actual redemption of the world from its evil; to the Resurrection as covering the whole essential nature of man; to Judgment as involved in the development of a moral nature. . . . It does not explain away from these doctrines their substance, nor minimize them, nor aim to do else than present them as revealed in the Scriptures and as developed in history and in the life of the church and of the world.[6]

How innocent these attempts to state the "substance" of the faith now appear to the lay believer! And yet each phrase is packed with polemics. Few of his fellow theologians would see in it "a constructive, not an iconoclastic temper." And even a reader in 1950 might become a little suspicious when he read, at the end of this "substantiation" of the faith, that "Revelation is not so much *from* God as *of* God." Whether the new theologians tried as Munger did to be conciliatory or whether they relied more modernistically on idealistic philosophy and evolutionary doctrine, they all agreed with Munger's eloquent dictum:

If Christianity has any human basis it is its entire reasonableness. It must not only sit easily on the mind, but it must ally itself with it in all its normal action . . . . It deals with human life as do the poets and dramatists: it views humanity by a direct light, looks straight at it, and into it, and across its whole breadth.[7]

What it means to conceive theology thus humanistically is made very plain by Munger: "The New Theology seeks to recover spiritual processes from a magical to a moral conception. It regards faith as a moral act, a direct acceptance and laying hold of God in trusting obedience, a simple and rational process."[8]

Though such doctrine was being preached from Christian pulpits and being given a biblical veneer, its substance was evidently taken from the philosophy of science. During the last decade of the nineteenth century, such doctrine had been genuinely a "new theology," a reinterpretation of the Christian gospel. But during the early decades of the twentieth century such preaching became definitely antitheological and there was clearly a longing for a faith more universal than Christianity. Biblical exegesis and credal interpretations became strained, tedious, and irrelevant. The specifically Christian or Jewish elements in doctrine were regarded as liabilities of faith, as restrictions upon the more universal and rational worship of God. There had been created during the Chicago World's Fair at the Parliament of Religions (1893) a genuine interest in oriental religions and a willingness to consider Christianity as one religion among others. Thus the question of "the finality of the Christian religion" became more than an academic problem even for Christian theologians, and they began to write books about religion in general at the expense of theology. For example, Lyman Abbott, though he kept the word "theology" in the title of his lectures, *The Theology of an Evolutionist*, and though he discussed revelation, sin, sacrifice, propitiation, miracles, and Christ, subordinated them all to evolution (for example, "the place of Christ in evolution"). Clearly the "New Theology" was now neither new nor theology. It had become, as it was later called in retrospect, a "new orthodoxy" or a "new dogmatism," whose chief aim was to rise above all theologies, creeds, and cults to a universal faith grounded in universal evolution.

This was modernism. Lyman Abbott, though he also preached in Henry Ward Beecher's Plymouth Church, Brooklyn, spread this gospel (as had Emerson) by giving lecture-sermons throughout the land, by editing the *Outlook*, and in general by using modernistic techniques of publicity. He stated frankly and repeatedly that the chief sources of his inspiration were the philosophers who expounded theistic evolution (Joseph Le Conte and Henry Drummond) and he made a slogan of John Fiske's "Evolution is God's way of doing things." For the benefit of younger readers who may not have heard such preaching, though it used to be common enough, I have put together a few selections from his lectures which may give an idea of the kind of gospel "enlightened" Christians heard not only from Lyman Abbott's pulpit but from hundreds of other pulpits and platforms fifty years ago. (See Exhibit XI.)

It needs no commentary to prove that this doctrine is only verbally Christian. It was the popular philosophy of the day translated into Christian language. By applying "natural law" to the "spiritual world" it used Christian doctrine and symbols to express such truths as "the struggle for existence," "progress through struggle," truth through trial and error, and the other commonplaces of evolutionary ethics.

Similarly for Reform Jews, practically the same ideas were being preached as the essence of Judaism by such "theologians" as Isaac M. Wise, Kaufman Kohler, and Emil G. Hirsch. Their famous "platform" remained for decades the basic statement of the Reform faith. (See Exhibit XII.)

The universalistic enthusiasm which inspired all these complacent radicals was expressed during its early days with all the naïveté of an evangelist by Rabbi Isaac M. Wise, whose *Cosmic God* was inspired directly by John Fiske's *Cosmic Philosophy*, as follows:

Scientist, here is your God and Lord, whom you seek, and whom to find is the highest wisdom. He is the God found by induction and felt by spontaneity. Philosophers, here is your God, whom to expound is the highest glory of human mind — Kant, and other thinkers have argued against the anthropomorphous God of theology; cosmic God is philosophy's first and last substance. Simple-minded men, here is your God, whom you need not seek, for He is everywhere, in you and about you, in every quality of matter and every motion of the mind; where you are, He is; where you observe or think, you think Him. Children, here is your God, in the fragrance of your flowers, in the beauteous hues of vernal blossoms, in the thunder and the whisper, in heaven's azure dome and earth's verdant garb, in your innocent smiles and your mother's sweet tenderness. Sage or fool, great or little, here is your God, you cannot escape Him, and He cannot escape you; He is in you, and you are in Him. Men of all future generations here is God in the Harmony of all human conceptions and knowledge, the God of all, and all eternity, the cosmic God, the GREAT I AM, and none beside Him.[9]

This kind of "modernism" had been cultivated among American Catholics, too, until the Pope's Encyclical *Pascendi gregis* (1907) put an end to it, at least in Catholic pulpits and presses. But the atmosphere of confidence, progress, and universal brotherhood, which modernism expressed, could not be much affected by papal prohibitions so long as it continued to be the pervasive tone of American culture. There are still Americans who with Minot J. Savage believe the following:

Here in America, for the first time in history on any wide scale, we have solved the problem of liberty and order under a popular form of government; a government flexible enough to adapt itself to all conditions, and capable of indefinite expansion and progress. We are more and more learning how, through knowledge and obedience, to control the forces of nature and make them minister to our physical, intellectual and spiritual life. But as yet we have only made a beginning. This is no old and worn-out world, hastening to decay; no "old wreck bound to sink, and from which we must save as many of the crew as we can and let her go," as Mr. Moody has described it. The long night is past; the eastern sky blushes red with dawn; but the day is all ahead of us, — a day of wiser and better and happier peoples, a veritable "kingdom of God" on earth.[10]

Though few preachers gave it the outspoken and radical formulations which we have just cited, the American unity-in-complacency was then more conspicuous than the division into biblical and evolutionary theists which had disrupted theology in the nineteenth century. Theodore Munger stated the situation concisely when he said:

Earnest and intelligent men to-day do not discuss the apostolic succession, nor the forms of baptism, nor endless punishment, nor the verbal inspiration of Scripture. The banners that used to wave with vigor over these doctrines are still carried, but the battles do not rage around them; indeed, there are no battles beyond slight skirmishes, — only questions as to what is best to be done . . . .
To cut out of ancient creeds intolerable parts, leaving a mangled remainder to live on, is a weak expedient which, if persisted in, results in a degenerate church and ministry; for strong men shrink from feeble measures. If it is true that the pulpit is degenerating, it is in no small degree due to the fact that clear-eyed candidates will not put new wine into old bottles, and are equally unwilling to enter a ministry where there are neither wine nor bottles.[11]

Common Sense Liberalism

Sensing this danger for the ministry and in general for organized religions, the leaders of religious thought in America looked about for some more "constructive" message. This new life which began to be felt among technical theologians during the early years of the century did not become a general intellectual force until the middle of the second decade, when it came to be recognized as a new "liberalism" among Christians, and as "conservatism" among Jews. Roughly speaking, the years 1915–1930 were as intellectually dominated by liberalism as 1900–1915 had been intellectually dominated by modernism.

Liberalism had two wings: the social gospel and the appeal to critical common sense. The appeal to common sense instead of to either philosophy or science was a characteristically American simplification of what in Germany was a sophisticated theology. Hence a few words of explanation of the theology behind the antitheological movement are in order. In philosophy, stimulated by William James's great treatise on *The Varieties of Religious Experience* (1902), there was a widespread reaction against "scientism" and toward "empiricism," but the kind of clinical treatment to which James subjected religious experience and belief was obviously not calculated to be a suitable foundation for any theology; it was too individualistic, too mystic, too "sick-souled" to be useful for "constructive" sermons. But in Germany, as usual, the American liberals found what they were looking for — a school of neo-empirical theology whose founder was Albrecht Ritschl (d. 1899).

Ritschl looked for religious truth neither in natural science nor in pious sentiment, but in the "Christian consciousness," that is, in the successive and cumulative revelations of God in the experience of the church or community in its historic development. This emphasis on the historical experience of a religious community, more outspoken even than in Catholic theology, made it possible to determine the "essence" of a religion in terms of its history (or social evolution, as our Americans were apt to say). In this process God is revealed and divine judgment takes place, but the revelation is not of God's essence (which transcends human knowledge) but of God's value or meaning in history. Dr. Gordon, the modernist leader, had spoken of "the humanity of God" as "an infinite mystery," and he used the term "humanity" as a vague equivalent for humaneness, incarnation, and personality. The Ritschlians, by taking their theology out of the cosmological and metaphysical context, were able to give a historical definition of God-related-to-man. Thus the essence of Christianity could be defined and defended empirically (historically) without making a pretense of the kind of cosmic knowledge of God which both orthodoxy and evolutionary modernism claimed to possess. Adolf von Harnack's *What is Christianity* (1901) became the most popular exposition of this historico-empiricism in Christian theology. The first major American works to take up this theme were David Swing's *The Theology of Albrecht Ritschl* (1901), Henry C. King's *Reconstruction in Theology* (1900) and *Theology and the Social Consciousness* (1902), William Adams Brown's *Essence of Christianity* (1902), and George B. Foster's *The Finality of the Christian Religion* (1906). A long series of similar works followed rapidly. The general spirit of this approach to the "essence" of the Christian faith is stated succinctly by Foster:

> As moral teaching is not morality, artistic ideas not art, and patriotic precepts not patriotism, so religious teaching is not the whole of religion. If religion be life, then life, and not ideas, is the criterion of life; and to measure religious life by religious ideas is to measure the whole by a part. What is thus true in general is true also of the Christian religion.[12]

The Germans had developed this theological method by elaborate studies of the history of Christian thought in the context of Christian institutions, and the upshot of it all was to substitute for the Bible as central authority the historical or "living" Christ. Or, as Lewis F. Stearns put it, "We are trying to 'Christologize' our doctrine of God."[13] Such an enterprise, of course, gave almost endless opportunities for the reinterpretation of the New Testament in search of "the historical Christ."

But many of the liberals cut short this painstaking historical inquiry by appealing to a more contemporary version of the "Christian consciousness." There was a long tradition of empirical theology in America, beginning with the revivalistic, "experimental religion" of Jonathan Edwards and his followers, cropping up again in the Andover school's appeal to a "personal encounter with Christ,"[14] and culminating in the individualistic psychology of religion which grew out of William James's interest in analyzing religious experience. Consequently it was an easy jump for these American liberals to interpret Ritschl's "Christian consciousness" more practically and "teleologically" than he had conceived it. Thus Henry C. King wrote:

Christ is thus not only morally and spiritually at one with God, and so absolutely unique in his perfect response to the will of God, but also may be said to be metaphysically at one with God, when essence is interpreted teleologically. The newer and the older, the personal and the metaphysical, forms of statement would thus fall together; but there can be no doubt that the personal and practical form of the confession of Christ's divinity is, for the vast majority of men, much the more rational and surer test.[15]

And it was another easy jump from this practical or teleological location of Christ's authority in men's present-day confession of Christ's divinity to a more pragmatic disregard of the problem of authority entirely. Imagine, for example, the following coming from the Episcopalian Bishop of Michigan in 1909:

The mind of to-day is intensely practical, if not pragmatic. It insists that for it, at least, a valid Christianity is to be known, not by its *roots*, but by its *fruits*. It is saying, somewhat impatiently sometimes, to the advocates of religion, "Granted for the sake of the argument (though we are by no means sure of it), the genuineness of your ancient springs and reservoirs and the unbrokenness of your aqueducts, what of it? The one question that concerns us is, What is the character of the stream which reaches *us* from these sources and through these channels? Is it 'the water of life' to-day as it was of old? Can it quench the thirst of *our* souls? Can it still cleanse the uncleanness of the human heart? Can it invigorate our moral and ethical life?" . . . If it can do these things, we will accept it as valid for to-day. If it cannot, we must reject it, no matter how authentic its origins and traditions.[16]

This American version of Christian experience with its openly pragmatic appeal to "fruits," when coupled with the imported Ritschlian appeal to the historical experience of the Christian churches, provided a perfect foundation for liberal theology. The pragmatic empiricism gave it a forward-looking perspective, the historical empiricism a background of tradition; combined, the two furnished both scientific method and religious authority.

Thus American liberal preachers and teachers arrived at what I am calling a critical common sense attitude and appeal.

The literature of this liberalism is so voluminous and so familiar that I shall not describe it in detail.[17] It culminated in the immensely popular sermons and devotional books of Harry Emerson Fosdick, whose words are still fresh enough in our memories and whose influence is still evident enough, to make an exposition of his common sense appeal unnecessary. Though he traveled widely and preached in the pulpits of many denominations, he was best known as the builder and preacher of Riverside Church, New York, which became a national source and symbol of interdenominational liberalism. His plain eloquence and common sense made him the favorite spokesman for a large and growing body of middle-class Protestants who were indifferent toward theology but devoted to the life of their churches as a normal and central part of their culture. Probably the most influential of Fosdick's books in popularizing the "modern-positive" gospel was his *The Modern Use of the Bible* (1924); here he explained that the fundamental use of the Bible is to bring men to Christ, who as a living reality is the true foundation of Christian faith and that the power of the Bible to lead us to such "abiding experience" of Christ is more important than the "changing categories" of biblical criticism.

This same point of view can be found expressed with the same simple eloquence which Fosdick used in a very early collection of sermons preached in 1903 by Charles E. Jefferson and published under the title *Things Fundamental*. I have chosen a few passages from these sermons to represent liberalism in its early prime. (See Exhibit XIII.)

Social Theology

While a distinguished group of liberal preachers were thus making the Christian faith reasonable to men of common sense and good will, another group was appealing even more directly to action by preaching the Social Gospel. In the foregoing chapter we have already told the story of the development and meaning of social Christianity. It remains here only to tell how the theology which the promoters of the Social Gospel gradually developed reinforced the doctrines of liberalism which we have just been considering.

Religious social action was even less theoretically conceived in America than was religious liberalism. In its early formulations it was not only antitheological but antiecclesiastical. One reads, for example, in many of the early appeals that the church is merely one of the human institutions into which the Kingdom of God must come and that instead of keeping itself aloof from a hostile or "worldly" society, the church must also be transformed along with the rest of the social order. A Christian society will transform all institutions into channels of grace and the world will be saved collectively. The appearance of two works clearly marked this theological trend: in 1913 Gerald Birney Smith of Chicago published *Social Idealism and the Changing Theology* and in 1917 Walter Rauschenbusch published *A Theology for the Social Gospel*. These two were very different answers to the question of what kind of a theology is implied by the Social Gospel, but together they gave to the movement a broader intellectual expression, which proved useful to both its friends and its foes.

G. B. Smith's theology was the more American of the two and closer to modernism. It was a frank appeal to Christians to cut loose from traditional "aristocratic" and exclusivist attitudes toward the world which have haunted them since their earliest ages, and to ally themselves with the "secular," modern forces of moral and technical progress. He called this a democratic theology, and since such theologizing is still a novelty for most readers, it will be well to give here a substantial specimen.

. . . The empirical attitude toward human problems suggested by the method of Jesus was supplanted by the belief that moral principles were to be determined, not by observation and induction, but by exegesis of authoritative scriptures. This ideal has persisted through the centuries, and is still the fundamental presupposition of religious education in most churches. . . .

But the time came when the growing intellectual powers of men reached out in new experiments; and some of these experiments met with surprising success in enlarging the borders of human knowledge and in improving the conditions of life. Little by little the moral claims of these new "natural" doctrines began to make themselves felt . . . .

Now the religious consciousness trained in the older fashion does not easily discover in this manipulation of "secular" and "material-istic" resources the spiritual significance which it ought to possess. The means of grace have been conceived essentially as miraculous provisions for our eternal welfare . . . . If no religious interpretation is given to the scientific ideal, it will come to constitute a formidable rival to the church; but if the latent religious significance of scien-tifically directed effort be clearly brought out by Christianity, the territory of Christian aspiration and activity will be so expanded as to create boundless enthusiasm.[18]

Smith then points out that theology has not kept pace with such changes in religious experience and that it is high time that "divinity be defined in accordance with the dictates of our re-ligious experience."

We still picture it as something essentially belonging to an "other" world, and needing to be brought into this world by a special process. We feel that, in order to recognize it, it must be so set apart from the "natural" order that it shall appear as something unique. But, at the same time, we are compelled by the scientific and the moral demands of our culture to pare down and to modify those miraculous characteristics which formerly stood as the signs *par excellence* of divinity. The next step in the development of an ethical theology must be the translation of the categories of divinity into terms compatible with democratic ethics. We must learn to think of God as the immanent co-worker always toiling with his children rather than as the sovereign to whom they are subject, and from whom they receive special benefits and favors as from a patron . . . . For in this wonderful world with its infinite resources there is room for all that the human spirit holds dear. God is found working his marvels of transformation in the many varied processes of growth which lead to beauty and to moral life and to worship. Nothing is to be despised which leads to awe and reverence and moral aspiration.[19]

In sharp contrast to this enthusiastic reception of the modern world and its morals, stands the theology of Walter Rauschen-busch. He takes the stand of a prophet judging the world, calling it to repentance in view of the imminent coming of "the King-dom." The apocalyptic note is reasserted vigorously, and in addi-tion there comes the reassertion of collective guilt, sin, and redemption. However, Rauschenbusch does not preach the wrath of God. God is a loving father, who in Christ's life and in

Christ's "mystical body" of the church, becomes a collective reality. Christians are a community in and with God for the collective salvation of the world. This historical process of salvation is the Kingdom of God on earth, and it "comes" whenever men assume their collective burdens and work for the "Christianizing of the social order."

It is obvious that Rauschenbusch's type of theology would dominate "evangelical liberalism"; and as times grew harder and tougher his prophetic appeal forced into the background the more complacent and secular preaching of the philosophically radical liberalism of the Chicago group, George Birney Smith, George B. Foster, and Shailer Mathews. However, Shailer Mathews himself, in an autobiographical sketch, explains succinctly the forces which transformed his own thinking from the social implications of speculative modernism into an ideology for social work:

It became increasingly clear that theology was a phase of a religious movement and that as such it could not be understood as if detached from the operations of social groups. A theology which serves as a basis and test for the integrity of a group life is very different from truths abstractly considered. It must be approached from the social and historical fact rather than from metaphysics . . . .

Years of experience in committees composed of all sorts of men of Christian and non-Christian faith inevitably affect one's attitude toward religious beliefs. One comes to feel that in religion one is dealing with highly complicated social situations and histories. The history of doctrine becomes the history of people who make doctrines. The theologian seems to be less a philosopher and more a social engineer and, one had almost said, a social psychoanalyst. Christianity as a religious social movement comes to have a wider meaning than a religious philosophy or a body of infallible beliefs.[20]

During the twenties such Christian liberalism had its heyday. (See Exhibit XIV.) With a few exceptions the leaders of theological and of social reform within the churches combined forces and by organized coöperation gave an amazing momentum to the movements for institutional and moral reconstruction which we have already surveyed. Before we turn to tell of the attacks on this powerful liberalism, we ought to tell briefly of the analogous movement within Judaism.

Like their Christian neighbors Jewish religious leaders recognized the advantages of a historically oriented ideology over the naturalistically inclined theology of Reform Judaism during the late nineteenth and early twentieth centuries. Leading Reform rabbis recognized the need for the shift to a more Judaistic theology. Though it clings to its modernistic faith in the need for "expressing itself anew," Reform Judaism is now much more concerned to emphasize distinctively Judaist ideas and heritage and shares much of the cultural nationalism of Conservative Judaism. At the meeting of the Institute on Reform Jewish Theology, March 19, 1950, Rabbi Samuel S. Cohon said:

Reform, like the older expressions of Judaism, must continually reorient itself in the ever varying cultural and intellectual climate of the times . . . . Judaism has a character of its own and its own sources of insight and of strength, which we must explore, with the aid of the tools offered us by modern knowledge, for a fuller understanding and richer reformulation of our religious heritage. The renewed interest in theology, noted serious-minded laymen and rabbis, can be a blessing to Judaism if it does not align itself with the anti-liberal forces that despair of human nature, and disparage reason and freedom.

Out of this reorientation came the movement known as Conservative Judaism, which is too liberal for the Orthodox and too nationalistic for the Reform. We have already traced the importation and growth of this movement in America until it now holds a central position in Judaism; but we should point out here that the theology and ideology of this movement have won acceptance far beyond the ranks of the Rabbinical Assembly and have emerged as clearly the most influential trend in the religious thinking of American Jews today. However, being a trend, it is still fluid and no one can tell at present how far it will go. The left wing of the movement, known as Reconstructionism, has adopted an extremely modernist position in theology and is philosophically so liberal that the Orthodox have condemned it. But among the ranks of the Conservatives there is a wide tolerance on doctrines about the Torah, the Prophets, revelation, God — all within the framework of modern historical and biblical criticism. The "fundamentals" are not so much doctrinal as historical, a faith in or loyalty to the continuity and distinctiveness of Jewish tradition and culture. Accordingly Zionism has become for this type of Judaism not only a symbol of the continuous historical existence of the Jewish people, but a hope that Jewish literature, law, and piety will again take on the form of a living culture, instead of being regarded as merely a variant expression of monotheistic and universal religion. In short, the restoration of the Homeland of Israel is the focus of contemporary Jewish piety, much as the person of Christ is the focus of Christian liberalism — both tendencies being a repudiation of the overemphasis on the authority of the Bible.

The Fundamentalist Attack

The intellectual attack on liberalism came from various directions and created a many-sided battle which is still being waged and whose outcome will probably be decided by nonintellectual forces. Meanwhile it is possible to distinguish four main lines of attack: (1) Fundamentalism (which, intellectually speaking, can be identified with orthodoxy); (2) Neo-orthodoxy (which in America at least would better be called Neo-radicalism); (3) Existentialism (which is a form of theological realism); and (4) Humanism (which is liberal but not theological).

The social and moral significance of fundamentalism as a movement of the twentieth century we have discussed in other chapters. As a theological argument or standpoint, however, fundamentalism is a continuation of the repeated attempts made during the nineteenth century by orthodoxy to resist any change in doctrine. The "heresy" trials centering around such notable scholars as Charles A. Briggs (Union Theological Seminary, 1891), Henry Preserved Smith (Presbyterian ministry, 1892), A. C. McGiffert (Presbyterian ministry, 1900), Borden P. Bowne (Methodist, Boston, 1904), and A. S. Crapsey (Episcopalian, Rochester, 1906) are analogous to those at Andover Seminary several decades earlier, and, for that matter, to the long and tragic list that goes back at least as far as Socrates. And the attempts to keep the ministry of the major Protestant denominations free from modernist innovations has proved to be a losing cause. The culmination of orthodoxy's stand came in the case of Princeton Seminary, and resulted in the retreat of the orthodox faction, which established Westminster Seminary, Philadelphia, as an interdenominational headquarters for the old-fashioned type of biblical exegesis. Though Professor Gresham Machen was in many ways a competent New Testament scholar, his attempt to make such scholarship serve the cause of fundamentalism has by this time shown itself to be quite futile. Bible study is increasingly being established on the general principles of historical criticism, even though there is no general agreement on the ultimate implications of these principles.

The grounds on which the Pope attacked modernism in his Encyclical *Pascendi gregis* (1907), his reference to "curiosity and pride" as sources of the trouble, were even more *ad hominem* than those of the Protestant champion of Biblical authority. However, the real grounds that moved both the Pope and the fundamentalists were their realization that anyone who took modernism very seriously would have difficulty in explaining why the Christian faith should be taken authoritatively, and that a churchman could, therefore, not be loyal wholeheartedly to both the historical faith and to modernism. If one asks, "To *what* are 'the fundamentals' fundamental?" the differences of interest immediately emerge. The "things fundamental" in Charles E. Jefferson's liberalist sermons involved the very beliefs on which the fundamentalists insisted, but in Jefferson's treatment the "things" rather than the beliefs were fundamental to religious living; in other words, the Bible is more fundamental than belief in the inspiration of the Bible, miracles more fundamental than the belief in certain miracles, sin and forgiveness more fundamental that theories of atonement, and so on. But popes, bishops, father confessors, and preachers must speak with authority, and to religious authority, the validity of certain beliefs is fundamental, even if they are not fundamental for religious living. From their point of view the church itself is undoubtedly fundamental if authority itself is fundamental. But the liberals were undermining authority. When President Eliot of Harvard could proclaim, "The world has had too much of authority!" (see Exhibit XV), there was cause for worry.

Fears for authority were well-grounded, but authoritarian attempts to refute modernism scientifically and morally were pitiful. Modernism could be stopped, perhaps, but intellectually orthodoxy could not be defended so easily. The Catholics immediately and the Fundamentalists gradually realized that some more scholastic methods would be needed. The development of neo-Thomism as a defender of the Catholic faith is an important modern achievement which has served the Church well because it has exploited the Thomistic appeal to reason rather than the ecclesiastical appeal to authority. The story of this development would take us outside the United States, for until very recently American Thomism has but followed feebly the paths blazed by European scholars. In any case it is obvious that the kind of systematic orthodoxy which Scholasticism has erected is very different from the fundamentalist appeals to the Bible.

There are signs here and there that an evangelical scholasticism may arise among American Protestants. Certain evangelical theologians are attempting to defend the basic doctrines of orthodoxy by empirical argument rather than by biblical authority. For example, in Louisville, Kentucky, not far from the disgraceful performance of the Scopes trial, where William Jennings Bryan and the fundamentalists tried to defend the Tennessee law that prohibited the teaching of evolutionary doctrines, Edgar Y. Mullins, President of the Southern Baptist Theological Seminary, was making a more lasting impression on students by his serious attempts to present "the doctrinal expression" of Christianity as a reasoned account of Christian experience. *Why is Christianity True?* (1905) is the title of one of his most popular books; and it reflects his attempt to give to evangelical doctrine at least a philosophical form and to defend it by the methods which its opponents have used in their attacks. However, relatively few orthodox teachers are willing to rest their faith on empirical grounds, or, more accurately, to risk their faith in empiricist argument.

The Revival of Theology

So-called neo-orthodoxy or neo-radicalism in theology met modernism and liberalism more effectively by exhibiting their shortcomings, charging that they did not go far enough; liberalism failed to keep pace with the religious needs and experiences of a world in crisis. The experience of crises was indeed something for which liberalism was not prepared. The optimistic faith in progress and evolutionary providence survived the First World War because many liberals convinced themselves, as did their Presbyterian leader, Woodrow Wilson, that "a war to end war" could be justified on Christian as well as on pragmatic grounds and that their faith in the coming of the Kingdom might have this dramatic, though not anticipated, culmination. But in the light of the failure of the League of Nations, the failure of various church "world movements" and reforms (notably Prohibition), the Depression, the deepening conflicts with secular authoritarianisms and brutalities, it seemed that the sermons of liberal preachers and the efforts of social reformers were a voice from the past. The world had changed and needed a different gospel. Reinhold Niebuhr's *Reflections on the End of an Era* (1934) not only expressed the new mood, but made preparations for a new era. According to these reflections man has little chance for redemption if he follows either the resources of human nature or the logic of history. Hence a religion of grace or a gospel which holds out hope of a transcendent source of redemption can bring some comfort, if not strength, to the "human spirit in its inevitable defeat in the world of nature and history." [21] This might be interpreted by Marxists as political and moral defeatism sugarcoated by spiritual "opium." But it was intended to recall the churches from their complacent social politics to a more pious trust in God, despite the difficulties which the logic of history were raising for the liberalist faith in historical Providence.

The prophets of the crisis came from the ranks of liberalism itself; and this is a significant fact. Liberalism was reforming itself ("under God," of course). The attack seemed to come from the outside. Systematic lamentations, imported from Germany during the twenties and thirties, descended on America like the voice of doom. After Spengler came Karl Barth, then Emil Brunner, then Karl Jaspers, and Paul Tillich; meanwhile, lamentations in another key were coming from the disciples and translations of Kierkegaard. A new vocabulary, a strange philosophy of history, a sophisticated use of the "Word of God," a trumpeting of transcendent judgment overwhelmed not only the spirit of American complacency but also the voices of American idealism. Thus the atmosphere became charged overnight with apocalyptic judgment. This sound and fury of "dialectical theology" was a theological thunder that rolled out over an exploding culture. It was an expression of the crisis that ended liberalism's dream. Its philosophy was foreign, but it was used among American liberals to describe a fate which also seemed to have overtaken them from the outside. It did not seem plausible to Americans at first that the cruel task to which this generation is doomed should be in any sense a consequence of their own sinfulness or blindness, and like Job they were inclined at first to defend the validity of their idealism, charging that "demonic" forces from abroad had precipitated an undeserved tragedy. But gradually during the last two decades, the self-confidence of Americans has been undermined and at least their religious leaders have been viewing collective human sin more radically and critically than the earlier prophets of the Social Gospel had done. In any case, however true it may have been in 1903, when Gordon wrote "optimism is a faith that has good foundations," [22] it has now become clear not only that the foundations of optimism are gone, but that the Christian faith has little to do with optimism. In a sensational "confession," preached in 1935, Harry Emerson Fosdick repudiated humanistic tendencies in liberalism and proclaimed his belief in a theology "beyond modernism." (See Exhibit XVI.) Other liberalist leaders, too, were ready to return to a more theological and doctrinal message.

The neo-radicalist message, however, was clearer in its denunciations than in its positive directions; its doctrine of sin was more conspicuous than its doctrine of grace. Certain positive features, however, could readily be discerned. It was militantly Protestant or a "neo-Reformation" theology. Liberalism had minimized the doctrinal differences between Catholics and Protestants, hoping to achieve some basis of practical coöperation with Catholics on social questions. Now, with the revival of theological discussion, came an insistence on the Lutheran and Calvinist view of man, on the "pessimistic" and antirationalist view of human nature, in contrast to the "rationalism" and "perfectionism" of Thomism. The attack on Catholic theology coincided with the attack on Catholic politics for abandoning the cause of socialism. The neo-radicals were for the most part militant socialists and hoped to win the leadership of Christian socialism after Rome had announced its own social philosophy. Since Marxism was relatively weak in the United States the Protestant Christian socialists hoped to win the sympathy of American labor, and they moved decidedly "to the left" of the platform on which the Social Gospel had stood. But as militarism grew and socialism became increasingly complicated both in theory and in practice (as was noted in the preceding chapter), these neo-radicals were compelled to use vague, if not rhetorical devices to designate their "frontier" radicalism, and often the "left" hand hardly knew what the right hand was clasping. In such a mixed-up world of affairs, about all that the social interpretation of religion could hope to do was to maintain the faith that there is a practical relation between human history and the Divine Kingdom, while admitting that the "plan" of salvation is indiscernible. Or, as one of the leaders put it frankly, "Many of us are seeking for a basis for loyalty to the purposes of God in history which does not depend upon expectation of results in our time." [23]

There is a significant theme that runs through the theological thinking of the whole half-century — the doctrine of atonement. The New Theology of the late nineteenth century fought its stormiest battles over this doctrine, and it was largely because of these bitter controversies that the modernist reaction against all theology set in; but in the midst of the reaction Josiah Royce revived its philosophic discussion in his *Problem of Christianity* (1913) and made a social theory of atonement basic for a theory of the church. Rauschenbusch preached the social interpretation of the cross of Christ as "bearing our sins" of bigotry, graft, corruption, militarism, and inequality. One of the late works of the veteran liberal, Shailer Mathews, was entitled *The Atonement and the Social Process* (1930) and revealed his ability to sense the need for a revival of this fundamental doctrine of Christian theology. Vicarious suffering, whether or not it is accepted as the primary form of redemption, is now regarded as a tragic but essential element of the moral life. This return of "the cross" to a central position in ethics has meant a return of Christianity and

Christian theology in many liberalist circles which during the early decades were not specifically Christian. In general, the attempt to conceive a social theology on which Protestants, Catholics, and Jews could agree has lost much of its attractiveness to all three parties. Wherever there is active theological construction there is a strengthening of the walls between religions, for however universal the themes of theology may be, each system has its peculiar idioms and is part of a particular faith. The community of tragedy which has engulfed all mankind has given all religions new life insofar as they meet or interpret this universal tragedy, but the systems of interpretation necessarily diverge. The return of the cross and martyrdom has driven Protestant, Catholic, and Judaist theologians to revive their different ways of reconciling such suffering with monotheism, but at the same time it has created a "community of suffering" that transcends all conventional boundaries and induces the various theologians of tragedy to share in this universal fellowship. The huddling together of Christians into an ecumenical movement under these distresses has its parallel in the recognition within each religion that all are being tested and that consequently all should respect religious devotion in general.

Theological Realism and Existentialism

These trends in radical social theology have been accompanied by a transformation of the philosophical orientation of religious thought. The absolute idealism which had nourished liberalism gave way to a theological realism, and the evolutionary enthusiasm to existentialist analyses of man's relation to the world. Though any theologian is aware of this basic shift in current philosophy, it is not easy to define clearly the change that has taken place; for in part the change is not so much intellectual as emotional, a change of attitude both toward the world and toward God.

The reaction against absolute idealism which had grown steadily since William James had launched his attack in the field of technical philosophy and metaphysics, was beginning to take shape as a positive world-view. Whitehead popularized a theory of cosmic process which was a version of emergent evolutionism. Whereas previous evolutionists like Samuel Alexander had followed the conventional pattern of regarding "Deity" as a culminating emergent in the process, and whereas the Hegelians had conceived the eternal "Reality" to be the *object* of the process of "realization," Whitehead regarded God as the principle of *actuality* within the process. This putting of God into time and assigning to him the continuous, creative function of making ideal objects concrete, made a considerable theological difference. "Actualization" in the sense of bringing "eternal objects" down to earth, permitting them to "ingress" into history, is the reverse of the idealistic "realization" which assumes that particulars are gradually being transformed into "concrete universals" as the progress of freedom and knowledge advances to its final "objectification." This actualistic God of Whitehead's made it possible to relate the historical theology (taken over from Ritschl) to natural philosophy, and to give a cosmic framework to a theory of incarnation that previously had appeared to be all too human. This realistic theology was further encouraged by the publication of John Dewey's *A Common Faith* (1934), which also gave an empirical, realistic account of the continuity between the real and the ideal.

Theologians now began to construct a general philosophical theology, which might reconcile the newer "process philosophies" of secular realism to actual religious practices and faiths. The most notable attempts in this direction have been made by Douglas C. Macintosh, Walter Horton, Henry N. Wieman, and Charles Hartshorne. It is impossible to give here an adequate account of their systems and it would be confusing to elaborate the differences among them. In general, however, the realistic reaction undermined the humanistic strains in liberalism. As moral optimism collapsed, the doctrine of the "humanity" of God lost its hold on philosophical theologians. God was now represented by the "faith-realists" (as Tillich called them) as the absolutely other, the ultimately encountered ground of being, the principle of actuality, the awakener from dreams and illusions. God, they explain, stands over against man and man's world; God's realm is neither natural nor social. In the words of one of realism's champions, Robert L. Calhoun of Yale: "Over against the minds of all men is an other, one or many, of such nature that it may suitably be called the divine, or God. For religious realism it is no human construct, but an obdurate environmental factor having ways of its own that condition, sustain, and, in part, set at naught the wishes and ways of men." [24]

Existentialism, which on the continent of Europe had achieved considerable proportions in secular philosophical circles, where it had undermined idealistic metaphysics much as realism had done in America, was imported into America as a distinctly religious philosophy. The Danish Protestant critic of Hegel, Sören Kierkegaard, and his Spanish, Catholic disciple, Miguel Unamuno, were introduced during the thirties as radical critics of the Social Gospel and as romantic exponents of an anxious and agonized conscience. They made available for religious reflection the kind of personal concern and analysis which had become fashionable in secular literature and important in medical and moral science. But their analyses of "the human situation" were not taken to be realistic in America or for Americans; they were eagerly read by many Americans as symptoms of disintegration elsewhere. Gradually, however, as American idealism lost its confidence, a sober worry about the human situation in general began to take on major proportions; there arose among theologians and philosophers a critical literature which brought into relief the more personal aspects of maladjustment, isolation, frustration, guilt feelings, which used to be displayed in religious revivals. These were now presented as prevalent facts of modern experience and culture, and as empirical evidence that the Christian and Jewish theologies which represent man as a lost or estranged creature in a hostile world were based on fact, and that they apply as much today as ever. Thus there grew what Unamuno called "the tragic sense of life," and among theologians there grew a respect for the tragic themes in the theologies of sin, damnation, election, and "salvation from above."

Existentialist analysis, which seemed for a few years to be bringing Jewish, Catholic, and Protestant theologians within listening distance of each other, now seems doomed to a largely Protestant career. The papal condemnation of existentialism (Encyclical *Humani generis*, 1950) will no doubt confine public teaching and theological publication to the conventional patterns of neo-Thomism. Behind this Roman façade, however, there will certainly continue to flourish in private those experiments in reconstructing orthodoxy in view of modern thought which have enriched Catholic thought in all ages. It takes more than a papal encyclical to prevent the thoughts of Martin Buber, Gabriel Marcel, Jacques Maritain, Paul Tillich, and Nicholas Berdyaev from influencing each other.[25] In America especially this inter- play of international and inter-faith ideas must continue to bear fruit and to prevent the kind of dogmatic purity which popes and fundamentalists pray for and which is incompatible with theological or any other growing science.

If, as seems quite possible, the realistic tendencies in philosophi- cal theology become more closely related with existentialist doctrine on the one hand and with historical and social theology on the other, a significant school of American theology may emerge as one of the major intellectual reconstructions of our time. In other words, during the last two decades Americans have been made aware that they have a share in the European agony out of which existentialist theology came, and they no longer regard this religious expression of tragedy as the senti- mental ravings of a few disjointed spirits. The theologies of tragedy (including, by the way, the revival of ancient Greek tragedy) have become realistic, even if exaggerated, portraits of our own age and situation. The realization that our "historic doom" is not an unintelligible experience, that it is an inherent phase of centuries of human struggle, and that our theology, if it is to be adequate, cannot be merely "new" but must relate us to the historic careers of other peoples and alien faiths, gives to our religious ideologies inherent dignity and enduring meaning. And it also makes it easier for us to understand prophetic literature in general. The voice of prophets must be biblical, though the hands be rough with modernism; such preaching of the ancient "Word of God" as an ever new revelation of what "passeth under- standing" need not be hypocrisy, as the liberals assumed it to be, but may be the most articulate groaning of which a world in travail is capable.

Among Judaist scholars this realistic integration of religious thought has progressed further than among Christians. The Reconstructionist Movement which the Society for the Advancement of Judaism has promoted combines the historical, philosophical, and social aspects of Judaism in a remarkable and radical way. But being specifically a theory of Jewish civilization and national aspirations, it is not directly applicable to a more universal theology, except as an illustration of method; and, besides, the rabbis are far from agreed as to how far this kind of reconstruction can be carried without being destructive.

The New Humanism

One more phase of the critique of liberalism must be mentioned to round out our account of the present intellectual situation. A minority of the liberals, their modernist wing, has concluded from the course of events that liberalism fell into disrepute because it was not liberal enough, because it made compromises all along the line: compromises with theism, with nationalism, with supernaturalism, with ecclesiastical politics, and with sectarian interests. To them the chief enemies of free religion are the flight from reason, the defense of historical creeds, the institutionalization of faith, and the lack of fraternal respect among religions. Discouraged by the revival of theology and intolerance among religious bodies, these modernists from many faiths have banded together under the banner of humanism. Though they are trying desperately not to become one more sect, and therefore are cultivating an informal fellowship among humanists of many religions, they are inevitably becoming militant and are organizing for missionary activity. Intellectually humanism has not yet achieved an orthodoxy of its own, though humanist creeds are being circulated, and a "fourth faith" is in the making. In *A Humanist Manifesto*, first published in 1933 but still used by the group as an anticreedal creed, the most striking affirmation is the seventh, containing the following definition of religion:

Religion consists of those actions, purposes, and experiences which are humanly significant. Nothing human is alien to the religious. It includes labor, art, science, philosophy, love, friendship, recreation — all that is in its degree expressive of intelligently satisfying human living. The distinction between the sacred and the secular can no longer be maintained.

Though this statement could readily be criticized as a definition of religion, it serves admirably, as most creeds do, not to define religion in general but to exhibit the import of a particular faith. Basic to this faith is the attempt to substitute for the distinction between the sacred and the secular, the distinction between the humane and the inhumane.

There are among the humanists left-wing Unitarians who reflect the liberalism of Emerson and who like him do not wish to be confined to Christian limitations. There are materialists who are no longer "doctrinaire" materialists, but who are suspicious of theologians who use terms like "soul," "immortal," "transcendental," "God," and "Spirit"; they prefer more secular language for more secular truths. There are naturalists who are disgusted by the sophisticated use of supernaturalist symbols and myths among neo-radical theologians, who find no use for organized religions, but who have a "religious" concern for the life of reason. There are still a few old-fashioned rationalists, freethinkers, or professional atheists, who mourn the failure of humanitarianism as a universal religion, and who are therefore willing to call themselves religious humanists. There are many liberal spirits in the ranks of Christian churches, Judaism, Ethical Culture, and other distinctive religious bodies, who resent the exclusiveness of their organizations and join the humanist fellowship in order to bear witness to their personal, broader faith. And there are many individuals who cannot be labeled, since they do not feel at home either in any religious body or in the cold world of secular interests; nevertheless they seek some expression for their passionate desire to promote "the complete realization of human personality" and "a free and universal society." The humanist societies have succeeded in bringing these various kinds of liberals together for fellowship, instruction, publication, and promotion of their common interests. The reappearance of humanism as an independent religious movement is significant in spite of its small numbers. It gives proof through the night that modernist liberalism still lives as a positive religious faith, that the demand for religious expression exceeds the supply offered by conventional religious bodies, and that philosophers are not as hopelessly individualistic as they appear to be to more conformist minds. Those who share the comforts of a conventional religious home are continually confronted in a free country with free religion. Though freethinkers are apt to appear as religious orphans or vagabonds to those whose intellectual lives are more comfortable and sociable, these free spirits in their wanderings and seekings produce their fair share of prophets, and usually serve the causes of enlightenment and brotherhood which no religion worthy of the name would now dare to deny, since all are ashamed when they betray them.

There exists also in a form less organized and evident than the religious humanist movement a significant number of religious secularists. For them secularism represents neither irreligion nor religious indifference, but a positive concern (as near to "absolute" concern as they dare come) for certain values and institutions, which they wish to defend as sacred, if necessary, against all organized religion. They regard themselves as the champions of democracy, freedom, and science, and they often appeal to the spirit of Thomas Jefferson as their American patron saint. They are usually anticlericals and believe that it is possible to express a "common faith" to which all free spirits are loyal and which unites those whom organized religion divides.

How many reformers and prophets have suffered persecution and martyrdom in their efforts to do away with the cramping survivals of religious infantilism! How childish do the trappings of orthodoxy seem to the mature mind! How eagerly do the traditionalists and the fundamentalists cling to the doctrines and forms of religion which have lost their power to enlist the hearty support of modern man! Is it not high time that we unite in the endeavor to define and practice a religion of adults? [26]

Horace M. Kallen has given an able and representative expression of such religion in his *Of Clericalism and Secularism in Religion*.[27] For how many of the approximately 30 per cent of Americans who are religiously "unaffiliated" he speaks it is difficult to say. But it is necessary to recognize that secularism or its equivalent exists as a positive faith, that it is not necessarily "Godless," though unorganized and theologically inarticulate, and that it is not religiously illiterate. It is strongly represented among the literary intelligentsia, in political circles, among social scientists, and ex-Marxists. To have religion without benefit of clergy is indeed getting it free if not easy, but the common prejudice expressed by churchmen that such religion reflects a too "easy conscience" is in most cases without foundation. The chief difficulty that confronts the observer is knowing where to draw the line between such religion and irreligion. For, as Meyer Schapiro well says, "Religion now has its fellow-travelers." [28]

5.

TRENDS IN
PUBLIC WORSHIP
AND RELIGIOUS ART

Theology has a double duty: it must keep religious faith abreast of the growth of knowledge, and it must make a particular mode of worship intelligible. The dawn of the century found theology more conscious of its duty to science than to worship. There seemed to be a mutual estrangement between doctrine and cultus, doctrine fraternizing (as has been shown in the preceding chapter) with science and philosophy, while cultus threw in its lot with social service. In their wanderings both have learned their need for each other, and their present reconciliation has given new vigor to both. Theologians as well as laymen now realize that worship is the very life of religion and have ceased to think of it merely as an "external" means to internal grace; they conceive it as an end in itself, as one of the "humanities," dignifying life and enriching American culture. The creation of this conscious will to worship is for Americans an achievement of the twentieth century and a product largely, I should think, of the agony of our times. It was a wise Frenchman who said, "Experience teaches us that we must sooner or later bend the knee, and it is before God that it is least humiliating to bow." Americans too have come to feel the religious *need* rather than the ecclesiastical *duty* of worshiping, and have returned to their churches and temples in devotion to a God whom they have learned to fear and love. Thus sobered, and, as it were, driven to their knees, Americans are demanding more of public worship than their fathers did.

Traditional Distrust of the Art of Worship

It is necessary to explain the prejudices and handicaps under which worship suffered even among religious persons fifty years ago, and which still survive in large segments of the population; for only if one understands these obstacles to the conscious cultivation of the art of worship, can one get a just appreciation of the creative work which has been done in recent years.

First of all there is the long-standing Puritan prejudice against formalities, ceremonies, and sacraments, which all smacked of "popery." The papal theory of worship has been reasserted recently in the Encyclical *Mediator Dei* (1947). The general purpose of worship is defined as being "the greater glory of God and the sanctification of men" and the pope explains further: "Although public liturgical prayer has a greater excellence than private prayer, yet through the latter the faithful become properly disposed to receive the sanctifying action of the liturgical rites."

That worship is for the glorification of God was universally accepted, but that liturgical prayer is more "excellent" (presumably meaning "for the greater glory of God") than private was an offensive idea to the Puritans, and that sacramental worship is sanctifying rather than "of the saints" was a peculiarly polemical issue. Not only did Puritans strip their churches bare until they were little more than schoolhouses, or as they called them, meetinghouses, but they refused to participate in the public or corporate celebration of feasts and fasts, of marriage and funerals. They cultivated simplicity, austerity, integrity; and their arts (especially their architecture and sermons) express these ideals. Accordingly they devoted their congregational assemblies largely to instruction, their ministers being regarded as primarily teachers. The public service was largely didactic; it was not so much a coming into the presence of God (for they worked daily in the presence of God) as a coming together to hear the Word and the Law interpreted.

In this they consciously resemble the Jews, who make a sharp distinction between the temple rites of worship, and the synagogue rites of study. Hence in practice the priesthood and the ancient sacrifices are subordinated to a different form of piety, to "the love of the Law." Such moralistic and didactic conceptions of congregational life are widespread in America, even among those who are ignorant of the ways of the Puritans or of ancient Israel. Precisely because meetinghouses and synagogues are "man's inventions," not biblical institutions, they are regarded as external to "true" religion. And the pomp of ecclesiastical celebration or of sacramental liturgy, being, even more clearly, man-made, seems to these persons a perversion of piety, a transformation of artificial ornaments into ecclesiastical obligations. "What doth the Lord *require* of thee?" All else is excess. "It needs to be emphasized that ritual is not religion, but only a recognition of the importance of religion, and an aid to the formal observance of it, — a technique of organized religion." [1] These words though written by a liberal Unitarian, Harold Scott, reflect the opinion of the great majority of American Protestants. I remember hearing a Fundamentalist preacher at the climax of his sermon shout, "I tell you, brethren, God *hates* religion; he wants faith!" This notion that religion is religiosity, and that a cultus is either idolatry or foolishness, is shared by some of the most pious and the most impious Americans.

The didactic conception of worship militates against the impersonality which is required in a liturgical service. And this is more than a matter of taste. Protestant ethics in America has been personalistic and individualistic, and the relation between man and God has been interpreted personally. Impersonal "channels of grace" and forms of mediation consequently appear to be not merely uncongenial formalities but positive intrusions into an intimate, personal relationship. To put worship into the context of the "amenities and courtesies" [2] of polite society is offensive to the "shirtsleeve" informality and equalitarianism of American life and smacks of hypocrisy. A ceremonial sacrifice is not a real sacrifice and a ritualistic penance may not express real contrition.

For similar reasons Protestant ministers abhorred the "professionalism" necessary in the administration of the sacraments and in formal prayer. "A good priest does not publicly tell God or the people how rotten he feels on many a morning when he must deal with the holiest of holies. Yet it is a very short step from this necessary discipline to a routine of dissimulation." [3] This hatred of dissimulation (which drove Emerson out of the ministry) is still a serious obstacle to the priestly office, and to anything in worship that resembles professional "acting."

This attitude among Americans also explains the power which preaching missions and evangelistic appeals still wield over large sections of the population. Preachers like Billy Graham can exhort men by radio, press, or transecclesiastical pulpit to "come to Christ" personally and individually, relying on "Bible study" rather than on church ceremonies or religious education. It is significant that such appeals are now made in terms of "the old time religion," and that such preaching is now treated popularly as closer to entertainment than to worship. In these times the gospel of olden times, though its content may be the same, has a new meaning; it has acquired the value of an antique. Such sentimentalism is a genuine trait in the American people, and their worship will naturally reflect this trait.

The distrust of conventional worship because it is essentially "organized" religion is also prevalent among what the sociologists call "the cults." Few cults have any use for cultus. The possession of a special revelation carries them beyond the pale of ordinary worship; they are chosen peoples, proclaimers of esoteric truth. "Organized religion stands exposed as being not of the Lord God," declares Judge Rutherford in behalf of Jehovah's Witnesses; "religion is revealed as the unchangeable foe of Christianity." [4] Like Christianity when it was newly born, such prophetic movements and mysteries repudiate "organized religions," and proffer a universality of vision or revelation which, if accepted, would make conventional worship obsolete. The frequent expressions in these movements of disillusionment, of the failures of churches to satisfy the demand for truth, make them important, if not eloquent, witnesses to the inadequacies of public worship. There is an inherent, native wildness in being God-possessed, and this religious frontier has by no means disappeared in America. It makes those who are willing to cultivate "organized religion" as such and who have a will to worship aware of the vast difference between believing in God and believing in religion.

It is widely believed that worship arises naturally or spontaneously, and that education in worship may spoil it. "Worship arises as spontaneously in the heart of the religious devotee," writes Professor Josey, "as love arises in the heart of the youth who has found in the maiden beauty, inspiration, and understanding. . . . Lack of the spirit of worship is therefore a symptom of a serious defect in one's religion which cannot be met merely by stressing the value of worship."[5] This may be true enough, but it may overlook the fact that if "the heart of the religious devotee" is allowed to be as unreflective as "the heart of the youth," worship may be too much like "natural" passion, and adoration may be as romantic as in an "adoring" youth. Worship normally begins, if an individual is born into a religious environment, as a habit (conventional rather than "spontaneous") and like all habits it comes under the eye of criticism when a person achieves intellectual maturity. It must then be evaluated "in the spirit of worship" and not, as Professor Josey goes on to explain quite correctly, in terms of "enriching life" or "strengthening character." But many believe that the attempt to cultivate consciously the spirit of worship is both impractical and an impious interference with the work of the Holy Spirit. It is quite typical of the American sentimental and individualistic tradition that the last stanza of Coleridge's poem should be very familiar:

> *He prayeth best, who lovest best*
> *All things both great and small;*
> *For the dear God who loveth us,*
> *He made and loveth all.*

whereas the first stanza has a foreign sound:

> *O sweeter than the marriage-feast,*
> *'Tis sweeter far to me,*
> *To walk together to the kirk*
> *With a goodly company!*

Of a very different sort is the conviction found chiefly among Catholics and Greek Orthodox that God himself has prescribed fairly rigid limits for the art of worship, since he has divinely ordained a particular cultus — a "divine office" for public prayer and a group of sacraments and sacrifices, culminating in the Eucharistic sacrifice which is a divine *action*. Even those liturgical churches which do not believe that their liturgy is a divine action have so great a respect for traditional forms, that their ideals for liturgical art are essentially conservative. For the great body of the faithful the forms of worship are taken for granted as established once and for all, so that their observance is a religious duty rather than a form of religious expression. Added to this is the widespread popular belief in the magical efficacy of rites, which gives to worship a utilitarian sanction.

Most serious of all, perhaps, is the growing opinion among persons of cultivated taste and education in the arts, that the techniques of worship are hopelessly antiquated. The churches being as they are, such anticlericalism cannot be ascribed wholly to malice or prejudice. Of what use is it to pour new wine into old bottles? A little modernistic church architecture here, a modern anthem there, a bit of religious drama or dancing, an occasional "streamlined Station of the Cross" — these are but artificial intrusions of the spirit of art into an enterprise which as a whole is no longer creative and makes no pretense of competing with the secular arts in the field of aesthetic expression. During the early years of the century many of the liberal clergy themselves felt such skepticism, and no longer tried to make church services attractive, but sought modern substitutes for traditional worship.

Growth of Interest in Liturgy

Despite these serious handicaps, religious artists (if I may so call them) have achieved remarkable results in raising the level of appreciation for the intrinsic values of worship, and in rebuilding rituals to make them expressive forms appropriate to our culture.

The initial impetus in the rebuilding of worship came from abroad. The Liturgical Movement in Catholicism is over a century old, having received its inspiration from the Oxford Movement and from the work of Dom Prosper Guéranger. The former emphasized the "corporate adoration of God" by the church as "the Mystical Body of Christ," the latter, with Solesmes, France, as a center, spread the revival of Gregorian music and other ancient liturgical forms, especially among Benedictine monasteries. With papal patronage the movement took hold in America early in the twentieth century. Its American headquarters is the Benedictine Abbey of St. John, Collegeville, Minnesota, and the movement is publicized by the Liturgical Arts Society (formed 1930), by its fine magazine *Liturgical Arts*, and by the Catholic Art Association, which publishes *The Catholic Art Quarterly*. The movement has generated two distinct aims whose confusion is apt to interfere with the success of either: one is the promotion of the liturgical arts for the enhancement of worship, the other is the patronage of Catholic artists and development of a Catholic school of art criticism and appreciation. The combination of these two aims has led to the attempt to revive the art of sacred drama — such as passion plays, miming of the Stations of the Cross, morality plays, and oratorios. These combinations of worship and entertainment were, of course, important elements of medieval culture, and there is no reason why they may not live again in modern dress. But for the time being they are somewhat pathetic — a too obvious attempt to make worship compete with the secular arts of entertainment. That the structure of the Eucharistic sacrifice is dramatic is true enough, and that there must be an intrinsic aesthetic value in worship is also true; but it takes a genius to combine the art forms appropriate to liturgy with theatrical techniques without spoiling both. When plays become "strictly conventional" as liturgies must be, and when worship becomes operatic as dramatic music tends to become, the results are neither religiously nor artistically impressive. It takes a greater genius than Wagner showed in *Parsifal* to put the essence of Christianity on the stage. (Wagner may have intended it as satire more subtle than Nietzsche's.) T. S. Eliot's *Murder in the Cathedral* is an effective religious drama, especially when performed in a church, but the author would probably be the last person to regard it as a form of worship. The passion plays I have seen have some interest as folk art, but they are pathetic tableaux rather than passion plays. Still, it would be absurd to

deny the theoretical possibility of using masques, dances, drum-
ming, tragic drama, chamber music, and any other form of expression as techniques of worship or of religious celebration.
But such ritual forms must come from the gradual hallowing
of genuine forms of a living culture, not from the attempt to
introduce archaic and primitive forms even though these have
enduring aesthetic value. Dean Sperry, commenting on the revolt
against sentimental worship, sums up the problem very well:

> The occasion for the antivanilla revolt was and remains a sound
> one. But the familiar solution, in the form of a retreat to medieval
> modes and Latin texts, though probably the simplest and most obvious
> at hand, sometimes seems too easy a solution of this whole problem.
> One has the suspicion that the choice of much of this music is
> prompted in part by a pedagogic attempt to improve our musical
> taste. That improvement must take place gradually; it is never a sudden
> conversion. In any case, when the pedagogic attempt to inform and
> improve us supersedes the endeavor to find fitting vehicles to express
> what we already think and feel, the nature of the resulting act of
> worship is subtly altered. By going to a church which has good music
> my taste may be developed in the course of time, but I do not go to
> church in the first instance to have it developed, even though such
> development may ultimately ensue.[6]

Religion may use as much art and as many arts as it can, but
the art of worship remains a distinct achievement. On the whole,
the Catholic Liturgical Movement has been most successful in
spreading popular appreciation for this distinctiveness of worship, even among those for whom the Catholic rites remain
"medieval." In fact one of the dangers in the cultivation of the
liturgical art is the love of archaicism and primitive forms, and
one of the purposes of the Encyclical *Mediator Dei* was to protest against archaic revivals such as the use of "table" for "altar"
and the use of vernaculars. On the other hand, such legislation
is apt to serve purely conventional standards, so that the progress
of liturgical art is confined within too narrow limits. By its
very nature the art of "sanctification" is less free than the secular
arts, and it must respect what is *de facto* hallowed. This fact
tends to throw the emphasis toward folk art, toward congregational participation in Gregorian chants, toward popular festi-
vals, novenas, and other traditional devotions.

In this connection, however, we should mention a significant American liturgical movement among the Evangelical Reformed Churches. It arose in connection with the "Mercersburg Theology" (Mercersburg Academy, Pennsylvania) about 1870, which, in turn, was inspired in part by Philip Schaff's acquaintance with the Plymouth Brethren. The critical and creative liturgical emphasis created by Nevins, Schaff, and other members of the Mercersburg School seemed to be a purely local phenomenon, but within the last two decades it has taken on new life and inspired a general liturgical development in the Evangelical Reformed Churches and may well spread beyond them.[7]

The High Church Movement in the Episcopal Church is also a liturgical movement and has contributed much toward restoring the sacramental conception of worship to Protestant churches in America. The history of this movement in the United States would take us back to the early nineteenth century, to the days of Bishop Hobart, but it is only since 1916, when a commission on revision of the Prayer Book emphasized constructive liturgical changes, that many Broad Churchmen have coöperated with High Churchmen. This coöperation produced not only the Prayer Book of 1928 but also the so-called "Liberal Catholic" trend in theology, which implies an acceptance of modernism in the field of historical criticism and ritualism in the art of worship. Thus the new Prayer Book made a critical selection among the Psalms "so that the more notably un-Christian portions of the psalter could be practically disused in public worship. In the lectionary, a much larger use was made of the Apocrypha, once the detestation of all good Protestants. And even in the Epistles and Gospels, there was throughout a decided freedom in the treatment of Scripture, and a large amount of textual correction." [8] The Catholic Breviary form of absolution was inserted after the Confession, and prayers for "thy servants departed this life" were added, indicating a conscious trend toward "communion of the saints." At the same time the recommendation of the Catholic party to substitute the title "The Holy Eucharist" for "The Holy Communion" was rejected. Likewise rejected were frequent proposals to take "Protestant" out of "Protestant Episcopal Church." But in their Catholic zeal

some of the Episcopalians have exceeded even the Roman Catholics in championing the "corporate" channels of grace or sacraments. Thus Theodore Wedel writes: "The Holy Spirit is hence
forth a corporate, not an individual possession. Church and Holy
Spirit are from this point on inseparable. . . . Apart from this
corporate community, there is no gift of the Holy Spirit." [9]

The Episcopalian combination of Apostolic authoritarianism
in worship and in church government with modern liberalism
in biblical and theological doctrines has set a popular pattern
for Protestant priests in several denominations who welcome the
liturgy as an expression of the Christian tradition and of the
freedom to use the pulpit for modest observations which make
no pretense to oracular authority or prophetic message. The
"Word of God" thereby gains an impersonal dignity and authen-
ticity which is usually lacking in sermons. The attempt has been
made to put social doctrines as well into the liturgical context,
which is again being more Catholic than Rome. Thus in the
Episcopal Church there was founded in 1939 the Society of the
Catholic Commonwealth, composed of priests and laymen for
the purpose of "applying Catholic liturgical analysis to the secular
and economic process."

Meanwhile the Methodist Church staged its own type of liturgical revival. It repudiated the apostolic succession as a theory of
church government and became explicitly democratic. At the
same time the Methodists made a few timid moves in the direction of Anglican worship, or as they say, in the direction of
the "primitive" Methodism of the Wesleys. The General Conference of 1916 urged greater congregational participation in
Communion Service and stricter adherence to the formulas. In
1932 the term "Communion" was given preference over "The
Lord's Supper" and the ceremonial act was defined as "partaking
in the divine nature through Him [Christ]." In 1944 the *Book
of Worship for Church and Home* was greatly enlarged, bringing it closer to a prayer book. Meanwhile the music, vestments,
and order of service in the larger churches were becoming increasingly ritualistic.[10]

There is a curious paradox in the current tendency of the
Roman Catholic church toward an evangelical emphasis in wor-

ship and the current trend among the evangelical churches toward liturgy. They may be learning from each other or they may both be yielding to the popular tastes of American folkways. But the historian must smile at the spectacle of a conservative, conventional community of Southern Baptists being invaded suddenly by a caravan of Franciscan Tertiaries in autotrailers or trucks labeled "The Outdoor Apostolate," "Evidence Guild," "Motor Pulpit," or "Catholic Campaigners for Christ." Some of them advertise that they are "converts from Marx to Christ." They set up street-meetings, distribute tracts, and give "information" to souls hungry for the true gospel. I have heard from Catholic pulpits plain, pastoral preaching such as would make an old Methodist recall the good old days of biblical simplicity. Similarly the historian must smile when he sees side by side a Baptist Gothic cathedral and a Catholic "colonial" meetinghouse.

Silent worship has become an increasingly popular form of public rite. Respect for the Quaker technique of being "quiet before the Lord" has grown far beyond the confines of the Society of Friends. Especially in college communities, mixed services, and occasions on which traditional rites seem impractical or inappropriate, a brief "silent prayer" is frequently employed. This form is not necessarily a mere confession of inarticulateness or diversity, but may be a positive confession that the emotional and intellectual content of an occasion exceeds the abilities of speech or image or music to express; meaningfulness and uncommunicativeness often go together in both mystic and nonmystic communion. On the other hand, the resort to silence has its dangers. As Dr. Felix Adler has pointed out: "The great thinkers may be silent because their thought is too vast for them to express; but depend upon it, if silence become the rule in the world with respect to an idea, then that idea will soon utterly perish." [11]

Changes in Religious Architecture and Music

The cultivation of the art of worship is reflected in the changes which have come over church architecture. (See Exhibit B.) There are a few changes which have little to do with religion and which reflect changes in the art of building. Modern materials and architectural forms are beginning to be used in religious buildings, but in general the "hallowed" forms are apt to survive longest in sacred art. Modernist design is resisted for much the same reason that modernist thought is resisted — fear of infidelity. But a few distinguished modernist churches have been built during the last decades. Rexford Newcomb states:

As early as 1900 Bernard Maybeck erected a unique and original church for the Unitarians in Berkeley, California. A half dozen years later came Frank Lloyd Wright's Unity Temple in Oak Park, this to be followed by other works by Wright and his pupils, Bruce Goff and Barry Byrne, who have made significant contributions to modern church design. Among the more interesting American churches designed in a modern vein are the Boston Avenue Methodist Church (1929) at Tulsa, Okla., by Goff; Church of Christ the King, Tulsa, (1930), Saint Francis Xavier, Kansas City, Mo. (1948), and Saint Thomas More (1948) at Iowa City by Byrne; the Tabernacle Church of Christ (1940) at Columbus, Indiana, by Eliel Saarinen; and Saint Vincent's Archabbey at Latrobe, Pennsylvania (1948) by Emil Frei.[12]

But there are significant changes in style that are the outcome of the religious reconstruction. During the early years of the century the functional demands of the larger institutional churches required an establishment for the various activities of the congregation — educational, recreational, social service. The result was a type of building which has been described by a prominent minister as "our modern streamlined garages that go by the name of churches" and that give "one more evidence of how the church is capitulating to the culture and secularism of our society." [13] The central feature of these buildings was an auditorium, like a theater except that curved benches were used instead of curved rows of seats, facing a platform whose central furnishings were a pulpit and three chairs, a pipe organ and choir seats (curtained off below the hat line), and, below or behind the pulpit, a small altar or communion table. Surrounding the auditorium were sliding doors for segregating Sunday School classrooms, or for overflow. In the basement, the tower, or the rear of the building — or in all three — were club rooms, kitchen, dining room, gymnasium, stage, offices, and so forth.

Such buildings are now out of style and out of favor. A well-ordered congregation has these separate buildings: a house of God for worship, a parish house or its equivalent for the activities, and a rectory or parsonage for the priest's or minister's residence. The houses of worship have become more visibly and sincerely monuments to God as well as places of assembly. The Gothic style, which was revived earlier in academic architecture, has now become the most popular standard, especially among Protestants. It even invaded Reform Judaism (witness Temple Emmanuel on Fifth Avenue in New York) and the Swedenborgian Community at Bryn Athyn, Pennsylvania. At least a score of notable Gothic monuments have been built recently. The architectural and also the ideological leader of the recent Gothic revival was Ralph Adams Cram. Here and there a little Romanesque and Byzantine has crept in. (Notable is the Methodist "Christ Church" in New York.) This return to the consecrated styles of Christian history was, of course, part of the liturgical movement. Altars, open chancels, stained glass, sculpture, and the rest were accepted even by those liberals who used a minimum of liturgy.

With it there came a revival of liturgical music. Quartets gave place to genuine choirs, and semisecular, operatic anthems gave place to sacred music. The standard for church music both Protestant and Catholic now came closer to the standard which had been defined in the Encyclical *Motu proprio* (1903) of Pope Pius X: the music must be "true art" and "holy" and "universal." The musical form should be subordinated to the "general characteristics of sacred music" in such a way that "nobody of any nation may receive an impression other than good on hearing them." The musical performance of an average American choir cannot be called "good," but it may nevertheless make a "good impression" if the music attempted is appropriate to the ritual. The sentimental "gospel hymns" were excluded from newer hymnals. A very austere, almost Gregorian, standard was set by the Harvard Hymnal and the Harvard choir under the direction of Professor Archibald T. Davison. These standards are in fact so severe and antisentimental that they have received only limited approval and application among a sentimental populace; but they mark an unmistakable beginning of the trend toward the objective and "universal."

Meanwhile those denominations and sects to whom such "organized religion" is anathema, have gone to the opposite extreme. Especially in our large cities there has been a mushroom growth of "store-front" churches; gospel missions, and tabernacles, in which old-time religious business is being carried on with a vengeance. Here the gospel hymns and the sentimental religious ballads flourish, while evangelists of the "full gospel" make their highly rhetorical and emotional appeals.

In short, what has happened to worship during this half century is that the mediocrity which characterized worship early in the century has given way to both the better and the worse. Whether there is a class distinction underlying these aesthetic extremes is a moot question, which involves the general sociology of art and education.

The lines are not always clearly drawn between the objective and the sentimental. For example, there is in the new Episcopal hymnal among the "Hymns for Children" a "hymn" set to a rollicking balladlike tune by an American composer (John Henry Hopkins, 1940) and marked to be sung "with vigor." It is very popular and reflects in many ways the genial, democratic spirit of American culture in Christian dress. (See Exhibit XVII.) I might also recall in this connection having heard a children's sermon delivered by an Episcopal priest in connection with a liturgical morning prayer on the Sunday after Ascension Day. He explained that the Ascension is a very important feast of the ecclesiastical calendar and concluded by saying, "Children, the lesson which the Ascension teaches us is that there is always room at the top." No doubt it was such modernism which the Pope had in mind when he condemned it. But the popes are not in a much stronger position when they explain that it is important that the body of the Virgin should be with her soul in the heavenly presence of God, while they leave the idea of "bodies in heaven" a complete mystery.

Theories of Worship

Liturgical movements have overcome to a large extent one of the popular prejudices against public worship, the fear of formalism, except insofar as these movements themselves have become "attitudinarian." Formalities when they are composed of significant forms need not be screens for empty heads or weary souls. Another deep-seated prejudice in American culture is being overcome — the notion that the daily work of "service" is a more adequate service to God than are public "services" of worship. A philosopher friend of mine is devoting himself to preaching what he calls "the gospel of workship." George Albert Coe, one of the pioneer liberals who tried to make the "life of prayer" intelligible in terms of modern psychology and value theory, proclaimed the doctrine that "Monday is as holy as Sunday, because all our time belongs to God; . . . doing the duties of life with hand or with mind is as religious as prayer." [14] Similarly, Dean Sperry cites with approval the old saying, *Laborare est orare.* He proceeds to qualify his approval, however, as follows:

The act of worship, while it may not be divorced from the life of work, is an act which may be distinguished from the manifold forms of human helpfulness. Christianity holds that the practice of the brotherhood of man is a necessary consequence of a profession of faith in the fatherhood of God, and that without that practice such a faith is vain and dead. But this does not mean that the initial ascription of divine fatherhood to God is a gratuitous and unreal act, with which we may safely dispense. On the contrary Christianity holds that the inclination and the will to practise the brotherhood of man depend upon the constant adoration of God as father. If men were to cease the worship of God the greatest single incentive to fraternal ways among men would be withdrawn, since no social compacts entered into for mutual advantage, or for the greatest good of the greatest number, have the moving power which inheres in the thought and love of God as the father of all men.

If the church does nothing else for the world other than to keep open a house, symbolic of the homeland of the human soul, where in season and out of season men reaffirm their faith in this universal fatherhood of God, it is doing the social order the greatest possible service, and no other service which it renders society can compare in importance with this.[15]

The "principle of alternation" between work and worship has been developed most fully by William Ernest Hocking both as a general philosophy and as an argument for worship. In his *The Meaning of God in Human Experience* (1912) he outlined a new theory of mysticism and linked mystic experience with worship. In ordinary practical experience, Hocking explains, we must attend to details or "parts"; in worship our attention shifts to "the whole" which is implied by our dealings with parts but of which we are not conscious while at work.

There is something about our practical attention to any part or parts which turns self-defeating, and requires such complete abandonment of the parts, and reversion to the whole as religion has demanded, that whole which is different from all parts. And there is also something about practical attention to the whole which turns self-defeating, and can only be recovered by occupation with the parts. Hence the movement of our temporal life must swing between them . . . .
We are by "our finite situation," bound in a predicament from which our active selves cannot shake free, though the ultimate knower in us is not involved in it. Ambition and duty, all use of conscious freedom, all *work*, in short, develops of itself an inner opposition, or spiritual checkage. For this loss of margin, as the artificial self becomes identified with its own assumptions and objects, is a progressive impoverishment of that *whole-idea*, whose use, . . . gives all objects what value they have. In order that my various practical enterprises should go on well, it is necessary that my various ends should maintain their worth; and in order that they may hold their worth and interest, my whole-idea must be active in all my occupations . . . . And whatever recovers the worth of living by *recovering the natural vigor of the whole-idea* is worship, or a part of worship . . . . Worship, we may say, is *the self-conscious part of the natural recovery of value;* it is that part, therefore, which assigns all other parts their place and meaning.
Worship cannot last; it also has its type of self-defeat and death. The worshipper who persists in his contemplation of the whole, thinking to establish himself permanently in the immediate presence of God, becomes an automaton, precisely as the determined worker becomes a machine.[16]

This argument has provided a reasonable justification for the periodic shift from workday to sabbath, from "week-day self-assertion to Sunday self-abasement," from doing God's will to adoring the divine majesty, and from the thinking which solves problems to the meditation which promotes moral perspective. It also gives a reasonable argument against the professionalization and isolation of worship as in monasteries or among mystical ascetics: worship overdone is worse than none, for it fails to sanctify man's work.

It can readily be seen why such analyses of worship would be seized upon by moralists and educators to justify religion by its use in character formation. In breaking down the resistance of secular moralists who deprecated any obstacle to "integration," and who regarded any appeal to the sacred as an insult to the secular and as incipient schizophrenia or "vicious dualism," the theory that "alternation" is a normal, healthy, mental process and that man must periodically make "total responses" was very effective. After Hocking, Charles A. Bennett, Henry N. Wieman, Hugh Hartshorne, and other philosophers paved the way for a more tolerant attitude on the part of rational moralists toward worship or toward what they loosely called "mystical" experience. Gradually educators tried to make place for religious rites as an aid in the creation of an adequate "sense of values" and conversely, religious education was patterned on the principle that worship centers in "the realization of value."

Though this defense of worship on moral grounds was an effective entering wedge, in the long run it proved disastrous for theology, because it subordinated religious experience to moral education. It assigned a "subjective" being to God, and a pragmatic value to religion. Catholics ridiculed it as being merely one more evidence of the individualism and subjectivism inherent in Protestantism. Accordingly there arose a need for some more objective and religious conception of worship. Several objective idealists (notably Hocking himself) and several objective realists (notably Professor James Bissett Pratt of Williams College) came to the rescue. They showed that worship did not achieve its aim unless it brought the worshiper into an objective or "real" presence of God. This theory of "the real presence" was taken up by Dean Sperry of Harvard and given a very impressive exposition in his *Reality in Worship*, a book which has dominated American discussion of worship ever since its appearance in 1925. The importance of this approach to the theory of worship lies in its treatment of symbolism. According to this view religious symbols are not merely indicative of their objects, they are revelatory; an icon is not a representation of the divine, it is a "channel of grace" or a means of making the divine a present reality. The value of worship is its ability to take us consciously into the presence of God.

In a reminiscence Professor Pratt gives us a delightfully frank statement of the kind of considerations which led him to attach greater importance to public worship:

It is now nearly thirty-five years ago that I first thought of writing a book on the question, "Can We Keep the Faith?" I was then at the beginning of my work as a college teacher . . . . I decided on the title and I wrote one chapter. The chapter was about *sincerity in religion*. Last year I unearthed the ancient chapter. . . . I was impressed when I wrote the chapter, with the need of greater frankness in the expression of Christian beliefs; and my hope was that if the churches and their leaders would drop those portions of their creeds which are no longer living beliefs and would express outspokenly their sincere faith, Christianity would find itself in an unshakable position. I still believe in the pressing need of sincerity; but I am less sanguine than I was about it as a cure-all, and I have (as I now believe) a deeper insight into the nature and use and value of religious symbols . . . . The American scene has changed considerably, in part certainly for the better, but not without some loss as well as gain. There has been a growth of insight and of sincerity, but also a growth of indifference. And indifference is the greatest danger that Christianity, or any other religion, has to fear. . . .

A large proportion of us keep on repeating the old and blessed formulas when, to use James' words, "the sincere heart of us is elsewhere."

The proper place of symbols in religion is thus a question as difficult as it is important. . . . The thoughtless, conventional use of religious symbols may be not only dishonest but deadening. There is nothing that suffers more from being made merely polite, conventional, and second hand than does religion. There is nothing that more needs to be thoroughly empirical — a firsthand immediate experience of the individual, a living force abreast of and in advance of the times. Religion indeed wishes to be useful and beautiful: but it also means to be true. It is not, to be sure, a theology, but it must have a theology, a genuine belief about ultimate matters. And this theology it must not consider as poetry.[17]

Pratt then goes on to explain that the proper use of symbols in worship is not their value as instruments of communication, but their power to move the emotions and imagination of the worshiper beyond his capacity to define and to communicate. A religious symbol leads to communion rather than to communication. And he cites a passage from Professor Wilbur M. Urban of Yale, an influential Anglo-Catholic layman, which sums up admirably the "objectivist" theory of worship:

> The reason why the religious symbol, even in its most developed forms, never loses the character of poetry is that religious language must be lyrical and dramatic or it is nothing. . . . The religious symbol distorts the intuition to suggest and represent the infinite and the transphenomenal. It is always supernatural in all the possible meanings of this word. An extreme, but in a sense typical, illustration of such distortion is [the common Hindu image of a god]. When Hindu religious art symbolizes the infinity of divine activity by the figure of a god with innumerable arms and legs we have a distortion of nature in order to express that excessivity which is a necessary character of the infinitely other. Such distortion, like that of art, is a fiction, but it never is felt as such, either by artist or worshipper, for it is apprehended as a symbol and not as a literal picture, and expresses "values more real than the real values.[18]

Pratt has stated clearly the shift which has come over religious thought on the subject of worship since the early years of the century: the hope of the early years was that by cultivating sincerity religious men might achieve clarity of faith, but the experience of subsequent years taught them that even though God is not known clearly, his power and glory can be felt indubitably once the indifference to worship has been overcome. And indifference to worship can be met only by making worship worthy of its objective.

Another type of religious philosophy which encouraged the reform of worship was the "religion and art" school. It became popular under the general reaction against theology and "scientific religion" early in the century. And it became a controversial issue during the period of the heresy trials when young ministers were given the choice of being "sincere" in rejecting the creeds or of admitting a merely aesthetic interpretation of worship. Professor Kirsopp Lake of the Harvard Divinity School stated forcefully the reasons why the younger or "experimentalist" generation could neither subscribe to any of the creeds as statements of their "opinions" in doctrine nor reject them as elements of worship.

The Creeds are not merely official statements of doctrine, but part of the Liturgy, and in dealing with the Liturgy those born in the English Church, and still more those who, like myself, were ordained in it long before they realized any of these theological problems, perceive that the difficulty is to preserve, not to destroy. . . . "The Histories of Christianity" are all full of doctrines which have been dropped and forgotten. . . . To drop the creeds would be to register a fact, not to introduce a revolution. . . . This is because the Creeds are not mere statements of doctrine. Their use as theological statements for the prevention of wrong opinion or heresy is antiquated, and ridiculous because ineffective; it ought to be abandoned. . . . For theologically the Creeds are all Fundamentalist, and they cannot be anything else. . . . The creeds which were not taken into the liturgy have irrevocably perished, but those which are recited in the services of the church live on. . . . It is perfectly true that the theology of this liturgy is quite alien to mine, or to that of any Experimentalist. . . . Nevertheless the liturgical art of the services of the church, like the architectural art of its cathedrals, rouses a response in me which cannot be wakened by any modern service or by any modern building. . . . The Institutionalist . . . ought surely to say frankly . . . "The creeds do not represent our belief; the 'I' in them refers only to the author; but the service is our heritage, which we will neither give up nor mutilate." . . . To retain the creeds as part of an uplifting and inspiring liturgy, to abandon them as statements of thought is a possible programme for the Experimentalist, and may, I believe, be adopted before long by many Institutionalists.[19]

This clear statement of antifundamentalist institutionalism is limited to a theory of liturgical art, but it indicates a willingness to assign to art in general a greater scope within religion in general than the more rationalistic spirit of early American liberalism did. This attitude among the liberal clergy was given abundant support by social scientists, whose anthropological studies of religious symbolism in the context of folk art and collective mentality supplanted the earlier, less informed accounts of the evolution of religion out of "animism."

The most vigorous champions among the clergy of this point of view came from the Chicago radicals. The Chicago group

Creation of the National Council of Churches of Christ, Cleveland, Ohio, November 28, 1950 (Photo supplied by the National Council of Churches)

Unity Temple, Oak Park, Illinois, 1907, Frank Lloyd Wright, Architect (Courtesy of the Museum of Modern Art, New York City)

Blessed Sacrament (Roman Catholic) Church, Stowe, Vermont, 1948, Whittier and Goodrich, Architects. Painted glass windows by André Girard represent thirty scenes from the life of Christ. Exterior panels painted on wood represent the work of Brother Joseph Dutton among the lepers of Hawaii. (Photo supplied by Liturgical Arts Magazine)

*Tabernacle Church of Christ, Columbus, Indiana, 1940, Eliel
Saarinen, Architect (Hedrich-Blessing Photo)*

Millburn Synagogue, Millburn, New Jersey, Percival Goodman, Architect (Photo by Alexandre Georges supplied by the Architect)

Church of St. Clement (Episcopal), Alexandria, Virginia, Erected 1948, Joseph H. Saunders, Architect. The strong liturgical effect is achieved by the central altar and exclusive downlighting through a dark ceiling. The altar is surrounded on the two ends by the congregation and on the one side by the reading-desk pupit-lecturn unit and on the other side by the font and main entrance, over which is the choir balcony. (Courtesy of the Reverend Darby Betts)

were influenced as theologians by Schleiermacher's emphasis on celebration (*Das Festliche, Das Feierliche*) in religion. One of their leaders, Gerald Birney Smith stated the theory as follows:

> The intellectual understanding of religion is admirably provided for. But as yet there is little appreciation of the fact that religion at its best furnishes a noble aesthetic interpretation of the meaning of life. Religion at its best brings poetry and music and pageantry and adoration into the life of men. Growing religion is always creating these characteristic means of expression. . . . In the last analysis, religion is an art rather than a science.[20]

Smith's colleague, Von Ogden Vogt, wrote two influential volumes, *Art and Religion* (1921) and *Modern Worship* (1927), in which he developed this theme in detail. Worship, said Vogt, is "the celebration of life"; ceremonial is life's holiday. By formalizing the facts and values of human existence religion expresses the meaningfulness of the world. These themes were further pursued by Edward Scribner Ames, Henry Nelson Wieman, and Bernard E. Meland among religious leaders and by a much larger group of anthropologists and sociologists. They think of religion not only as "the mother of the arts" but as the culminating form of human self-expression. In addition, therefore, to recommending a religious use of the other arts, as Vogt and some of the more conservative members of the group do, these so-called humanists want religion to become again the chief of the humanities, the central art of our culture. From humanists and theorists such doctrine may be accepted as nothing new, but there is a real revolution in religious thinking when a Methodist minister in Michigan can formulate and promote a "Copernican Revolution" in the art of worship. (See Exhibit XVIII.)

Without attempting to adjudicate the claims of these various theories, we might summarize the net outcome of all this philosophical critique for the better understanding of the nature and aims of worship. Ideally worship should embrace at least four functions. (1) It should give formal and symbolical expression to the basic aspects of human existence in general and to the values of a culture in particular. (2) It should provide standard mediums for self-criticism and moral instruction (such as confession, thanksgiving, prayer, meditation, praise, the use of

Scriptures and sermons). (3) It should promote a distinctive kind of fellowship or "communion of saints," as well as a sense of human brotherhood. (4) And it should bring each worshiper as an individual into the presence of God. Clearly there are subjective as well as objective factors in worship. The current attack on the subjective aspects is owing largely to the association of "subjective" with "sentimental" in the languages of art criticism and moral idealism. But where there is not a union of subjective and objective, of need and power, of love and glory, there is neither art nor worship. Dean Sperry maintains two important theses regarding worship: that "the act of worship is itself the process by which we first define God," and that worship is the celebration of the "kingdom of ends in human experience." [21] The former statement calls attention to the "objective" factor, the latter to the "subjective." Adoration and celebration are neither identical nor incompatible; they are complementary.

Trends toward Public Worship

There are four chief modes of worship: personal, family, communal, and ecclesiastical. It is difficult to say with confidence what has happened to personal devotions during these fifty years. Practically everyone takes for granted that there has been a marked decline, but it is difficult to measure the extent of this decline and more difficult to determine its causes. A survey made by Lincoln Barnett for the *Ladies Home Journal*, the report of which was published in the November 1948 number under the title "God and the American People," indicates that about 95 per cent of those responding professed to believe in God, 75 per cent were church members, 40 per cent were regular attendants, and about 25 per cent acknowledged a devout, personal religious life. Usually those who admit that their personal or private devotions have lapsed are not willing to admit that they are no longer personally religious. An Anglican visitor to the United States recently reported that there prevails a "shocking personal religiosity among Americans." It is probably true that both when compared with Europeans and on the strength of their own testimony Americans take religion more personally than

other peoples do; but it is practically impossible to tell what
Americans mean by being religious but not devout. They are,
in the words of Dean Sperry, "imperfectly irreligious." Relatively few profess to be atheists, and of those who do, few are
militant; they are, as Jacques Maritain calls them, "not practic-
ing atheists." Among philosophical theologians consciously and
among many others half-consciously there may be a belief in
God, but no impulse or habit of worship. A distinguished philosopher when chided by his university chaplain for not worshiping, replied quite seriously, "I am a High Churchman, and
as I pass chapel I often thank God that we have a chapel and
that a chaplain is praying for us." There may be a few more
who, if compelled to rationalize their indifference to worship
personally, would take the position that there is a professional
class of *religiosi*, monks, priests, clergymen, rabbis whose business it is to perform the devotions for the people, and that it
is the people's duty to "support" religious institutions without
participating in them, except on special occasions when worship
is a form of expression rather than a duty. But the vast majority
take religion for granted as a ready help in time of trouble, not
as something requiring a daily regimen. Until the twentieth
century the maxim expressed by Shakespeare,

> Poor soul, God's goodness hath been great to thee:
> Let never day nor night unhallow'd pass,
> But still remember what the Lord hath done.
>   [*King Henry VI*, Part II, Act II, Scene 1]

might have passed as an elementary religious duty, but now
such advice would probably be regarded as Elizabethan. Worship
is for most laymen not a daily diet, and in their personal experience they show, whether they admit it or not, that religion
is not as central in their lives as the clergy claim it must be.

Many are not able, or believe themselves not to be able "to
get out of the harness" of affairs for periodic relaxation, recreation, and meditation, and accordingly they prefer "church work"
to worship. To many the rhythm of work and sabbath is a
nuisance, especially when they need physical rest, and to more
it is preposterous to think that there is time for devotions dur-

ing the modern working day. Neither morning, noon, nor night is "free." I know several energetic businessmen who profess a profound religious concern and expect to spend their "last years" religiously. The fact is that even among the devout, devotions are usually performed out of a sense of duty to a church rather than out of a feeling of personal need; consequently when they discover that worship is a privilege rather than a duty, they renounce the privilege.

It is of course true that religion need not take a form which would be recognized as worship. There has been of late considerable interest in devising "methods of private religious living" [22] which are more appropriate for modern man. In the next chapter we shall have more to say about "religious experience" as distinct from private worship. Suffice it here to note that one of the chief reasons for this search for new forms of religious expression is the decline in personal devotions such as are prescribed or taken for granted by the major organized religious bodies.

Family devotions have declined for similar reasons, except in Judaism. For Jews the family is still the primary center of religious observance. The Seder Feast continues to be celebrated and enjoyed far beyond anything the synagogue can offer. And many other rites are performed to sanctify the daily round of life in the home. The reasons for this strength of family worship in Judaism are not to be sought in peculiar characteristics of Jewish family life, which, if they exist, tend to vanish in American Jewish homes, but lie rather in the historic character of the religion of Israel. Folk religion is naturally in large part composed of family rites, whereas a religion like Christianity (and a life like the life of Christ) is largely independent of family life. It is both more private and more public, but it is also less patriarchal and less national than the religion of Israel from which it departed. It may be corporate, but it is less collective. In its pastoral and agricultural settings there are obvious economic reasons for the centrality of the family in the cultus, but even in modern urban life and even under the revival of a political nationalism among the Jews, it is the family rather than the community or the national homeland which remains

the focus of celebration and memorial. Nothing short of a revival of ghetto conditions or pogroms, which seem impossible
in America, is apt to shift this focus to the community center
or synagogue. Congregational worship is, of course, integral to
Judaism, but the congregation and its rabbi is less vital to the
survival of Jewish piety than is the parish church and its priest
or minister to Christianity. Christian worship can manage without family devotion, but Judaism can not retain its hold without
the family rites.

There is a type of rite, such as burial rites, which concerns
primarily a family group, though it also may concern larger
groups and communities. The religious bodies have made some
progress in conducting funeral services, but there seems to be
a steady growth in the demand for simplified services which can
be conducted in funeral parlors. Some estimates by funeral di-
rectors indicate that more than half the burials in our large
cities are made from funeral parlors, neither apartment houses
nor city churches being suitable. The churches take some part,
to be sure, in the rites conducted in funeral parlors, but the
tendency is to construct rituals appropriate to the occasion and
circumstances with only secondary reference to ecclesiastical
tradition. Dr. Corliss Lamont, who has constructed a ritual primarily with the needs of funeral parlors in mind, and who has
published it under the title *A Humanist Funeral Service*, reports
an increasing demand for it.

Professor Elton Trueblood writes, how seriously I do not
know, that "houses of marriage" may be as familiar as funeral
parlors in the near future.[23]

Community cultus, which is public in the strict sense, has
grown during the twentieth century both among Jews and
Christians. And by "community" in this context I mean a *secular*
community, which gives both geographical location and moral
meaning to a religious congregation. It is only insofar as a religious body serves some secular public, giving "spiritual" expression to the unity of a temporal group, that the German
sociologists call it a "church" in the technical sense. This reflects a survival of "establishment" notions of what religion ought
to be, and is reminiscent of ancient Rome and Israel and Puritan

New England. Strongest in America is the local community or neighborhood, such as the New England town, the village, the suburban community, the city neighborhood. Congregations are strongest when they bring into communion such communities. There has been a steady growth of Protestant community churches or federated churches, which cut across denominational lines. They are especially popular in college communities and suburban towns. More widespread and significant is the growth of "comity" among denominations, which aims at avoiding useless competition within a community. If the members can agree on a mode of public worship, other issues are apt to be regarded as "unessential." The strength of many of the denominational lines is dependent on the fact that they reflect European communities and nationalities which still preserve some vitality in America. Different kinds of Lutherans come from different parts of Europe. The Scottish connections are still important to Presbyterians, and the English to Episcopalians and Congregationalists. Surrounded by such churches, the Baptists and Methodists are apt to feel like 110 per cent Americans. Local Roman Catholic churches, too, are apt to be less Roman than they are Italian, Irish, Polish, Mexican, and so on. These cultural differences, reflecting the cultural pluralism of the American people, are probably the most powerful cause for the variety and vigor of our churches. No doubt the European backgrounds are gradually receding, and European visitors are able to detect better than we ourselves the emergence of a "typically American" form of Christian worship.

Certainly the national life of the United States has become increasingly a religious concern, especially during the years of war. There is probably less of the fanatic philosophical idealization of the nation now than during the first decades, and certainly the aims of the Social Gospel are less nationalistic now than formerly. But the struggles of the people as a whole have contributed a wealth of religious emotion and meaning to American patriotism and politics. Political ceremonies, occasions of national consecration, and patriotic rites in the public schools have contributed something to a secular national cultus, but civic religion is negligible in the United States compared with the political cults of Europe and the Orient. On the whole the celebration of the spiritual life of the American people has been entrusted to their several religious bodies, and these have risen to the occasion eagerly, so that there seems to be little sentiment even among Catholics, that Americans need either a state church or the degree of spiritual unity which Europeans are inclined to think necessary for moral solidarity. Thus the national community is composed of many types of community with distinctive spiritual traditions and rites.

Lastly there is a type of public worship which characterizes strictly religious societies, that is, communities whose sole bond of unity is a religious faith, and whose faith is in competition with others and with secular communities. Such societies, like Augustine's "City of God," are supposed to have an invisible unity in God, and to be as essentially hostile to "worldly" societies, as heaven is "above" earth. They constitute God's own public and their aim is to redeem all other forms of community. Ecclesiastical worship, in this sense of the term, is the expression of a revelation, not of a culture. A church is "a community of solitude before God," [24] whether it is related to any other public or not. When churches expressly dissociate their service of worship from their cultural environment, believing themselves to be "called *out*" of the world and not merely assembled *in* the world, their worship takes on a supernatural status which makes it immune to human criticism. It is this superiority complex, "the chosen people complex" as it has been called, that is not only offensive to other societies but also the chief cause within the churches of the revolt known as the Social Gospel. Hence many churchmen were inclined to interpret the socialization or moralization of the gospel as an antiworship campaign. In any case, ecclesiastical worship not only cuts across the other communities but is a divisive kind of community. The quality of monotheistic worship, to say nothing of the quality of mercy, is strained when each religion, or even each church, in its efforts to chain the infinite spirit of Truth to the rock of some particular church prays for militant strength against the others and against their common world. Worship has a tendency to lose its humanity when it becomes missionary.

A fighting faith certainly has its place in the world, but militancy seems out of place at the altar.

Churchmen have attempted to overcome the evils of ecclesiasticism by promoting ecumenicity, but in the sphere of worship unity seems a hopeless, if not a foolish ideal. By this time it seems fairly clear that "ecumenical" unity among Christians is important less for worship than for concerted work or fight. The leaders of the movement for Christian unity have nourished a hope that all Christians might unite their prayers before God and thus symbolize the "invisible" unity visibly. But this hope seems more sentimental, possibly even more political, than Christian piety really demands. In any case, Christian unity, like interfaith coöperation, is practical now and then for concrete objectives, and like the ideal of human brotherhood in general is more effective when operating among men than when being proclaimed before God ecclesiastically.

If we trust the empirical evidence and if we follow the type of criticism suggested by the concern for improving the *quality* of worship, there is every reason to believe that American culture with its many modes of worship, each susceptible of great improvement in its own way, may contribute more to the greater glory of God if it continues to cherish the opportunity given in America for many faiths to make their distinctive contribution to the variegated religious life of a variegated people, than it would if it forced its religious energies into a single mold. As there are many choirs in heaven, so it may be well to preserve many on earth; for both God and man may enjoy the "alternation" of varied hymns of praise in "one world."

Does the King of Kings have to explain why He delights in His creation and the continuation thereof? . . . God delights in having His creatures do some creating of their own, and that is why it says in Genesis: "He created man in His own image." Here is man's greatest title to nobility, and all human activities can be rated to the extent to which they contribute to the perpetual recreation of the world.[25]

6

VARIETIES OF RELIGIOUS EXPERIENCE SINCE WILLIAM JAMES

James's Analysis of Religious Experience

When in 1900 William James began to compose the two series of Gifford Lectures which he delivered in Scotland, he intended to discuss in the first series "Man's Religious Appetites" and in the second "Their Satisfaction through Philosophy." He never wrote the second half, and when in 1912 he wrote *The Pluralistic Universe*, which was suggested by the first series, it turned out to be not on how philosophy could satisfy religious "appetites" but on how metaphysics must be reconstructed in view of the facts of religious experience. This change of mind in James is significant not merely for his own intellectual career, but for the general transformation which was taking place in religious thought and in thought about religion. In the background of the Gifford Lectures and in James's own background was a tradition vaguely identified as "natural religion." The faith of this tradition and the theme to which James as "Gifford Lecturer on Natural Religion" was supposed to devote himself was that man has natural religious "propensities" and that a philosophy which shows them to be natural can satisfy them better than can the conventional beliefs and practices of revealed religions. The "absolute" philosophical idealisms which surrounded James in both Scotland and America were not merely philosophies of religion; they were religious philosophies, substitutes for institutional religions and theologies. Many of James's friends, Thomas

Davidson, Dickinson S. Miller, William Torrey Harris, Josiah Royce, Principal John Caird, James Martineau, to say nothing of his own father, were all religious philosophers in this sense. They found religious satisfaction in philosophy; their relation as individuals to God was mediated by an idealistic system of doctrine rather than by ecclesiastical channels of grace. It was against such "gnosticism" that James revolted, for despite his anticlericalism he was confident that man's "religious appetites" could never be satisfied by philosophy. A few of his variations on this theme are worth quoting here, since they indicate not only James's own turning from rationalism but the beginning of a general revolt in America against idealistic as well as mater-ialistic absolutisms.

There is a crasser and a more refined supernaturalism, and it is to the refined division that most philosophers at the present day belong. . . . Refined supernaturalism is universalistic supernaturalism; for the "crasser" variety "piecemeal" supernaturalism would perhaps be a better name. . . . Notwithstanding my own inability to accept either popular Christianity or scholastic theism, I suppose that my belief that in communion with the Ideal new force comes into the world, and new departures are made here below, subjects me to being classed among the supernaturalists of the piecemeal or crasser type. Universalistic supernaturalism surrenders, it seems to me, too easily to naturalism. . . . In this universalistic way of taking the ideal world, the essence of practical religion seems to me to evaporate. Both instinctively and for logical reasons, I find it hard to believe that principles can exist which make no difference in facts. But all facts are particular facts, . . . and yet . . . refined supernaturalism [says] . . . it is only with experience *en bloc* . . . that the Absolute maintains relations. It condescends to no transactions of detail.[1]

These passages throw light on the extremely personal or in-dividualistic emphasis in James's account of religious experiences. He was trying to prove that there are two types of consciousness more basic to religion than the type of "universalistic," rational, and philosophical consciousness in terms of which theologies usu-ally defend faith: these are religious feeling and religious illumina-tion, the emotional and the mystical aspects of religious experience.

His account of mystic illumination emphasizes certain Ameri-can characteristics. He gives much space to nature mysticism and says about "mystical moods" that "most of the striking cases which I have collected have occurred out of doors." [2] He explains that his aim in beginning with the more naturalistic and secular types of mysticism is to show their continuity with the ecclesiastical types, but he ·expends so much of his sympathy on the secular mystics and on "cosmic consciousness," that by the time he comes to the traditional and classic mystics his account lags. Among the American mystics he gives special mention to Benjamin Paul Blood's description of "the anaesthetic revelation," Ralph Waldo Trine's *In Tune with the Infinite*, and Walt Whitman's "soul-sight of that divine clue and unseen thread which holds the whole congeries of things . . . like a leashed dog in the hand of the hunter." [3] In the writings of Benjamin Paul Blood and of his Amherst companion, Xenos Clarke, James finds emphasized the point which is of chief theoretical importance to him, namely, that mystic illumination is *not* an emotional experience. In contrast to feeling, which is an attitude without cognitive claims, the mystic experience is "privately authoritative," a form of nonintellectual grasping of truth. He quotes the following remarkable dialectic from Blood and Clarke, more remarkable now than then since it contains the essentials of existentialism:

> The revelation is, if anything, non-emotional. It is utterly flat. . . . It is an *initiation of the past*. . . . The Anaesthetic Revelation is the Initiation of Man into the Immemorial Mystery of the Open Secret of Being, revealed as the Inevitable Vortex of Continuity. Inevitable is the word. Its motive is inherent — it is what has to be. It is not for any love or hate, nor for joy nor sorrow, nor good nor ill. End, beginning, or purpose, it knows not of.
>
> It affords no particular of the multiplicity and variety of things; but it fills appreciation of the historical and the sacred with a secular and intimately personal illumination of the nature and motive of existence, which then seems reminiscent — as if it should have appeared, or shall yet appear, to every participant thereof. [4]

James, the clinical psychologist, listens sympathetically to all this, but he is primarily interested in what the *"fruits"* of such experiences are. From this point of view, too, Benjamin Paul Blood is of special interest to him, since he exemplifies the individualistic salvation which mysticism brings and supports

James in his impression that such personal illuminations bring peace of mind to those who have been afflicted by ecclesiastical tortures and "Jehovan thunders." Thus Blood confesses:

The lesson is one of central safety: the Kingdom is within. All days are judgment days: but there can be no climacteric purpose of eternity, nor any scheme of the whole. . . . The world is no more the alien terror that was taught me. Spurning the cloud-grimed and still sultry battlements whence so lately Jehovan thunders boomed, my gray gull lifts her wing against the nightfall, and takes the dim leagues with a fearless eye. . . . I know — as having known — the meaning of Existence: the sane centre of the universe — at once the wonder and the assurance of the soul.[5]

Similarly, James's own interest in mysticism proceeded from experimenting with "cosmic consciousness" and with various forms of nature-mysticism to attempting to explain how mysticism could illuminate the "meaning of personal existence" and destiny without resorting to the illusions of reason or emotion. He believed that mystic experience, being an immediate contact with an objective reality or fact, is (as a type of consciousness) essentially a sensation or an observation, neither logical nor emotional.

Turning now to the emotional varieties of religious experience, we find James discussing them under two heads, "healthy-mindedness" and "sick-soul." Among the healthy-minded type of persons, in whom "happiness is congenital," he mentions Emerson, Theodore Parker, Edward Everett Hale, Walt Whitman, and the devotees of New Thought and Christian Science. And he adds:

The advance of liberalism, so-called, in Christianity, during the past fifty years, may fairly be called a victory of healthy-mindedness within the church over the morbidness with which the old hell-fire theology was more harmoniously related. . . . In that "theory of evolution" which, gathering momentum for a century, has within the past twenty-five years swept so rapidly over Europe and America, we see the ground laid for a new sort of religion of Nature, which has entirely displaced Christianity from the thought of a large part of our generation. The idea of universal evolution lends itself to a doctrine of general meliorism and progress which fits the religious needs of the healthy-minded so well that it seems almost as if it might have been created for their use.[6]

In this passage James betrays the peculiar ambivalence in his mind, revealing that while he himself was a product of this "advance of liberalism" which had produced a new, relatively pagan, religion of optimism, he could also examine critically his own heritage. He might have joined Shailer Mathews in reporting that he grew up with no sense of the urgency of social problems and knew simply that "God had been good to New England." At the same time, like Shailer Mathews he had come to realize the hollowness of such healthy-mindedness, and he treated it with condescension as a form of childishness. I cite one of his satirical passages:

We all have some friend, perhaps more often feminine than masculine, and young than old, whose soul is of this sky-blue tint, whose affinities are rather with flowers and birds and all enchanting innocencies than with dark human passions, who can think no ill of man or God, and in whom religious gladness, being in possession from the outset, needs no deliverance from any antecedent burden. . . . In the Romish Church such characters find a more congenial soil to grow in than in Protestantism, whose fashions of feeling have been set by minds of a decidedly pessimistic order. But even in Protestantism they have been abundant enough; and in its recent "liberal" developments of Unitarianism and latitudinarianism generally, minds of this order have played and still are playing leading and constructive parts.[7]

It is clear that James disassociates himself from such "popular" religion and turns with more respect to the "twice-born" type of person with his "melancholy" and his "sick soul." To those who know of James's own youthful struggle against chronic depression this clinical acquaintance on his part with such religious experience will come as no surprise. But James leaves his own experience out of account and reflects rather the current interest among both psychologists and religious leaders in the phenomena of conversion. He also reflects the spirit of disillusionment:

There is no doubt that healthy-mindedness is inadequate as a philosophical doctrine, because the evil facts which it refuses positively to account for are a genuine portion of reality; and they may after all be the best key to life's significance, and possibly the only openers of our eyes to the deepest levels of truth. The normal

process of life contains moments as bad as any of those which in-
sane melancholy is filled with, moments in which radical evil gets
its innings and takes its solid turn.

Systematic healthy-mindedness, failing as it does to accord to sor-
row, pain, and death any positive and active attention whatever,
is formally less complete than systems that try at least to include
these elements in their scope. The completest religions would therefore seem to be those in which pessimistic elements are best developed.
Buddhism, of course, and Christianity are the best known to us of
these. They are essentially religions of deliverance.[8]

Despite this basic distinction between the healthy-minded and
sick-soul types of temperament, there is a significant passage in
The Varieties of Religious Experience which shows that even
more basic in James's diagnosis is the analysis of saintliness which
can be achieved by either type; accordingly he appends as a
footnote to his "conclusions" this important admission:

The contrasts between the healthy and the morbid mind, and
between the once-born and the twice-born types . . . cease to be the
radical antagonisms which many think them. The twice-born look
down upon the rectilinear consciousness of life of the once-born
as being 'mere morality,' and not properly religion. "Dr. Channing,"
an orthodox minister is reported to have said, "is excluded from
the highest form of religious life by the extraordinary rectitude of
his character." It is indeed true that the outlook upon life of the
twice-born — holding as it does more of the element of evil in
solution — is the wider and completer. The 'heroic' or 'solemn' way
in which life comes to them is a 'higher synthesis' into which healthy-
mindedness and morbidness both enter and combine. Evil is not
evaded, but sublated in the higher religious cheer of these persons.
. . . But the final consciousness which each type reaches of union
with the divine has the same practical significance for the individual;
and individuals may well be allowed to get to it by the channels which
lie most open to their several temperaments. . . . The severity of the
crisis in this process is a matter of degree. How long one shall continue to drink the consciousness of evil, and when one shall begin
to short-circuit and get rid of it, are also matters of amount and
degree, so that in many instances it is quite arbitrary whether we
class the individual as a once-born or a twice-born subject.[9]

It is characteristic of James the clinical psychologist as well
as of James the pragmatic philosopher that his analysis of religious experience should culminate in an evaluation of the "fruits

of saintliness." He uses the term "saintliness" in a broad sense to designate the totality of the various aspects of "the religious life," and he faces the task of a moralist estimating the peculiar contributions which religious virtues and vices make to civilized life. A glance at James's attempt to distinguish between what is normal and what is excessive in saintliness will give us a good idea of the kind of religious ideals which flourished in American life early in the century.

The first observation which James makes is that a religious experience is intensely personal, unpredictable, unorganized, and that therefore all orthodoxies are impositions, and all "saints" are more or less "lonely" in the world.

The religious experience which we are studying is that which lives itself out within the private breast. First-hand individual experience of this kind has always appeared as a heretical sort of innovation to those who witnessed its birth. Naked comes it into the world and lonely; and it has always, for a time at least, driven him who had it into the wilderness. . . . When a religion has become an orthodoxy, its day of inwardness is over: the spring is dry; the faithful live at second hand exclusively and stone the prophets in their turn. . . . The basenesses so commonly charged to religion's account are thus, almost all of them, not chargeable at all to religion proper, but rather to religion's wicked practical partner, the spirit of corporate dominion. And the bigotries are most of them in their turn chargeable to religion's wicked intellectual partner, the spirit of dogmatic dominion, the passion for laying down the law in the form of an absolutely closed-in theoretic system. The ecclesiastical spirit in general is the sum of these two spirits of dominion; and I beseech you never to confound the phenomena of mere tribal or corporate psychology which it presents with those manifestations of the purely interior life which are the exclusive object of our study.[10]

This diatribe against organized religion, which might have come from the pen of William's father, the elder Henry James, is motivated largely by James's eagerness to keep politics out of religious experience, and to judge saints individually not in terms of the articles of their creeds but in terms of the moral quality of their lives. If a saint carries his piety to excess, that is a fault chargeable to his own religious experience; if he organizes a movement or church which commits crimes, the fault is chargeable to religion only indirectly, if at all.

The direct fruits of religious experience, according to James's judgment can be summarized as follows.

(1) There is *devoutness* or devotion to God, which when carried to excess breeds fanaticism. James's list of the evils of fanaticism includes "saintship based on merits." [11]

(2) Closely related to devoutness is *purity*, which is also in danger of being "theopathic." In this connection James remarks:

> The Catholicism of the sixteenth century paid little heed to social righteousness; and to leave the world to the devil whilst saving one's own soul was then accounted no discreditable scheme. To-day, rightly or wrongly, helpfulness in general human affairs is, in consequence of one of those secular mutations in moral sentiment of which I spoke, deemed an essential element of worth in character; and to be of some public or private use is also reckoned as a species of divine service.[12]

(3) *Charity* or tenderness is another saintly virtue which when carried to excess yields an indiscrimination, "preserving the unfit, and breeding parasites and beggars." Whether nonresistance is excess tenderness James hesitates to say, but he makes this striking remark:

> If things are ever to move upward, some one must be ready to take the first step, and assume the risk of it. No one who is not willing to try charity, to try non-resistance as the saint is always willing can tell whether these methods will or will not succeed. When they do succeed, they are far more powerfully successful than force or worldly prudence. . . . This practical proof that worldly wisdom may be safely transcended is the saint's magic gift to mankind.[13]

(4) *Prayer*, if taken in the wide sense of inner communion with the divine, is the "very soul and essence of religion," but petition, when its "transactions" cease to be about matters of salvation of soul or health of body is in danger of fanatical "guidance." Religious "inspiration" James regards as a use of man's subconscious energies.

(5) *Confession* is dismissed with a few succinct observations which do not indicate clearly whether James thinks confession should be allowed to lapse further into its "decadent" state or whether confession should be more genuinely public. He writes:

For him who confesses, shams are over and realities have begun; he has exteriorized his rottenness. If he has not actually got rid of it, he at least no longer smears it over with a hypocritical show of virtue — he lives at least upon a basis of veracity. The complete decay of the practice of confession in Anglo-Saxon communities is a little hard to account for. Reaction against popery is of course the historic explanation, for in popery confession went with penances and absolution, and other inadmissible practices. But on the side of the sinner himself it seems as if the need ought to have been too great to accept so summary a refusal of its satisfaction. One would think that in more men the shell of secrecy would have had to open, the pent-in abscess to burst and gain relief, even though the ear that heard the confession were unworthy. The Catholic church, for obvious utilitarian reasons, has substituted auricular confession to one priest for the more radical act of public confession. We English-speaking Protestants, in the general self-reliance and unsociability of our nature, seem to find it enough if we take God alone into our confidence.[14]

It is to (6) _asceticism_ that James gives the most critical attention. At a time when philosophers were condemning it as immoral, James makes a special point of defending asceticism, provided it can be given an up-to-date form. The passage in which James recommends poverty as a needed discipline in a war-torn world is still worth reading as a religious expression of his "moral equivalent of war." [15] (See Exhibit XIX.)

These comments on the religious virtues are but a few striking instances of many that might be given which show James as a moralist evaluating religion in terms of its actual or possible fruits. But the most striking evidence of James's moralism is his repudiation of the aesthetic side of religious experience, which he usually refers to the "second-hand" aspects of religion. His satirical remarks on this subject are partly directed against liturgical practices in general, and at Cardinal Newman in particular, but they are also intended to keep the concept of religious experience free from extraneous interests, such as "aesthetic richness," politics, etc. Personal morality he regarded as internal to religious experience, but even the most personal aspects of art seemed to him extraneous. The following passages deserve close analysis:

The eloquent passage in which Newman enumerates [the scholastic list of attributes of the deity] . . . shows how high is their aesthetic value. It enriches our bare piety to carry these exalted and mysterious verbal additions just as it enriches a church to have an organ and old brasses, marbles and frescoes and stained windows. Epithets lend an atmosphere and overtones to our devotion. They are like a hymn of praise and service of glory, and may sound the more sublime for being incomprehensible. Minds like Newman's grow as jealous of their credit as heathen priests are of that of the jewelry and ornaments that blaze upon their idols. . . . Compared with such a noble complexity, in which ascending and descending movements seem in no way to jar upon stability, in which no single item, however humble, is insignificant, because so many august institutions hold it in its place, how flat does evangelical Protestantism appear, how bare the atmosphere of those isolated religious lives whose boast it is that "man in the bush with God may meet." . . . It pauperizes the monarchical imagination!

The strength of these aesthetic sentiments makes it rigorously impossible, it seems to me, that Protestantism, however superior in spiritual profundity it may be to Catholicism, should at the present day succeed in making many converts from the more venerable ecclesiasticism. The latter offers a so much richer pasturage and shade to the fancy, has so many cells with so many different kinds of honey, is so indulgent in its multiform appeals to human nature, that Protestantism will always show to Catholic eyes the almshouse physiognomy. The bitter negativity of it is to the Catholic mind incomprehensible. . . . The two will never understand each other — their centres of emotional energy are too different.[16]

This passage is usually cited to show James's Protestant bias, but strictly speaking it is written from an artist's point of view. James was an artist and he had an aesthetic distaste for Catholic pomp as well as for Calvinist scruples against religious art. He was an aesthetic modernist, who shunned the antique as he shunned hypocrisy. And his aesthetic dislike of conventional art probably had more to do with his satirical attitude toward Catholicism than did his Protestant and moralistic environment. Be that as it may, James kept his artistic and his religious experiences as far apart as possible.

Other Interpretations of Religious Experience

Following closely upon the publication of the *Varieties of Religious Experience* came another influential treatise on religion by James's colleague, George Santayana. Though it owed much to James, Santayana's *Reason in Religion* was an effective antidote, for it reflected a very different religious interest — aesthetic and institutional. In place of James's three types of consciousness (feeling, intellect, and illumination) Santayana distinguishes three stages in the growth of religious life: prerational (superstition), rational (philosophical faith), and postrational (imaginative constructions). This progress can be observed in each of the two dimensions of religion: *piety*, which in its rational form is loyalty to the grounds of our being; and *spirituality*, which in its rational form is the free pursuit of ideals. In its prerational form piety is reliance on authority and observance of tradition; in its postrational form piety is the glorification of necessary being. In its prerational form, spirituality is fanaticism (energy redoubled after the goal is forgotten); in its postrational form, spirituality is the cultivation through art and theology of divine forms, essences, or ideals. This progress from childish to rational to imaginative religion also involves the growth of civilized institutional forms of expression and of corporate religious interests.

In its immediate setting this volume was a justification of Catholic modernism, but in its enduring effects on the religious education of Americans it has been a tract for classicist enthusiasm. Especially when read in the context of Santayana's poems and his essays on *Poetry and Religion*, this poetic mixture of Platonism, Aristotelianism, and modern naturalism became among literate circles a bible of the new humanism, half Christian, half Greek. It reconciled young freethinkers to organized religion, and it liberated dogmatic minds from superstition. Above all it did what James, too, was trying to do — it put reason in its place. The "life of reason" could be pursued, according to this conception of it, without alienating the soul of man from his body, or opposing reason to faith. As in James's philosophy, reason is assigned an intermediate, interpretive role in human experience; but Santayana, more than James, conceived rational experience as opening the door to the world of the imagination or "spirit," which is boundless and free.

It now came Josiah Royce's turn to revise the idealistic conception of the absolute in such a way as to meet the criticisms of James and of theists. This he did in his last great work, *The Problem of Christianity* (1913), which is a more humanistic and social interpretation of religious experience, and which marks the beginning of the reconciliation between philosophy and theology which has characterized the movement of religious thought since James. Abandoning cosmological speculation, Royce tried to construct a universal theory of the kind of redemptive community which the church is supposed to be. According to this philosophy all religious men (all who are loyal to the spirit of mutual understanding and vicarious atonement) form an infinite "beloved community" whose spirit is God and whose faith rests on the effort made by all members to "interpret" and reinterpret each other's selves and experiences until they become, under God, sharers in a single structure of knowledge, suffering, joy, and achievement. Such a conception of the religious life practically deifies the church and goes much further in the direction of a "social theology" than most theists were willing to go. Nevertheless, Royce effectively called attention to *the* problem of Christianity during this century, and counteracted the radical individualism which then characterized both American philosophy and liberal theology. Royce also gave impetus to a tendency among those American idealists who tried to do justice to religious experience to conceive absolute experience or God less in terms of cosmic reality or Being per se, and more in terms of man's personal, social, and historical experience of good and evil; less in terms of eternal being and more in terms of temporal process and human values.

The works of William Ernest Hocking, George Plimpton Adams, Edgar S. Brightman, John E. Boodin, DeWitt H. Parker, Julius Seelye Bixler, all of them influenced by both James and Royce, have given more detailed expression to this tendency in idealism; and this tendency has been appropriated by liberal theologians, who, as one of them puts it, can pray to a God who is perso*nal*, even though he may not be *a* person.[17] Professor Gordon W. Allport expresses a little less vaguely this same interpretation of religious experience in terms of personal values by regarding God as a generalized expression of the value of personality:

Abstracting from my physical individuality the general concept of selfhood, I gradually come to value whatever makes for the conservation of personal integrity anywhere. . . . God Himself I may declare to be the supreme expression of personality, a necessary and final value *required* to explain and to conserve all other values of selfhood. . . . Thus it comes about that under conditions of fear, illness, bereavement, guilt, deprivation, insecurity, the restoration of values through religion is commonly sought.[18]

More revolutionary for James's approach to the theory of religious experience than these tendencies within idealism was the growth of more objective approaches to the theory of experience in general. The description of types of consciousness as "states" given for introspection has been practically abandoned not only by empirical philosophers but even by the psychologists themselves. The biological or Darwinian approach which characterized at least one half of James's *Principles of Psychology* paved the way for a general revolt against introspection, so that the studies of "the religious consciousness" which were prevalent in 1900 soon gave way to studies of religious behavior or conduct. And this in turn opened the door for anthropological and sociological investigations, so that today the empirical science of religion has become a combination of anthropology, sociology, and psychiatry. John Dewey among the philosophers and Reinhold Niebuhr among the theologians have turned the attention of observers of religion from the private and "solitary" aspects of experience to human history and culture, to man's institutions and customs, to vested interests and funded meanings. This revolutionary shift in the science of man has not implied the abandonment of self-knowledge or the concern for personal values. On the contrary, the growth in self-knowledge which the last fifty years have brought about is due primarily to the fact that "persons" are now studied not in isolation, but in their habitat, in their historical and social relations to each other and to their heritages. Organized religion is no longer regarded as "second-hand," for a man may be as far from "immediate" religious experience in his private life as in his public.

But the most significant consequence of this new social science of religion is its effect on theology. For, as we have noted in an earlier chapter, the "religious situation" or man-related-to-God is no longer conceived as it was by James as man-in-his-solitude facing God-in-his-cosmos, but as a cultural, historical episode or crisis in which men must face both each other and God in order to make their religious decisions and formulate their faiths. Religion is, of course, personal, but persons are social creatures, and God, too, is both in human history and above any particular movement. Few theologians have taken the trouble to deny that God is also a cosmic reality or "King of the Universe," but for practical, religious purposes God is no more natural than religion is natural. This becoming "history minded" on the part of theologians and philosophers is part of a larger transformation in American culture during this century, but for religious experience the change has been peculiarly significant.

The most evident and practical bearing of these new developments in the knowledge of personality and experience is the application of the ideas of health and disease to those types of experience which had been conceived exclusively in terms of sin and salvation. James was more prophetic than he knew when he described religious types as "healthy" or "sick." And he was very subtly prophetic in contrasting healthy *mind* with sick *soul*. For the basic aim of modern pastoral counseling as also of modern psychiatry is to provide even a sick *soul* with a healthy *mind;* that is, psychological analysis and psychiatric diagnosis have provided the means (to some extent, at least) for enabling a broken spirit to have a critical and clinical understanding of his own condition. Thus the general and traditional judgments passed on man's sinfulness by the word of God, by which a sinner becomes "convicted," can now be supplemented by detailed diagnosis and prescriptions. The sharp lines that used to be drawn between crimes and diseases, morals and religion, eternal and temporal welfare have become shadowy. Some distinctions no doubt will remain, but as the body-mind-soul complex is unified in the concept of the person or self, so the health-righteousness-salvation complex becomes a unified though complicated problem. The better understanding of "theopathic" persons is indicative that also in normal religious experience we know more than James did of what is actually being "transacted" in prayer, or what is actually present in mystic ecstasy, or whence come revelations. Such knowledge is still in its infancy but the progress of the last fifty years has been phenomenal. Anton T. Boisen's *The Exploration of the Inner World* (Chicago, 1936) was one of the first American works to question the conventional notions of religious "healthy-mindedness," and since then the writings of Eric Fromm and others have popularized the fact that religious practices have much to do with mental hygiene. No psychiatrist today would diagnose a patient as did Dr. R. M. Bucke in 1900 as suffering from "cosmic consciousness"; yet James was compelled to take this diagnosis very seriously.[19] The "sick souls" and "divided selves" whom James described in his book can now be distinguished much more accurately than James was able to do in terms of specific ailments. On the other hand, some of the treatments to which such patients are subjected are still derived from traditional pastoral techniques.

For the most part psychotherapists employ implements borrowed from the clergy. The reason is simple enough: until recent times the church alone dealt with troubles of personality. The borrowed devices include listening, encouragement, advice, and the relationship of transference wherein the applicant finds security in dependence upon his counselor.[20]

Certainly there is a growing coöperation between the psychiatric and the pastoral professions. Psychoanalysts can no longer dismiss religion and its escape mechanisms as infantile illusion, and priests can no longer deal with obsessions as "spirit possessions." Ever since 1923 there has been organized clinical pastoral training involving clinical seminars for theological students at mental hospitals and courses for ministers in psychiatry. There are several journals of pastoral psychology and clinical training, and numerous discussions of the general problem of religion and health, notably Seward Hiltner's *Religion and Health* (1943), David E. Roberts' *Psychotherapy and a Christian View of Man* (1950), and the "Symposium on Religion and Health" published by the University Seminar of Columbia University under the direction of Horace L. Friess.[21]

What appears to be emerging from this growing coöperation between the pastoral and psychiatric professions is a recognition that neither has had an adequate training to deal effectively with the problems that confront both. A new art of moral counseling, perhaps a new profession is taking shape which includes in its technical equipment a clinical understanding of mental diseases and health, a critical evaluation of moral needs and ideals, and a practical interest in social reconstruction. Certainly the "mind-cure" movements of James's day now appear primitive, though they did much pioneering. Their sectarian value has declined because their insistence that "salvation" implies "healing" is now generally accepted.

Christian Science, for example, which late in the nineteenth century was a sensational creation of New England idealism, has become a settled and stable denomination, holding its own in a fairly rigid fashion. It takes its place now as an outstanding American representative of a "layman's church" which "permits no professional clergy or priesthood." The professional or full-time practitioners, who in the early days were the whole life of the movement, and who now number about 10,000 have become a subordinate phase of the work of the church. The religious services — public worship, Wednesday testimonial meetings, Sunday Schools — constitute the basic activities of the Church of Christ, Scientist. And even the personal services of the practitioners are now as a rule much closer to the "spiritual counseling" or "healing help" which is a normal part of pastoral and priestly duty, than to literal healing. It is significant that a separate profession of "Christian Science nursing" has arisen, and that in Christian Science literature and practice, specific diseases are taken seriously and are recognized by their medical names, even though they are not believed to be material. Thus, though the teaching continues to be a rigid theology derived from immaterialistic philosophy, the practice is now much closer to the work of the other Christian churches.

The same general trend applies to Spiritualism. During its nineteenth century career, it gained strength because of the amazing feats of its mediums, and then prided itself on being a "scientific" development rather than a religion. But during the twentieth century the wonders performed by individual mediums decreased, whereas Spiritualist churches grew rapidly.

Similarly among the other "new thought" and healing cults the Unity Movement has been the most successful and the closest to an ecclesiastical organization. A few exceptional preachers, like Emmett Fox, have been able to gather fairly stable congregations about their pulpits, but on the whole, New Thought is giving ground to secular thought and psychiatry. For similar reasons the Emmanuel Movement in the Episcopal Church proved to be of brief duration.

In general, religious therapy is now more interdenominational and more medical than it was, and its theology is more closely related to the theory of salvation. For no matter how important it may be for theology to maintain the doctrine that the salvation of souls is a matter of "eternal life," it still remains true that the concern for such salvation takes place in this life, and that the hopes, fears, and longings which it engenders must be dealt with here and now. Furthermore, they must be dealt with not by dismissing this world as insignificant when compared with another, but by making a knowledge of that other world contribute to man's welfare in this world, otherwise religion becomes an immoral fanaticism and a mockery in the eyes of reasonable men.

The experience of social crises, anxieties, and insecurities with which this century has made us all too familiar has also brought about a wide extension and transformation in the concept of religious experience. First of all it has brought back as daily experiences the insecurities, anxieties, tortures, persecutions, and martyrdoms which our fathers had dismissed as "medieval," and which in all ages have driven men to their knees. In the face of such cruelty man is also immediately face to face with God; he does not need to seek God, but finds himself driven to God. This means in the language of Santayana, that "piety" takes precedence over "spirituality"; that basic human loyalties are being tested so severely that the positive efforts in the pursuit of happiness and other ideals are pushed into the background. The problem of *facing* evil (internally and externally) is real to us, over and above the problem of *abolishing* evil. Americans were especially unprepared spiritually for this turn of events, having imagined the twentieth century to be naturally destined to be "the century of progress." That the progress of invention should be accompanied by progressive misery was incredible except to the small band who followed the teachings of Henry George. American socialists, few of whom were radical Marxists and most of whom were "white collar," were perhaps the most blindly confident of progress through technological advance and universal coöperation; to them "national socialism" seemed a veritable kingdom of heaven. The fool's paradise of the 1920's which blinded speculative Americans, with or without capital, to the facts of social conflict and chaos made the disillusionment of the 1930's all the more pathetic. The situation was ideal for apocalyptic visions; prophets of all kinds appeared and were received with open ears and ready stones, as always.

Obviously "society" was itself a sick soul doomed both to being damned verbally and to eternal damnation. William James could not have imagined, and few of his contemporaries could have foreseen this socialization of insecurity and "divided selves." The curious specimens of "varieties" of consciousness which found their way into James's psychological laboratory, have become familiar sights to us, so familiar in fact, that our theological sociologists have begun to use them as examples of "*the* human situation," whereas James had used them as specimens of "radical expressions" of religion.[22] In short, what has happened since the days of William James is that the religious phenomena which were then examined as vagaries of consciousness, have now become objective material for existential analysis. Existentialism represents the de-psychologizing of mystic and sinful states; the existentialist account of the human situation is not as introspective and as sentimental as was James's psychology, but is socially introverted and socially romantic. The divine presence and the personal "transactions" with God in prayer, which James interpreted psychologically, are the same experiences which the existentialist theologian describes as "objective encounters with the transcendent Other." The experiences described are equally personal, but the context of the experiences has shifted from states of consciousness to social situations. What to James was a conversion of religious appetites is now a cultural transformation. Thus the analysis of religious experience has followed the same trend toward objective, social, realistic analysis that has characterized philosophy in general during the period.

But the temper or temperament of existentialist analysis is quite different from that of James's psychology, and reflects the tragedies that have intervened. James, like a true scientist, could stand off from his religious patients and their passions, dispassionately evaluating their reasonableness, but the existentialist of today shares a holy concern for the cause of religion among the surging of secular interests. In those days religion was trying to make peace with science and to prove its own reasonableness; today religion is fighting for its life against strong cultural forces which treat it with indifference and disdain. During the first quarter of the century there were many books on "religion in an age of science" and "science" meant primarily natural science. In this context the most reasonable religion seemed to be the spirit of dispassionateness. It was Walter Lippmann who, writing under the influence of James and Santayana, praised the spirit of disinterestedness as "high religion." [23] To be above partisanship, above special pleading, to love God as Spinoza did with an *amor intellectualis*, and to find peace in understanding, seemed then the height of both piety and spirituality. How different the context of religion now! Religion is commitment, decision, faith, personal responsibility. To be religious is to take a serious part in historical decisions.

The more important our knowledge the more important is not only directness of meeting but also the companionship of fellow knowers. . . . It is not in lonely internal debate but in the living dialogue of the self with other selves that we can come to the point where we can make a decision and say, "Whatever may be the duty of other men this is my duty." . . . We must make our individual decisions in our existential situation; but we do not make them individualistically in confrontation by a solitary Christ as solitary selves. The existentialism that has emphasized the reality of decision and its free, individual character has also made us aware of the significance of the moment. The speculative, contemplative reason may live in past or future or in timelessness. . . . But the thinker must return from his journeys, for he is a man . . . and the time of decision is neither past nor future, but the present. . . . What makes the moment of crisis . . . so pregnant with meaning is not the fact that the self is alone here with the responsibility of decision, but that there is someone compresent . . . remembered and expected. . . . Our decisions must be made in the present moment — but in the presence of historical beings whose history has been made sacred by the historical, remembered actions of the one who inhabits eternity.[24]

Of course it is possible to reconcile theoretically the high religion of Walter Lippmann with this social existentialism of Richard Niebuhr, since it is possible to take the high ground of committing oneself disinterestedly yet wholeheartedly to God in a moment of "historical" decision. But in practice the two moods are incompatible and belong to different varieties of religious experience. The former is a "reflection at the end of an era," the latter is a call to action in the midst of a crisis; the former is detachment, the latter is involvement.[25]

Recent Varieties of Religious Experience

Turning from the *concept* of religious experience to the various kinds of religious life which have actually emerged in America recently, we face a bewildering variety, and a variety which is not adequately reflected in the numerous religious bodies to which we have given our attention in earlier chapters. For within many of these bodies there flourish distinct types of experience and those bodies which represent distinct types of experience in organized form usually conceal this fact under their official statements of belief, which are for the most part justificatory rather than descriptive. Like William James we might fix our attention on the more extravagant, "radical" types, intending thus to collect fresh specimens. But many of the less conventional types are decidedly "second-hand" and have several centuries of history behind them. Mr. Marcus Bach, in his delightful and informative collection of unfamiliar types of religion which he happened to find represented among his friends,[26] describes six such types: Trappist monks, who have recently attracted the attention of "worldly" Americans; Penitentes, who practice mortification of the flesh and who flourish chiefly in the Southwest; Vedantists, who have interpreted the theosophic meditation and literature of India to Americans in return for the Christian missions in India; Swedenborgians, who enjoy the privileges of a special revelation in book form and who have already entered "the New Jerusalem"; Hutterites, whose religion consists largely of communal work; and Mormons, whose special revelation and communal life in "the latter days" rivals that of the Swedenborgians. These types are all more than a century old, and all but one of them have origins foreign to American life and thought.

Of the thirteen "modern cults and minority religious movements" described in Charles S. Braden's *These Also Believe* (1949) the newest are: The Peace Mission Movement of Father Divine;[27] Psychiana, which might be called a mail-order variety of religious experience if it is really religion at all; the I Am Movement, and the Liberal Catholic Church, which are but the latest of many popularized versions of theosophy that have spread beyond California; Jehovah's Witnesses;[28] and the Oxford Group Movement, of which I shall say something below.

In view of these recent descriptions of the spectacular, bizarre, and unfamiliar elements in contemporary American religion, I shall confine myself here to describing a few types of religious experience that have emerged recently and that are directly related to the important changes in the concept of religious experience which I have been reviewing.

First should be considered the attempts to secure an authoritative revelation, prophecy, or self-knowledge to supplement empirical science on the one hand and the Bible on the other, both of which no longer exercise the kind of authority for practical guidance which is here being sought.

The conviction that religious knowledge is different from natural knowledge, having more authority and less rational evidence, has gained ground steadily. Many individuals and groups are willing to listen to the claims of fundamentalist authoritarianism that God can still give specific and detailed instructions. A good example comes to us from recent Mormon literature. Brigham Young had said in one of his discourses:

The majority of the revelations given to mankind anciently were in regard to their daily duties; we follow in the same path. The revelations contained in the Bible and the Book of Mormon are examples to us, and the book of Doctrine and Covenants contains direct revelation to this Church; they are a guide to us, and we do not wish to do them away; we do not want them to become obsolete and to set them aside. We wish to continue in the revelations of the Lord Jesus Christ day by day, and to have his Spirit with us continually. If we can do this, we shall no more walk in darkness, but we shall walk in the light of life.[29]

The faith in such guidance is, of course, difficult to maintain, even among Mormans. But faced with Modernist versions of revelation James E. Talmage reasserted the orthodox doctrine:

Current revelation is equally plain with that of former days in predicting the yet future manifestations of God through this appointed channel. The canon of scripture is still open; many lines, many precepts, are yet to be added; revelation, surpassing in importance and glorious fulness any that has been recorded, is yet to be given to the Church and declared to the world.[30]

In one way or another, by meditation, by esoteric learning, by self-analysis, by "realization," men are trying to acquire a "vertical" knowledge, which unlike scientific knowledge or any other form of "knowledge-about," is immediately and personally a form of power and illumination. There are many American followers and imitators of the English religious writer, Gerald Heard, who repeat with him: "Continually by daily rejuvenation and the renewal of humility, trust and wonder, I cast off the creeping shroud of complacency, indifference and concession to things as men maintain they must be." This is not a defiance of science but a companion or supplement to being informed; it is a need for knowing neither facts nor values, but knowing what-to-do-next; it is not objective certainty, but self-assurance, not erudition but confidence. Such saving knowledge has been sought by man in all ages, but by its very nature it must be continually recreated or rediscovered. It must represent a personal accomplishment in religious discipline. There are some, notably the group of naturalists led by Professor Henry N. Wieman, whose "methods of private religious living" are based directly on the latest scientific philosophies and who attempt to free themselves from anything resembling myth or misleading symbolism. But even they emphasize "qualitative meaning" and they hope by the cultivation of such meanings to appropriate God's "creative events" (as science and technology make them known) in such a way that men's lives will be "connected in mental support, vivifying and enhancing one another in the creation of a more inclusive unity of events and possibilities." [31] Thus there is a qualitative distinction between secular knowledge and religious faith, and the former fails to serve mankind insofar as the latter fails to lead men beyond empirical inquiry into "the deepest sources of human good." But by far the largest number of those who cultivate this personal, "vertical" form of insight or inspiration turn to the language and literature of religious traditions as sources from which they can secure power. They turn to myth and mysticism not for the sake of learning either, but for the sake of deriving from them something peculiarly "qualitative" which can better be expressed in terms of living than of thinking.

As an illustration of such saving knowledge I present (Exhibit XX) a composite sermon based on theosophic sources. It comes from the recent writings of members of *The Temple of the People*, a lodge at Halcyon, California, which was theoretically founded in 1898 but which has flourished more recently. It may be known to some readers through its connection with the life of Thorstein Veblen, but it is known reverently to a small community for whom it is a center of healing knowledge and spiritual power. The reader should note that such "knowledge" acquires its authoritative power by providing (a) a cosmic source, (b) a historical career, (c) a scientific intelligibility (at least by analogy), and (d) a sense of sharing in a group-creation.

The gospel contained in this sermon has many variations in many sects and among men of no sect, but the central appeals and motives are typical of the great effort which is being made in our generation to cure a "sick soul" by cultivating a "healthy mind." But it is not literally "mind cure"; it is "divine science," a tapping of the sources of spiritual power. The basic idea of such religious experience was put in popular form by Professor Chad Walsh in his *Stop Looking and Listen*. It is related to the other popular slogan created by Joshua Liebman's *"Peace of Mind,"* but what is aimed at is not mere peace of mind but rather a peaceful power through mental discipline.

For those who desire elementary versions of saving knowledge

I recommend the handbooks for self-improvement sold by "Sermon Publications, Inc.," composed by the Reverend Dr. Norman Vincent Peale with the coöperation of psychiatrists, and displaying such come-on titles as *The Art of Real Happiness, A Guide to Confident Living, You Can Change Your Personality Defects, Your Prayers Will Get Results, Happy Ending to Your Gloomy Feelings, The Wonderful Feeling of Security.* These secular-sounding titles should not mislead the reader, for any one of these books and tracts makes it perfectly clear that you can *not* help yourself literally; you must turn to Christ, to prayer, to the Bible, and to Dr. Peale's publications. But at least you can manage without public worship, if you must!

It is difficult to tell at present whether religious healing and counseling are tending toward the more conventional forms of worship and confession or whether they are creating religious treatments for individual "patients" analogous to medical practice. The experience of the older healing groups is inconclusive. It seemed in the early days of Christian Science that the "practitioner" would be its effective center. And for a generation or so, the Mother Church at Boston feared the inroads of dissident practitioners and of the more individualistic New Thought Movement. But under present conditions the worship services and ecclesiastical forms of Christian Science seem to have more importance than healing in the practitioner's sense. I remember the very acute observation which a New Thought leader made to me sometime in the early 1930's. She said that until the Depression came, individual practitioners or "metaphysical" teachers were able to meet the needs of those who came to them individually. They were content to leave upon payment of a fee for services rendered. The medical and teaching professions served as a practical model. But when the Depression made itself felt, many left the Movement for Christian Science or some other church because, she said, "they wanted to join something." In times of greatest insecurity it is probable that persons are more inclined to feel security by "joining" than by being "analyzed," and the healing value of the organized religious practices may be more generally appreciated now than it was at the time of William James. On the other hand, priests and pastors are worried because they are expected increasingly to help as psychiatrists, on an individualist basis, those whom the public services fail to attract or help.

The most conspicuous development in this connection is neither the growth of pastoral psychiatric counseling nor the revival of traditional confessionals, but the popularity of group movements, which encourage small groups to form intimate fellowships for mutual confession and encouragement. Such groups are naturally most conspicuous during what James called "the religious moult-ing time" of adolescence and youth, but they have spread to groups of all ages, classes and nations. The Oxford Group Move-ment, or First Century Fellowship, later known as the "Moral Rearmament" program is one of the more important of these groups. Though notorious chiefly for its glamorous financial con-quests and its fashionable "house parties," it concerns our story of moral reconstruction because of its ingenious attempt to combine the features of evangelical orthodoxy with techniques of modern psychotherapy. The fact that its founder, Frank Buchman, was thrown suddenly from settlement work in Philadelphia's slums to meeting with students at Oxford and Cambridge only par-tially explains this curious juxtaposition of Quaker quietism and Anglican sophistication. The "tipsy cocktail-party generation" that tried to lead its distracted life between the two wars found both release and relief in the kind of "quiet-time" fellowship which the Oxford Group Movement offered it. Here small groups of persons who were for the most part religiously illiterate but otherwise well-read and overstimulated, assembled alternately in silence and in reciprocal confession.

This combination of privacy, intimacy, and public confessions gave the members an opportunity, without benefit of clergy or analyst, to psychoanalyze themselves and each other, and to ex-perience both the pleasure of spiritual nudism and the sense of revelation or guidance. The theory was the Quaker theory of waiting upon the Holy Spirit for inspiration and guidance, plus the evangelical emphasis on absolute "surrender" to God; the practice was that of group-analysis (in a very amateur way) and of sublimating guilt-feelings, resentments, and other obstacles to happiness. These fellowships produced a number of spectacular conversions and created a kind of "familism" (as it used to be called several centuries ago) both within and without the churches; they gave an experience of communion and revelation which the conventional religious services failed to give. Such pietistic fellowships are no new phenomenon, but it is significant that they have achieved a distinctive modern pattern: small informal groups of both sexes, meeting preferably in homes at "protracted" evening sessions, sharing religious and moral problems frankly, confessing troubles sincerely, trusting each other's friendship and aid, restricting such fellowship to a confidential circle, and keeping clerical advisers or organizers either out altogether or else in the background.

Such group meetings used to be called "quietism" and were usually not welcomed by the clergy. Today the clergy are encouraging "lay leadership" in such movements. Youth fellowships are perhaps most cultivated among college students, and they operate on college campuses as religious "cells" — sometimes in conscious antithesis to communist cells and their tactics. There is a literature on Christian "cell culture." The Fundamentalist Inter-Varsity Fellowship operates in this way. In 1929 Baptist students organized a Master's Minority Movement. Though many of these college manifestations are kindled and fanned to inflammatory proportions by fundamentalist organizations, such as the Youth for Christ Movement, they should not be interpreted as essentially fundamentalist in nature. The orgy of mass confession which broke out recently at Wheaton College in Illinois is merely an exaggerated instance of the excitement and "idealism" generated readily among societies of young people when they are appealed to in the interest of commitment, sincerity, sacrifice, loyalty, and fellowship. These groups usually devote at least a part of their meeting to prayer and reading of the Scriptures but the distinctive appeal and value of the movements is the combination of personal devotion or commitment to a religious cause with personal devotion or commitment to each other in the fellowship. Among Christians such groups are apt to be interpreted as "First-Century Christianity." Educators have long struggled with the dangers arising from the over-sanctification of fraternity friendships. Religious fraternities (some of them even go under Greek letters!) and fellowships are also in danger of promoting exclusive, sectarian cliques, but such dangers are today less conspicuous than are the often pathetic interests of youth in devoting or sacrificing themselves to some cause that is authentically universal, humanitarian, and peaceful. The attempt to direct such religious devotion among Protestant students into useful channels has led to the formation of national agencies, such as the National Intercollegiate Christian Council (1934), the United Student Christian Council (1944), and the National Commission on Church Student Work (1948). The social appeal of such fellowship is, of course, universal and finds many secular expressions. Among the recent fellowships which are on the borderline between religious and secular communion is Alcoholics Anonymous.

Closely related to group movements are religious retreats, which are rapidly increasing in number and popularity. These usually have a more clerical leadership and more ecclesiastical aims. They combine features of the Catholic "third orders" of monasticism with features of the evangelical camp meetings and YMCA and YWCA camps. The majority are held during summer vacations at camps or resorts, in secluded homes or on small campuses. Some are week-end affairs, others last a week or more. Among Catholics brief retreats for laymen have been traditional, but their popularity in America has greatly increased recently. Some of the large Evangelical camp meetings, which under the decline of revivalism were in danger of becoming liberalist Chautauquas, have been gradually reorganized on the retreat plan. Several organizations are imported. The Catholic Worker Movement, which arose in America during the Depression as a radical offshoot of Third Order Franciscans, was inspired by the French Jocist Movement. The Quakers, whose whole movement is devoted to the cultivation of fellowship, have a center of adult religious education at Pendle Hill, Pennsylvania. They have also organized many work-camps and the institution of religious work camps has spread far beyond Quaker lines. I quote from an exposition by one of its leaders, Alexander Miller:

"Student-in-industry" camps retain the original conception that work alongside people is the best basis for understanding and solidarity with them; they depart from the original basis, where work was unpaid and volunteers met their own expenses, by putting young people into industry for a period on the same basis as other workers, including, of course, the weekly pay-packet. . . . The students live a common life of worship, study and common household labour, and from this centre they go out first to look for work and then to do their daily stint in factory and mill. These are students for the most part who would be working, in any case, at some manual or clerical job to earn money for their next college year. . . . They are sharing the life of a committed Christian group. . . .

The practice of daily worship in this kind of setting not only discovers resources in Word and Sacrament, which speak to new needs, but sets secular and industrial life in a perspective which their divine and human and social meaning can be taken in. . . . The regular study, which is part of every such camp — study on the Faith and on the facts of industry and society — has a vitality which springs out of living encounter with the stuff of contemporary life. . . . A group of this kind discovers out of this triple dealing with God and the situation a solidarity in community which is buttressed by their dependence upon one another for the wholesome handling of the daily life of the camp.

American Presbyterians, inspired by the Scottish Iona Community, began in 1944 a series of retreats for both young clergymen and lay groups (families) at Kirkridge, Pennsylvania, which rapidly became a popular interdenominational retreat center. The Episcopal retreat centers are for the most part connected with the recent growth of monastic communities (most of them of Anglican origin), such as the Cowley Fathers, the Order of the Holy Cross, the Sisters of St. Margaret, and others. Socially conspicuous, possibly intellectually as well, is the Trabico center for the spiritual life which has grown up in Southern California under the leadership of Aldous Huxley, Gerald Heard, and other literary figures who have become devoted to an adaptation of oriental mysticisms.

These various forms of religious retreat, for the most part seasonal, periodic, like the normal retreats for Buddhists into monasteries, do not all share the same motivations, and it would be misleading to generalize concerning them. From the most trivial point of view they may be sanctified picnics. They may be escape mechanisms of the sort which James called "taking moral holidays." On the contrary, they may be centers of inspiration for radical activity or for social services. They may also be little religious communes in the making. In any case they seem to prove that what James called "out-door mysticism" may be an American institution deeply rooted in the needs for rest, recreation, frontier atmosphere, and emotional dedication.

The following statements issuing from the Kirkridge "Retreats for Protestants" may formulate what many of these retreat programs are intended to do. They constitute a sort of retreat ideology, but scarcely reveal the many motivations and satisfactions which enter into these religious communal experiences.

At first Kirkridge's purpose is that of helping persons rediscover their own direction and vocation in God. Harried pastor, perplexed deacon, teacher consulting a psychiatrist, businessman with ulcers, social action enthusiast who no longer knows why, housewife dull in prayer, seminarian soft about his faith, college student groping for motive and meaning — their trouble, Kirkridge is convinced, arises from the fact that God's intention is not being fulfilled by what they do. Indeed, Kirkridge like many a prophet ancient and modern holds that until intelligent people deliberately withdraw from everyday life — ringing phones and roaring headlines and dizzying television — they will not recover their purpose and steadily realize why they were born. A primary Christian task is to reclaim perspective and destiny within individual lives. . . .

Kirkridge has evolved specific work-retreat procedures to achieve its purposes — borrowing from various Christian traditions. Its usual daily regimen embodies most of these. A group (never more than 20) rises at six, shares breakfast without speaking while one member reads, and sings its praise in brief Morning Prayer at the hearth. Three or four hours of corporate manual work usually follow (mixing mortar, making garden, felling trees, sewing, laying up masonry), with an hour-and-a-half of discussion before late midday dinner. Afternoons are free until another discussion at five. Silent supper with reading is followed by sunset singing at the ridge, or further discussion until Compline at nine. Relaxed corporate stillness then follows through the night until morning prayer. Variations of this general schedule usually maintain the emphasis upon group quiet, manual work, mutual friendly conversation and discussion. Scripture is ordinarily the basis for one of the daily discussion periods. Early-morning celebration of the Sacrament in simplest form around the long scrubbed tables is also a part of most work-retreats.[32]

In contrast to retreat-fellowships are a number of action-fellowships — but the contrast is more nominal than real. The ideologies of the social action groups are more aggressive; their aim is to transform religious "bodies" into religious "movements." In 1946 the Presbyterian Department of Evangelism of the Board of National Missions launched a "New Life Movement," designed primarily to win and organize young people for the church. The New Life groups promise formally: "I give my heart to thee, O Lord, willingly and sincerely." As a church extension scheme it is obviously successful, but it also serves the purpose of revivalism, putting new religious life or "movement" into the work of the churches. Similar organized efforts are being made by numerous other religious bodies.

This desire to put religion on the offensive is evident among Protestants, Catholics, and Jews, and among them jointly. They all feel that they have two basic forms of religious experience in common, which can be made a positive force in the contemporary social chaos: encounter with God and absolute commitment. These two experiences may, of course, be parts of a single act of religious devotion, but they have different connotations. The encounter with God signifies the receiving of revelation. The type of revelation which is now being emphasized is not the kind of "illumination" which James took for granted on the basis of traditional mysticism, but is an unexpected and uncontrovertible judgment. When a man "meets" God (and this is distinct from the more special Christian experience of "fellowship with Christ") he is "stopped" abruptly. Some "other," transhuman actuality (not clearly understood) imposes itself and reveals a man's limitations to him, frustrates his own aims, condemns his ways. A man when thus confronted with God realizes that he is not "the captain of his soul," that he is a creature among creatures more or less blindly groping his way toward goals of which he is at most dimly aware. The story of Job is cited repeatedly as the classic description of mankind's situation before God and of the futility of human counselors. There are, of course, many counselors like Karl Barth who distrust the "still small voice of God" under these circumstances and undertake to thunder in the name of God. But even discounting the theological versions and perversions of the man-face-to-face-with-God situation, the experience thus designated is common enough even among laymen of all faiths to make the mythologies of "the divine encounter" meaningful and important in the crises which have shattered human self-reliance and self-confidence. It is difficult to describe such revelation in terms of the types of consciousness which James distinguishes; it is neither pure emotion, nor sheer illumination, nor reasoned judgment. It is not "existential anguish," nor immediate union with God, nor knowledge of God's will. It merely proves, as John Haynes Holmes has said, "that reason is not enough." As the theologians say, God discloses his presence without adding any information.

Is it possible, then, to hold communion with God? Yes, but one gets no dictated answers. He turns to his Bible, but it must be interpreted. He turns to Jesus, but finds him acting a parable, which must be understood, or stating a principle rather than a rule applying to just the situation faced. He must reflect. He must grapple and brood. He must read, and inquire, and think and grow. Only as one consorts with the seers and prophets and poets of the faith shall he discover the secret of the Highest, shall he enter His inner courts. To the wrestling, searching, brooding spirit the answer comes; for him the light breaks; in him the truth lives again and asserts its mastery over men. God is not cheaply won. He is no Aladdin of the Lamp, to be summoned by some sure mechanical movement or device. He is like the measure which comes to the poet, the harmony born in the musician's soul, the love that shines in a mother's eyes, the strength of One on Calvary's cross.[33]

This sounds like theological teasing or obfuscation, but it is an honest attempt to denote an actual and common experience. Getting such a revelation is very different from getting an inspiration; it is usually a disconcerting, disorienting, shock-experience.

The second common experience today is that of "commitment." Men make many commitments, but a commitment to God is not made, it "comes" to a man. He accepts it, if he does not rebel, but not as something done by him consciously. He finds himself in a condition of voluntary servitude. It is now generally recognized by observant students of religious devotion that the accounts of "conversion" which were current fifty years ago and which represented man as more or less making a deal with

God, "covenanting" in an explicit, contractual way on the basis of explicit terms are as far from telling the truth as were the myths of the social contract, which tried to account for our basic social commitments in terms of an original, over-all contract. Both the encounter with and the commitment to God are relations with an infinite being, and such relations are difficult to define even when the facts are clearly reported. It is therefore absurd to continue James's quest and to try to define modern man's religious *consciousness*. The best the empirical observer of religion can do is to try to define man's religious existence; but given the difficulties which empiricists have had with both terms, "religious" and "existence," the prospect for a science of religious experience is none too promising.

The major concern of religious leaders today, however, is not with such a science but with promoting religious action. Their social-action programs are not merely secondhand religion and firsthand partisan politics, though they often may be that; they are programs for giving religious experience an active formulation, putting religion in motion as a force among forces. Whether such a force be frankly termed "occult" as it is in our theosophic sermon, or whether, like other forces it be explained in terms of its fruits, is a minor, technical issue. The aim of religious agencies, be they councils for Christian action, Catholic youth movements, Zionist clubs, Reconstructionist movements, fellowships of reconciliation, or fellowships of Christian socialists, always is some distinctive form of social conduct which is readily discernible. Therefore fundamentalists and secularists who charge such "movements" with being an exploitation of religious energies for secular programs fail to understand what is fundamental in such types of religious experience. These modern revelations and commitments are, necessarily and fundamentally, experiences of faith which lead men into action, and no amount of psychologizing about religious knowledge will make such movements more intelligible than they are in action. In other words, the act of communion is not separable from the actions of the fellowship precisely because such communion cannot be defined clearly in any other way; it is not feeling, nor mysticism, nor creed. For this reason, too, religion which thus takes the offensive as a distinctive mode of culture can be judged ultimately only, as James tried to judge the religious experiences which he analyzed, by the fruits. It can be described, as James tried to describe saintliness, in terms of devoutness, purity, charity, asceticism, confession, and prayer, but these terms are little more definite than "saintliness," and a large part of this volume has been devoted to showing how these terms have changed their meanings as American culture has changed.

As for the mystic experience, it is difficult to tell what has happened to it. For the term "mysticism" is the most abused term of all; James used it loosely enough and now it is used still more loosely. The concept of mystic knowledge, of course, has been discussed continuously by philosophical theologians, notably by Hocking, Lyman, and Macintosh. But practical mysticism in America seems to have been subordinated during this century to religious ethics and religious action. This implies a decline of interest in such experiences as "intuition" and "sense of at-one-ness with God." Even those who, like Professor Lyman, continued to defend religious institution gave the term a Bergsonian, practical twist which linked it to moral aspiration rather than to passive contemplation. There may be much genuine mysticism in private, where it should be, but judging by the recent literature of mysticism, it has not inspired "effability." Three current types of mystic writing should at least be mentioned: the sermons and other writings of Rufus M. Jones, who linked the practice of Quaker quietism to the more classic strains of mysticism; the meditations of the Trappist monk, Thomas Merton, whose *Ascent to Truth* is a beginner's essay to follow in the steps of the medieval solitaries; and a beautiful volume by Abraham J. Heschel, entitled *Man is Not Alone*, which is a Chassidist expression of the individualism, the universalism, and "the noble nostalgia" that characterizes mysticism at its heights. An anecdote which Dr. Heschel tells gives succinctly the dominant tone of recent mysticism. A learned but newly impoverished Jew was asked by his congregation to lead them in their public prayers, but he was afraid, went to his rabbi, and told him of his fears. The rabbi replied, "*Be* afraid, and pray."

This traditional trait of pious and spiritual men and groups not to be afraid of fear, as so many of our secular, self-reliant organizations have become, may turn out to be one of the great contributions of religion to twentieth-century American culture, and may continue to give vitality and importance to praying in the fear of the Lord.

Religious Experience and Religious Existence

In the foregoing survey of the varieties of religious experience that have appeared on the American scene since William James, the emphasis has been put on variety. The "spontaneous variations" which were so conspicuous in the American environment during the nineteenth century continue to arise in abundance and in unforeseen ways and places. In spite of the fact that religious experience has become less subjective and individualistic since William James took it into his psychological clinic, it is today even less "secondhand" than it was then. Here is one of the world's great religious breeding grounds, and the diversity of new species continually defies classification and definition.

On the other hand, the large denominations which embrace over half our population have proved to be amazingly stable and have survived, despite many predictions to the contrary, a series of storms which have tested their intellectual and moral strength as severely as any "sifting time" in religious history. The revolutions of this century have left their marks on all our religious institutions and beliefs, but on the whole these revolutionary reconstructions have produced *renouvellements* rather than *bouleversements*. Whether the renewals are also "purifications by fire" does not appear in such an analysis as this. This has been primarily a narrative, not a judgment; a report, not a sermon.

However, the attentive reader may have noticed as he read the last three chapters that the three aspects of religion — theology, worship, and experience — seem to be less distinct today than fifty years ago. The psychological, mystical, and theological approaches to religion, which in the days of William James, Rufus Jones, and Theodore Munger were quite independent of each other, and quite critical of each other, have yielded to a general *rapprochement*. It is now less difficult to see religion whole, for its theory and its practice are better integrated. We need no longer abstract the religious consciousness from religious faith and both from religious institutions. It is more evident today what it means to *be* religious, and in this general pattern of religious existence, as it can be both observed and lived, the intellectual, cultic, and personal factors serve to make each other intelligible. But this growing reciprocity among the elements of American religious life is a tribute to the effectiveness of William James's heroic attempt to examine religion critically on the inside.

NOTES

NOTES

"Organized Religion in the United States," *The Annals of the American Academy of Political and Social Science*, volume 256 (March 1948), is one of the most comprehensive attempts at a survey of the American religious situation and contains articles by a score of authoritative writers: J. O. Hertzler, Winfred E. Garrison, Bernard Harrison, John Courtney Murray, William W. Sweet, Charles S. Braden, Kenneth Scott Latourette, Harry F. Ward, Liston Pope, Ray E. Baber, Paul Hanly Furfey, Ray H. Abrams, Alfred McClung Lee, Oliver L. Reiser, Blodwen Davies, G. Bromley Oxnam, and John Herman Randall, Jr. The first section, "Our Contemporary Religious Institutions," contains surveys of the major organized bodies by leading members. The second section, "Relationship to Other Institutions," discusses the relation of religion to political and economic institutions, the class structure, and the family. The third section, "The Churches and Social Action," outlines religious approaches to social work, to war, and to journalism. The fourth section discusses the relations between religion, science, and philosophy. Appended is a summary of religious statistics and a well-selected bibliography by the editor, Ray H. Abrams.

In Samuel McCrea Cavert and Henry Pitney Van Dusen, editors, *The Church Through Half a Century* (New York: Charles Scribner's Sons, 1936), essays surveying particular aspects of the subject were contributed by John C. Bennett, Julius S. Bixler, B. Harvie Branscomb, H. Emil Brunner, Adelaide T. Case, Edmund B. Chaffee, Henry Sloane Coffin, Olive Dutcher Doggett, Phillips P. Elliott, Daniel J. Fleming, Charles W. Gilkey, Walter M. Horton, Henry S. Leiper, Arthur C. McGiffert, Jr., Mark A. May, and Hermann N. Morse.

In a volume edited by Arnold S. Nash, *Protestant Thought in the Twentieth Century* (New York: The Macmillan Company, 1951), are contributions by Waldo Beach, John Bennett, Floyd Filson, C. W. Gilkey, Seward Hiltner, Walter Horton, H. S. Leiper, John Mackay, H. Shelton Smith, George Thomas, George Hunston Williams, Ernest Wright. Other recent works which are informative in this connection are: *American Jewish Year Book, 1948–1949*, compiled and edited by the American Jewish Committee (Philadelphia: The Jewish Publication Society of America, 1949); Gaius Glenn Atkins, "Memories and Movements of Fifty Years," *The Minister's Quarterly*, IV (November 1948), 34–40; Andrew Drummond, *Story of American Protestantism*

(Edinburgh: Oliver and Boyd, 1949), Book V of which contains an interesting description of the American religious scene by a visiting British Protestant; Vergilius Ferm, editor, *Religion in the Twentieth Century* (New York: Philosophical Library, 1948); John Knox, editor, *Religion and the Present Crisis* (Chicago: Chicago University Press, 1942), containing contributions by Edwin E. Aubrey, William Clayton Bower, Ernest C. Colwell, Charles W. Gilkey, Charles T. Holman, John Knox, John T. McNeill, Wilhelm Pauck, Henry N. Wieman; Kenneth Scott Latourette, "The Religious Situation in the United States," *World Christian Handbook* (London: World Dominion Press, 1949); Frank S. Mead, *Handbook of Denominations in the U.S.* (New York: Abingdon-Cokesbury, 1951); *The National Catholic Almanac.*

Of special value is Willard L. Sperry's *Religion in America* (Cambridge, England: The University Press, 1945). This description of American religion to a British audience is one of the best general characterizations of American religious variety and informality.

1 RELIGION IN A REVOLUTIONARY AGE

1. Minot J. Savage, *Religion: Its Changing Forms and Its Eternal Essence* (2nd ed., 1905), pp. 21 f.

2. Joseph Haroutunian, *Lust for Power* (1949).

3. H. Paul Douglas and Edward Brunner, *The Protestant Church as a Social Institution* (1935), p. 66.

4. Herman Nelson Morse, "The Church's Mission at Home," in *The Church Through Half a Century*, edited by Samuel McCrea Cavert and Henry Pitney Van Dusen (1936), p. 281.

5. R. A. Schermerhorn, "Salvaging Secularism," *Journal of Religion*, XV (1935), 54–56.

6. The latest figures available are summarized and interpreted in *Information Service* for March 8, 1952 (published by the Central Department of Research and Survey, National Council of the Churches of Christ). This tabulation amplifies a report made in the *Christian Herald*, August 1951. It observes among other trends: that among the large religious bodies The Salvation Army has gained 180 per cent and the Southern Baptists 100 per cent since 1926, whereas the average gain during this period among the large bodies was about 60 per cent. Though numerically small, the Fundamentalist churches gained during this period from 400 per cent to 900 per cent.

It is important to note that "the Roman Catholics, the Protestant Episcopal Church and many Lutheran bodies report all baptized persons. Jews estimate all Jews in communities having congregations."

7. *Information Service* for June 11, 1949. "Christianity and the Economic Order," Study No. 11, pp. 1–2.

8. See the report prepared by Dr. H. Paul Douglas and the Committee for Cooperative Field Research for the National Convocation on the City Church, Columbus, Ohio, January 1950. See also the excellent summaries in *Information Service* of the Federal Council of Churches for January 21, 1950, February 4, 1950, and June 16, 1951.

2 INSTITUTIONAL RECONSTRUCTION

1. *Religious Bodies, 1936, Selected Statistics for the United States,* Federal Bureau of Census, p. 9.
2. According to the report of the Youth Department of the National Catholic Welfare Conference, "The Catholic Committee on Scouting endeavors to 'aid the supernatural' by means . . . of cooperation with the Boy Scouts of America." *National Catholic Almanac* (1949), p. 435.
3. The full text of this manifesto is reprinted in *The National Catholic Almanac* (1949), pp. 86–91.
4. John Courtney Murray, S.J., "Contemporary Orientations of Catholic Thought on Church and State in the Light of History," *Theological Studies*, X (1949), 214, 220, 229.
5. Joseph Perkins Chamberlain, "The Mutual Obligations of Church and State," *Church and State in the Modern World*, Henry Pitney Van Dusen *et al.*, 1937, pp. 114 f.
6. See the excellent discussion of secularism in *Information Service*, National Council of Churches, January and February 1952. Other important discussions of this issue are contained in: *The Teaching of Religion in American Higher Education*, Christian Gauss, editor (New York: The Ronald Press Company, 1951), with contributions by Christian Gauss, Howard B. Jefferson, J. Hillis Miller, Kenneth W. Morgan, Robert Ulich; Alvin W. Johnson and Frank Yost, *Separation of Church and State* (Minneapolis: University of Minnesota Press, revised and enlarged edition, 1948); Conrad H. Moehlman, *The Wall of Separation between Church and State* (Boston: Beacon Press, 1951); James Milton O'Neill, "Church and State in the U.S.," *Historical Records and Studies*, United States Catholic Historical Society, XXXVII (1948); Wilfrid Parsons, *The First Freedom: Consideration on Church and State in the United States* (New York: Declan X. McMullen Co., Inc., 1948); Leo Pfeffer, "The Supreme Court as Protector of Freedom of Religion," *The Annals of the American Academy of Political and Social Science* (May 1951), pp. 75–85; Leo Pfeffer, "Church and State: Something Less Than Separation," *The University of Chicago Law Review*, vol. XIX, no. 1 (Autumn 1951), pp. 1–29; *The Relation of Religion to Public Education — the Basic Principles* (Washington, D.C.: American Council on Education, April 1947); *Religion and Education*, Willard L. Sperry, editor (Cambridge:

Harvard University Press, 1945), vol. IV of *Religion in the Post-War World*; *The Attack Upon the American Secular School*, V. T. Thayer (Boston: Beacon Press, 1951); Gerald Groveland Walsh, S.J., "Church and State in the United States," *Historical Records and Studies*, United States Catholic Historical Society, XXXVII (1948).

7. "There are today in this country about 635,000 plus Jewish children of elementary school age. About 42.0 per cent of this number are currently reported as attending some recognized Jewish school. This percentage is larger in smaller communities and smaller in larger communities. This figure does not mean that the remaining children never receive some kind of Jewish education. Actually, it is estimated that more than 80 per cent of Jewish children *do attend* one or another type of Jewish school during the course of their elementary school years, except that they *do not all attend at the same time or stay long enough* to complete their elementary courses of Jewish study. Of the High School age group, only about 10,000 pupils or 3.8 per cent are reported in attendance. Of the elementary school children who are enrolled, 50.2 per cent are in one-day-a-week schools (usually referred to as Sunday Schools), 41.8 per cent are in afternoon weekday schools, and 8.0 per cent are in private and congregational all-day schools (erroneously referred to by some as 'parochial schools')." *Jewish Education: Register and Directory* (1951), p. 11.

8. Horace M. Kallen, "Jewish Education in the American Scene," *Jewish Education*, XXI (1949), 30.

9. Wesner Fallaw, *The Modern Parent and the Teaching Church* (1946), pp. 42 f.

10. Statement of Catholic Bishops at the National Catholic Welfare Conference, November 15–17, 1950, in Washington, D.C.

11. Howard Mumford Jones, "Religious Education in the State Universities," *Religion and Education*, edited by Willard L. Sperry (1945), pp. 62–66, 70 f.

12. Paul Ramsay, "Religious Instruction Problematically Christian," *Journal of Religion*, XXVI (1946), 255 n. See also *Liberal Learning and Religion*, edited by Amos N. Wilder (New York: Harper and Brothers, 1951).

13. *Christian Unity: Its Principles and Possibilities* (1921), p. 140.

14. *Ibid.*, p. 143.

15. John C. Bennett, "The Next Period in Christian Missions," *Union Seminary Quarterly Review*, vol. VI, no. 4, (June 1951), p. 13.

16. Willard L. Sperry, "Our Present Disunity," *Religion and Our Divided Denominations*, by Sperry, *et al.*, pp. 22 f., 24 f.

17. Cf. R. E. Wolseley, "The Plight of Religious Journalism," *Crozer Quarterly*, XXIII (1946), pp. 215–221.

18. Alfred McClung Lee, "The Press and Public Relations of Re-

ligious Bodies," *The Annals of the American Academy of Political and Social Science* (March 1948), p. 121.

19. *Ibid.*, p. 124.

20. Luke Ebersole, *Church Lobbying in the Nation's Capital* (1951), pp. 44 f.

3 MORAL RECONSTRUCTION

1. Donald McMillan, "The Salvation Army," *Religion in the Twentieth Century*, edited by Vergilius Ferm (1948), p. 343.

2. *Ibid.*, pp. 345, 344, 343.

3. Bishop William T. Manning at the convention of the Diocese of New York of the Protestant Episcopal Church, summer, 1941. Quoted by Ray H. Abrams, "The Churches and the Clergy in World War II," *The Annals of the American Academy of Political and Social Science* (March 1948), p. 114.

4. *Ibid.*, p. 115, quoting editorial by Clayton W. Morrison, "An Unnecessary Necessity," *Christian Century* (December 1941).

5. From an editorial in *The Living Church*, December 17, 1941. Quoted by Abrams in *Annals*, p. 114.

6. *The National Catholic Almanac* (1949), p. 411.

7. On the relation of religion to mental health see: Anton T. Boisen, *Exploration of the Inner World* (Chicago: Willett, Clark & Co., 1936); Seward Hiltner, *Religion and Health* (1943); "Religion and Mental Health," two symposia, *Review of Religion* (May 1946 and March 1949); David E. Roberts, *Psychotherapy and the Christian View of Man* (New York: Scribner's Sons, 1950).

8. See: Willard L. Sperry, *Religion and Our Racial Tensions* (Cambridge: Harvard University Press, 1945), vol. III of *Religion in the Post-War World*; Henry C. Vedder, *The Gospel of Jesus and the Problems of Democracy* (New York: Macmillan Co., 1914); Frank S. Loescher, *The Protestant Church and the Negro* (New York: Association Press, 1948). The appendices include an analysis of denominational and interdenominational pronouncements on race religions from 1908 through 1947.

9. H. F. May, *Protestant Churches and Industrial America* (1949), p. 236.

10. Woodrow Wilson, "The Ministry and the Individual," Address before the McCormick Theological Seminary at Chicago, November 9, 1909, in *The Public Papers of Woodrow Wilson*, Ray Stannard Baker and William E. Dodd, eds. (authorized ed., New York, 1925–1927), I, 186–187.

11. Woodrow Wilson, "Militant Christianity," Address at Y.M.C.A. Celebration, Pittsburgh, October 24, 1914, in *The Public Papers of Woodrow Wilson*, Ray Stannard Baker and William E. Dodd, eds.,

I, 200; cited in Henry F. May, *Protestant Churches and Industrial America* (1949), p. 230.

12. Beryl H. Levy, *Reform Judaism in America* (New York, 1933).

13. Walter Rauschenbusch, *Christianity and the Social Crisis* (1907), p. 265.

14. *Ibid.*, p. 398.

15. Walter Rauschenbusch, *Christianizing the Social Order* (1912), p. 56.

16. Harry F. Ward, "Organized Religion, the State and the Economic Order," *The Annals of the American Academy of Political and Social Science* (March 1948), p. 78. The literature on the social gospel is voluminous. A few titles in addition to those mentioned in the text should be noted here: John C. Bennett, *Christian Ethics and Social Policy* (New York: Scribner's Sons, 1946); Winston Churchill, *The Inside of the Cup* (New York: Macmillan Co., 1913); Dorothy L. Height and J. Oscar Lee, *The Christian Citizen and Civil Rights* (New York: Federal Council of Churches, 1949); James Hastings Nichols, *Democracy and the Churches* (Philadelphia: Westminster Press, 1951). The last half of this book deals with the political aspects of American churches during the twentieth century and concludes with a critical statement by a leading Protestant historian on the relation between Roman Catholicism and democracy; Reinhold Niebuhr, *Moral Man and Immoral Society* (New York: Scribner's Sons, 1932); Justin W. Nixon, *Responsible Christianity* (New York: Harper & Bros., 1950); Francis G. Peabody, *The Christian Life in the Modern World* (New York: Macmillan Co., 1914); Walter Rauschenbusch, *A Theology for the Social Gospel* (New York: Macmillan Co., 1917); Gerald B. Smith, *Social Idealism and the Changing Theology* (Chicago: University of Chicago, 1913); J. M. Yinger, *Religion in the Struggle for Power* (Durham: Duke University Press, 1946).

17. Quotations are from the testimony of the Church League's executive secretary, George Robnett, before a Special Sub-Committee of the Committee on Education and Labor, House of Representatives, 81st Congress, first Session, pp. 340, 342. Cited in Luke Ebersole, *Church Lobbying in the Nation's Capital* (1951), p. 136.

18. F. Ernest Johnson, *The Social Gospel Re-examined* (1940), pp. 126–127.

19. *Ibid.*, p. 131.

20. Willard L. Sperry, *American Religion* (1945), p. 260.

21. N. H. Knorr, "Jehovah's Witnesses of Modern Times," *Religion in the Twentieth Century*, edited by Vergilius Ferm (1948), pp. 384, 389 f., 391.

22. Herbert H. Stroup, *The Jehovah's Witnesses* (Columbia University Press, 1945), p. 132. Cf. also the vigorous language in the Watchtower Tract entitled *One World*.

23. *The Spoken Word*, III (July 3, 1937), p. 21, cited by Charles S. Braden in *These Also Believe* (1949), p. 41.

4 INTELLECTUAL RECONSTRUCTION

1. George A. Gordon, *The Witness to Immortality* (1893), p. 6.
2. Lewis F. Stearns, *Present Day Theology* (1893), p. 534.
3. Carl S. Patton, "The American Theological Scene Fifty Years in Retrospect," *Journal of Religion*, XVI (1936), 456.
4. Walter Horton, "Authority without Infallibility," chapter X of *Religious Realism* edited by Douglas C. Macintosh (1931).
5. Theodore T. Munger, "The New Theology," in *The Freedom of Faith* (1883).
6. Munger, "The New Theology," in *The Freedom of Faith*, pp. 8–11.
7. *Ibid.*, p. 30.
8. *Ibid.*, pp. 32 f.
9. Isaac M. Wise, *Cosmic God* (1876), p. 164; quoted by Beryl Levy, *Reform Judaism in America* (1933), p. 46. Though this exposition dates from 1876, its ideas and even its rhetoric continued to be heard well into the twentieth century.
10. Minot J. Savage, *Evolution and Religion from the Standpoint of One Who Believes in Both* (1886), pp. 13 f.
11. Theodore T. Munger, *Essays for the Day* (1904), pp. 7, 21.
12. George B. Foster, *The Finality of the Christian Religion* (1906), p. 290.
13. Lewis F. Stearns, *Present Day Theology* (1893), p. 534.
14. Lewis F. Stearns, *The Evidence of Christian Experience* (1890), p. 143.
15. Henry C. King, *Reconstruction in Theology* (1901), pp. 248 f.
16. Charles D. Williams, *A Valid Christianity for To-Day* (1909), pp. vii–viii.
17. It is impossible here to give an account of the intellectual range and geographical spread of liberalist preaching as distinguished from theology, but some of the leaders of the movement should be mentioned. Minot J. Savage (1841–1918), Unitarian, Boston and New York; cf. especially his famous sermon, "Religion: Its Changing Forms and Its Eternal Essence" (1905). Henry Van Dyke (1852–1933), Presbyterian, New York and Princeton; he was an eloquent defender of liberal theologians who were tried for heresy. George A. Gordon (1853–1929), Congregationalist, Old South Church, Boston. Frank Wakeley Gunsaulus (1856–1921), Congregationalist, Chicago. Newell Dwight Hillis (1858–1929), Congregationalist, Plymouth Church, Brooklyn; he was an embarrassment to liberals during World War I because of his militancy. Charles E. Jefferson (1860–1937), Congregationalist,

Broadway Tabernacle, New York; he was a leading pacifist. Charles D. Williams (1860–1923), Episcopalian, Bishop of Michigan. Edwin McNeill Poteat (1861–1937), Baptist, North Carolina and South Carolina. S. Parkes Cadman (1864–1936), Congregationalist, Brooklyn. John Herman Randall (1871–1946), Baptist, New York, later in Community Church, New York. Henry Sloane Coffin (1877–   ), Presbyterian, New York. Joseph Fort Newton (1878–1940), Universalist, New York and Philadelphia. Harry Emerson Fosdick (1878–   ), Baptist, Union Theological Seminary and Riverside Church, New York. John Haynes Holmes (1879–   ), Unitarian, New York; he became a leader in the Community Church Movement. Charles W. Gilkey (1882–   ), Baptist, Chicago. Willard L. Sperry (1882–   ), Congregationalist, Harvard Divinity School; influential in promoting fellowship with Anglicans and in calling attention to the need for better forms of public worship in free churches. Ernest Fremont Tittle (1885–1949), Methodist, Evanston, Illinois; especially influential in liberalizing Methodism and a leader in pacifism. Justin Wroe Nixon (1886–   ), Baptist, Brick Presbyterian Church, Rochester, and Colgate-Rochester Divinity School.

18. Gerald Birney Smith, *Social Idealism and the Changing Theology* (1913), pp. 18, 45–46, 123–125.

19. *Ibid.*, pp. 227–228.

20. Shailer Mathews, "Theology as a Group Belief," *Contemporary American Theology*, edited by Vergilius Ferm (New York: Round Table Press, 1933), pp. 169–171.

21. Reinhold Niebuhr, *Reflections on the End of an Era* (1934), p. 279.

22. George A. Gordon, *Ultimate Conceptions of Faith* (1903), p 248.

23. John C. Bennett, "The Social Interpretation of Christianity," *The Church Through Half a Century*, edited by Samuel M. Cavert and Henry P. Van Dusen (1936), p. 119.

24. Robert L. Calhoun, "Plato as Religious Realist," *Religious Realism*, edited by D. C. Macintosh (1931), p. 197. Among other works in realistic theology we should mention at least the following: Vergilius Ferm, editor, *Contemporary American Theology*, 2 vols. (New York: Round Table Press, 1933), autobiographical statements by religious leaders, whose statements thus put together constitute a lively and informative account of intellectual developments during the twentieth century; George Hammar, *Christian Realism in Contemporary American Theology* (Uppsala, Sweden, 1940); Charles Hartshorne, "Theological Values in Current Metaphysics," *Journal of Religion*, XXVI (1946), pp. 157–167; Walter Horton, *Realistic Theology* (New York: Harper & Bros., 1934); "Liberalism in America, A Symposium," *Journal of Religion*, XV (1935), with contributions by A. C. McGiffert,

"The Future of Liberal Christianity in America," pp. 161–175, Wilhelm Pauck, "What Is Wrong with Liberalism?", pp. 146–160, and Paul Tillich, "What Is Wrong with the 'Dialectic' Theology?", pp. 127–145; D. C. Macintosh, *Religious Realism* (New York: Macmillan, 1931), with contributions by Arthur K. Rogers, James B. Pratt, Julius S. Bixler, Alban G. Widgery, Hugh Hartshorne, Henry N. Wieman, George A. Coe, Robert L. Calhoun, Eugene W. Lyman, Walter M. Horton, Douglas C. Macintosh, H. Richard Niebuhr, William K. Wright, John E. Boodin, William P. Montague; Reinhold Niebuhr, *Nature and Destiny of Man*, 2 vols. (New York: Scribner's, 1943); H. Richard Niebuhr, *Christ and Culture* (New York: Harper's, 1951); Paul Tillich, *The Protestant Era* (Chicago: University of Chicago Press, 1948), especially chapter V, "Realism and Faith"; Henry N. Wieman, *Source of Human Good* (Chicago: University of Chicago Press, 1946).

25. Such discussion has been stimulated recently by the appearance of a new Catholic periodical, *Cross Currents*, which contains existentialist contributions among others, and whose chief aim seems to be to encourage religious thinking outside the conventional forms of Thomism.

26. David Saville Muzzey, *Ethics as a Religion* (1951), p. 134.

27. Horace M. Kallen, *Of Clericalism and Secularism in Religion* (Boston: Beacon Press, 1951). See also many of the statements in the symposium, "Religion and the Intellectuals," *Partisan Review*, 3rd series (1950).

28. Meyer Schapiro, "Religion and the Intellectuals," *Partisan Review*, 3rd series (1950), p. 126.

5 TRENDS IN PUBLIC WORSHIP AND RELIGIOUS ART

1. Harold Scott, *Theological Terms in the Light of Modern Scholarship* (reprints from *Prospector*), 1944, p. 48 f.

2. Willard L. Sperry, *Reality in Worship* (1925), p. 204.

3. John B. Thompson in a sermon at the Joseph Bond Chapel of the Divinity School of the University of Chicago, August 10, 1948, "The Perils of Professionalism." Printed in *The Divinity School News*, XV (Nov. 1, 1948), p. 10.

4. J. F. Rutherford, *Religion Reaps the Whirlwind* (1944), pp. 58 f.; cited in Charles S. Braden, *These Also Believe* (1949), p. 358.

5. Charles C. Josey, "On the Decline of Worship," *Journal of Religion*, XV (October 1935), p. 471.

6. Willard L. Sperry, "Worship in the Academic Community," *Liberal Learning and Religion* (1951), pp. 215 f.

7. Cf. S. F. Brenner, *The Way of Worship* (1944), and D. Bard

Thompson, "Reformed Liturgies," B.D. Thesis, 1949, Union Theological Seminary.

8. George E. DeMille, *The Catholic Movement in the Episcopal Church* (2nd ed., 1950), pp. 198 f.

9. Theodore Wedel, *The Coming Great Church* (1945), p. 60.

10. Cf. Paul S. Saunders, "A Historical and Critical Study of the Order for Holy Communion in Episcopal Methodism," S.T.M. Thesis, 1947, Union Theological Seminary.

11. Felix Adler, "Changes in the Conception of God," *The Religion of Duty*, edited by Leslie W. Sprague (1912), p. 28.

12. Rexford Newcomb, "Church Architecture as an Expression of Culture in the United States," unpublished paper presented to a conference on "Religion and American Culture" sponsored by the American Council of Learned Societies, 1950; quoted here by permission.

13. Frederick Keller Stamm, *If This Be Religion* (1950), p. 37.

14. George Albert Coe, *The Religion of a Mature Mind* (1902), p. 332.

15. Willard L. Sperry, *Reality in Worship* (1925), pp. 164 f.

16. William E. Hocking, *The Meaning of God in Human Experience* (1912), pp. 411 f., 414 f., 419, 420, 425.

17. James Bissett Pratt, *Can We Keep the Faith?* (1941), pp. v–vi, 37 f.

18. W. M. Urban, *Language and Reality* (1939), pp. 580, 582; cited by James Bissett Pratt, *Can We Keep the Faith?* (1941), p. 4.

19. Kirsopp Lake, *The Religion of Yesterday and Tomorrow* (1925), pp. 100–104.

20. Gerald Birney Smith, "The Nature of Science and of Religion and Their Interrelation," *Religious Education*, XXIII (1927), pp. 308–310; cited by Bernard Meland, "The Genius of Protestantism," *Journal of Religion*, XXVII (October 1947), p. 285.

21. Willard L. Sperry, *Reality in Worship* (1925), pp. 230, 263.

22. Cf. especially the book under this title by Henry N. Wieman.

23. Elton Trueblood, *The Common Ventures of Life* (1949), p. 49.

24. Richard Hocking, "Right Pessimism and Right Optimism," *Bulletin of General Theological Seminary*, New York City (June 1951), p. 20.

25. Joep Nicholas in an address on "The Problem of Decoration in Church Buildings," Twenty-first Annual Meeting of the Liturgical Arts Society; cited in *Liturgical Arts*, XIX (May 1951), p. 57.

6 VARIETIES OF RELIGIOUS EXPERIENCE SINCE WILLIAM JAMES

1. William James, *The Varieties of Religious Experience* (New York: Longmans, Green & Co., 1903), pp. 520–522.

2. *Ibid.*, p. 394.

3. *Ibid.*, p. 396 n.
4. *Ibid.*, pp. 389–390 n.
5. *Ibid.*, p. 391 n.
6. *Ibid.*, p. 91.
7. *Ibid.*, p. 80.
8. *Ibid.*, pp. 163–165.
9. *Ibid.*, p. 488 n.
10. *Ibid.*, pp. 335–338.
11. *Ibid.*, p. 348.
12. *Ibid.*, p. 354.
13. *Ibid.*, pp. 358 f.
14. *Ibid.*, pp. 462 f.
15. His popular essay entitled "The Moral Equivalent of War" was published in 1910 in *McClure's Magazine* and *The Popular Science Monthly*, and in 1911 in the volume of *Memories and Studies*.
16. William James, *The Varieties of Religious Experience*, pp. 458 f., 460 f.
17. Justin Wroe Nixon in *Responsible Christianity* (1950).
18. Gordon W. Allport, *The Individual and His Religion* (1950), pp. 15 f.
19. William James, *The Varieties of Religious Experience*, p. 398.
20. Gordon W. Allport, *The Individual and His Religion*, p. 77.
21. See chapter III, note 7.
22. William James, *Varieties of Religious Experience*, p. 486.
23. Walter Lippman, *Preface to Morals* (1929).
24. H. Richard Niebuhr, *Christ and Culture* (1951), pp. 245–249. This is from the section on "Social Existentialism."
25. Cf. Edwin E. Aubrey, "Scientia, Scientific Method, and Religion," in *Liberal Learning and Religion*, edited by Amos Wilder (1951), pp. 52 f.
26. Cf. Marcus Bach, *Faith and My Friends* (1950).
27. Charles S. Braden, *These Also Believe*, chapter III, pp. 40–41.
28. *Ibid.*, pp. 38–39.
29. John A. Widtsoe, selector and arranger, *Discourses of Brigham Young*, p. 12.
30. James E. Talmage, *Articles of Faith* (1920), p. 311.
31. See especially Wieman's *The Source of Human Good* (1946) and his earlier work, *Methods of Private Religious Living* (1929).
32. *Intention at Kirkridge* (1949), pp. 2, 6 f. (Pamphlet published at Kirkridge, Bangor, Pennsylvania.)
33. Henry Burke Robins, "The Minister Himself: Six Paradoxes," *The Colgate-Rochester Bulletin*, vol. II, no. 5 (June 1930), p. 402.

APPENDIX

The Department of Research and Education of the Federal Council of the Churches of Christ in America (now the Department of Research and Survey of the National Council of the Churches of Christ in America) published in its weekly *Information Service* for May 15, 1948, a statistical study entitled "Christianity and the Economic Order — Social-Economic Status and Outlook of Religious Groups in America." Professor F. Ernest Johnson, the Executive Director of this Department of Research and Education, has given us generous permission to reprint a substantial part of this report. The report of the study as published gives a fuller account of the methods used and of the problems of statistical interpretation. It also includes several other tables.

RELIGION AND THE
CLASS STRUCTURE

An opinion-poll study was published five years ago by Professor Hadley Cantril, based on data for 1939–40.[1] Professor Liston Pope, who was given access to the data reported in this paper, writing on "Religion and the Class Structure" in the March 1948 issue of the *Annals of the American Academy of Political and Social Science*, comments thus on Dr. Cantril's study: "His material . . . indicates that there was at that time far less difference in class affiliation between Protestants and Catholics in the nation as a whole than had been commonly supposed, though differences become more apparent when data from the South are segregated. For every upper-class Protestant in the South, there were six lower-class Protestants; in the other regions of the country, the percentage classified as upper class ranged from 14 to 18 per cent, and the percentage in the lower class ranged from 25 to 32 per cent, leaving a majority in each region in the middle class.

"In comparison, the Roman Catholic Church was composed of a smaller percentage of upper-class members (ranging from 6 to 15 per cent in the various regions) and a larger percentage of lower-class adherents (varying from 30 to 51 per cent). But the net results of Cantril's study indicate that Protestantism had a larger representation from the lower class and Catholicism had more middle-class members than popular generalizations have assumed."

Comparing these findings with those of the present study Dr. Pope remarks that, assuming the reliability of this method of studying the relation of religion to class structure, the study here

[1] "Educational and Economic Composition of Religious Groups" by Hadley Cantril. *American Journal of Sociology*, Vol. 47, No. 5 (March 1943), pp. 574–579.

reported indicates "that a profound class realignment has occurred in religious denominations during the war years or that class lines themselves have shifted significantly."

The limitations involved in this procedure are obvious. We cannot, for example, go into the question, important as it is, whether educational level or a particular social attitude which is seen to characterize a given Protestant group has any direct religious significance or is but a reflex influence of class composition. In this paper we can only present data, with a minimum of interpretation.

The present study was made for INFORMATION SERVICE by Wesley Allensmith of Princeton University at the Office of Public Opinion Research of Princeton's Department of Psychology. The material from which the report was derived and the facilities for the work it entailed were made available by that office. Grateful acknowledgment is made to Professor Hadley Cantril, director of the Office of Public Opinion Research, and his staff, who gave thoughtful advice and full cooperation; also to Professor George Horsley Smith of the Department of Psychology, then managing editor of *The Public Opinion Quarterly*, who kindly gave consideration to special problems.

THE METHOD OF STUDY

The problem of determining status was approached as follows: Ballots on file in the archives of the Office of Public Opinion Research were combed for recent ballots which had obtained religious affiliation of respondents as a "control" item of information, and the cards for which had been punched properly and were available. Four suitable ballots were found. One, dated June 1946, totaled 3,073 cases; a second, dated March 1946, totaled 3,225; a third, dated December 1945, totaled 3,037; and a fourth, dated November 1945, totaled 3,086. These are all postwar, and the findings from ballot to ballot were consistent. Combined, the four ballots furnish information based on 12,421 cases.

Before presenting the statistical data we must caution our readers against drawing unwarranted inferences from small numbers and percentages. In order to show the full distribution of the sample, we have included categories into which only a few cases fall. Obviously, a group having only 16 cases has no statistical significance. As the lower end of each table is approached the significance from a statistical point of view becomes more questionable. Moreover, as social statisticians will see at once, each item is subject to technical treatment in order to establish the exact range of significance.

SECTION I

STATUS BY RELIGIOUS GROUPING

Social-economic status will be indicated by reference to data on "class" (upper, middle and lower), education, occupation, residence (rural and urban), political preference, and union membership. The reason for including political preference is that in recent years the national administration has been assumed to represent a "liberal" social philosophy and the opposition party a relatively conservative social outlook. Obviously, political preference is a less stable index than the others employed but it is illuminating in a comparative study at a particular time.

Union membership is revealing in terms of status, since it represents largely skilled labor, and also in terms of social-economic orientation.

Upper, Middle, and Lower "Class." The economic categories "Upper," "Middle," and "Lower" represent groupings in which respondents are placed by interviewers after a careful appraisal of the respondent's dress; home and its neighborhood and furnishings; ownership of phone and automobile; occupation; use of luxury items, possession of comforts as opposed to necessities; etc. Respondents on the ballots analyzed in this study were actually classified into the categories Wealthy, Average Plus, Average, Poor, Old Age Assistance, and On Relief; customarily the first two are lumped and called Upper; Average becomes Middle; and the last three are considered Lower. That procedure was followed in this study. Hence the data concern the tendency to economic stratification and no ideological connotations of the word "class" are here involved.

A person's *relative* economic status is presumed to be a more important determiner of his thinking and behavior than his *abso-*

TABLE I

Distribution of Religious Groups by "Class"

National Sample	Cases	Per cent	Upper		Middle		Lower	
			Cases	Per cent of group	Cases	Per cent of group	Cases	Per cent of group
	12,019	100.0	1,576	13.1	3,691	30.7	6,752	56.2
1. Roman Catholic	2,390	19.9	209	8.7	589	24.7	1,592	66.6
2. Methodist	2,100	17.5	266	12.7	748	35.6	1,086	51.7
3. Baptist	1,381	11.5	110	8.0	331	24.0	940	68.0
4. Presbyterian	961	8.0	210	21.9	384	40.0	367	38.1
5. Protestant, smaller bodies	888	7.4	89	10.0	242	27.3	557	62.7
6. Lutheran	723	6.0	79	10.9	261	36.1	383	53.0
7. Episcopal	590	4.9	142	24.1	199	33.7	249	42.2
8. Jewish	537	4.5	117	21.8	172	32.0	248	46.2
9. No preference	466	3.8	62	13.3	121	26.0	283	60.7
10. Protestant, undesignated	460	3.8	57	12.4	111	24.1	292	63.5
11. Christian	370	3.1	37	10.0	131	35.4	202	54.6
12. Congregational	376	3.1	90	23.9	160	42.6	126	33.5
13. No answer or "Don't know"	319	2.7	35	11.0	94	29.5	190	59.5
14. Latter Day Saints (Mormon)	175	1.5	9	5.1	50	28.6	116	66.3
15. Christian Scientist	137	1.1	34	24.8	50	36.5	53	38.7
16. Reformed	131	1.1	25	19.1	41	31.3	65	49.6
17. Atheist; Agnostic	15	0.1	5	33.3	7	46.7	3	20.0

lute economic status. Interviewers were therefore instructed to classify respondents "in relation to their own community, and not in relation to the country as a whole."

The distribution is shown in Table I.

The most striking thing about this table is the almost exact parallel between the Roman Catholic and the Baptist constituen-

TABLE II

Religious Distribution by Educational Level

	Cases	Per cent	Part H.S. or Less Cases	Part H.S. or Less Per cent	H.S. Grad. or More Cases	H.S. Grad. or More Per cent
National Sample	12,241	100.0	6,348	51.9	5,893	48.1
1. Roman Catholic ...	2,427	19.9	1,384	57.0	1,043	43.0
2. Methodist	2,162	17.6	1,069	49.4	1,093	50.6
3. Baptist	1,414	11.5	914	64.6	500	35.4
4. Presbyterian	974	8.0	361	37.1	613	62.9
5. Protestant, smaller bodies	886	7.2	562	63.4	324	36.6
6. Lutheran	762	6.2	429	56.3	333	43.7
7. Episcopal	595	4.9	210	35.3	385	64.7
8. Jewish	537	4.4	198	36.9	339	63.1
9. No preference	475	3.9	252	53.1	223	46.9
10. Protestant, undesignated	472	3.9	256	54.2	216	45.8
11. Christian	386	3.2	205	53.1	181	46.9
12. Congregational	381	3.1	110	28.9	271	71.1
13. No answer or "Don't know"	303	2.5	190	62.7	113	37.3
14. Latter Day Saints (Mormon)	178	1.5	79	44.4	99	55.6
15. Christian Scientist ..	138	1.1	46	33.3	92	66.7
16. Reformed	136	1.1	78	57.4	58	42.6
17. Atheist; Agnostic ..	15	0.1	5	33.3	10	66.7

cies, each of which appears to have two-thirds of its membership in the lower economic stratum.

The Methodist, Presbyterian, Lutheran, Episcopal, Jewish, "Christian," Congregational, Christian Science, and Reformed groups have a larger "middle-class" representation than is indicated in the national distribution.

The Presbyterian, Episcopal, Jewish, Congregational, Christian Science, and Reformed groups exceed their "upper-class" quotas.

Taking the twelve Protestant categories together the distribution is 13.8 Upper, 32.6 Middle, and 53.6 Lower. This is not far out of line with the national distribution. To the extent that these figures may be assumed to be representative, this is a noteworthy finding.

Educational Status. Since educational level is an important factor in determining social-economic status, we present a tabulation (Table II) in two groups: those whose education stopped short of high school graduation, and those who acquired more than that.

The Methodist, Presbyterian, Episcopal, Jewish, Congregational, Mormon, and Christian Science groups, as a glance at the table will show, have a higher educational level than the population as a whole.

Combining the 12 Protestant categories we get this distribution: Part High School or Less, 50.9 per cent; High School Graduate or More, 49.1 per cent. This is a slightly higher level than is shown in the national distribution.

Occupation. Occupational distribution is clearly important in the context of our inquiry. The data are shown in Table III. The categories need some clarification. In determining occupational status, the person's occupation, if a student or a housewife, is taken as that of the person who provides his livelihood. If the respondent is retired, or is unemployed, his former occupation is recorded.

The occupational category "Business" comprises both "executive" and "small business." "Service" is a combination of domestic servants, protective agents such as policemen, firemen, and soldiers, and people who are involved in providing personal services such as barbering and hotel maintenance. "Farm" denotes a heterogeneous group, including, as it does, farm owners, large and small, and farm laborers.

The large proportion of farm constituency in several of the Protestant, as compared with Catholic and Jewish, groups is what would be expected. The Mormons are outstanding in this respect.

TABLE III

Religious Distribution by Occupation

	Cases	Per cent	Professional		Business		White Collar		Service		Skilled and Semi-skilled		Unskilled		Farm	
			Cases	Per cent of group	Cases	Per cent of group	Cases	Per cent of group	Cases	Per cent of group	Cases	Per cent of group	Cases	Per cent of group	Cases	Per cent of group
National sample	11,671	100.0	1,220	10.5	995	8.5	2,383	20.4	1,310	11.2	3,175	27.2	640	5.5	1,948	16.7
1: Roman Catholic	2,332	20.0	166	7.1	153	6.6	537	23.0	317	13.6	823	35.3	136	5.8	200	8.6
2: Methodist	2,053	17.6	222	10.8	161	7.8	401	19.6	227	11.0	472	23.0	104	5.1	466	22.7
3: Baptist	1,344	11.5	82	6.1	76	5.7	195	14.5	209	15.5	392	29.2	90	6.7	300	22.3
4: Presbyterian	923	7.9	182	19.7	103	11.2	191	20.7	73	7.9	186	20.2	31	3.3	157	17.0
5: Protestant, smaller bodies	845	7.2	76	9.0	55	6.5	129	15.3	109	12.9	235	27.8	81	9.6	160	18.9
6: Lutheran	720	6.2	44	6.1	53	7.4	128	17.8	83	11.6	194	26.9	29	4.0	189	26.2
7: Episcopal	571	4.9	98	17.1	83	14.5	144	25.2	58	10.2	133	23.3	13	2.3	42	7.4
8: Jewish	515	4.4	74	14.4	112	21.7	188	36.5	22	4.3	115	22.3	1	0.2	3	0.6
9: No preference	453	3.9	53	11.7	37	8.2	105	23.2	48	10.5	128	28.3	32	7.1	50	11.0
10: Protestant, undesignated	439	3.8	41	9.3	33	7.5	87	19.8	50	11.4	146	33.3	30	6.8	52	11.9
11: Christian	365	3.1	36	9.9	23	6.3	51	14.0	35	9.5	93	25.5	20	5.5	107	29.3
12: Congregational	362	3.1	71	19.6	48	13.3	70	19.3	21	5.8	76	21.0	5	1.4	71	19.6
13: No answer or "Don't know"	305	2.6	28	9.2	20	6.6	50	16.4	24	7.9	95	31.1	29	9.5	59	19.3
14: Latter Day Saints (Mormon)	167	1.4	15	9.0	9	5.4	25	15.0	11	6.5	26	15.6	33	19.8	48	28.7
15: Christian Scientist	134	1.2	18	13.4	13	9.7	47	35.1	12	8.9	25	18.7	2	1.5	17	12.7
16: Reformed	127	1.1	9	7.1	14	11.0	30	23.6	11	8.7	34	26.8	4	3.1	25	19.7
17: Atheist; Agnostic	16	0.1	5	31.3	2	12.5	5	31.2	0	0.0	2	12.5	0	0.0	2	12.5

On the other hand, the Episcopal Church has fewer in this category than the Catholic Church.

The smaller and "undesignated" Protestant groups and the Mormons have a high proportion of unskilled workers. Here the Catholics are but slightly above the population average, and the Jews all but invisible.

In the Skilled and Semi-skilled category the Catholic representation is outstanding, though the Undesignated Protestant group approaches the same figure, and the Baptist group is not far behind.

In the Service category only five religious groups exceed the population average, the Baptists leading, with the Catholics second.

In the White Collar category six religious groups have an excess over their quotas, with the Jews and Christian Scientists in the high positions.

The Business category presents some impressive features. Six of the religious groups exceed the general population percentage for this category, with the Jewish group far in the lead. The same is true of the Professional category, except that the Presbyterian group is at the top, with the Congregationalists so close that in a larger sample the positions might be reversed. The Catholic Church has fewer than its quota.

The twelve Protestant categories taken as a whole present the following percentage distribution: Professional, 11.1; Business, 8.3; White Collar, 18.6; Service, 11.2; Skilled and Semi-skilled, 25.0; Unskilled, 5.5; Farm, 20.3. This is close to the national distribution, though the Farm group is 3.6 per cent larger.

Residence — Rural and Urban. The conflict between rural and urban interests and the important cultural differences underlying it make the residence factor important in this study. The distribution is shown in Table IV.

It will be noted that in the three population categories — Farm, small towns (Under 2,500), and communities 2,500 to 10,000 — the Catholics are substantially under their quota and the Protestants well above theirs. In cities from 10,000 up the preponderance is reversed. The Catholics, however, are proportionately more numerous on the farm than in small towns. They are also more numerous in cities of 10,000 to 100,000 than in those 100,000 to

TABLE IV
Religious Distribution by Residence — Rural and Urban

	Cases	Per cent	Farm Cases	Farm Per cent of group	Under 2,500 Cases	Under 2,500 Per cent of group	2,500 to 10,000 Cases	2,500 to 10,000 Per cent of group	10,000 to 100,000 Cases	10,000 to 100,000 Per cent of group	100,000 to 500,000 Cases	100,000 to 500,000 Per cent of group	500,000 and over Cases	500,000 and over Per cent of group
National sample	12,421	100.0	2,037	16.4	1,106	8.9	2,532	20.4	2,583	20.8	1,680	13.5	2,483	20.0
1. Roman Catholic	2,446	19.7	207	8.5	148	6.1	339	13.9	607	24.8	451	18.4	694	28.3
2. Methodist	2,191	17.6	500	22.8	283	12.9	536	24.5	418	19.1	231	10.5	223	10.2
3. Baptist	1,437	11.6	314	21.9	151	10.5	326	22.7	278	19.3	212	14.8	156	10.8
4. Presbyterian	985	7.9	160	16.2	81	8.2	259	26.3	202	20.5	123	12.5	160	16.3
5. Protestant, smaller bodies	909	7.3	169	18.6	77	8.5	231	25.4	188	20.7	111	12.2	133	14.6
6. Lutheran	766	6.2	194	25.3	73	9.5	150	19.6	154	20.1	81	10.6	114	14.9
7. Episcopal	601	4.8	47	7.8	60	10.0	123	20.5	138	23.0	111	18.5	122	20.2
8. Jewish	545	4.4	4	0.7	0	0.0	23	4.2	49	9.0	51	9.4	418	76.7
9. No preference	480	3.9	51	10.6	32	6.7	66	13.8	98	20.4	61	12.7	172	35.8
10. Protestant, undesignated	477	3.9	54	11.3	26	5.5	99	20.8	110	23.1	73	15.3	115	24.0
11. Christian	397	3.2	110	27.7	56	14.1	106	26.7	70	17.6	45	11.3	10	2.6
12. Congregational	388	3.1	74	19.1	37	9.5	89	22.9	124	32.0	28	7.2	36	9.3
13. No answer or "Don't know"	327	2.6	59	18.1	35	10.7	58	17.7	73	22.3	34	10.4	68	20.8
14. Latter Day Saints (Mormon)	179	1.5	49	27.4	27	15.1	64	35.8	21	11.7	13	7.3	5	2.7
15. Christian Scientist	141	1.1	17	12.1	7	5.0	24	17.0	25	11.7	31	22.0	37	26.2
16. Reformed	136	1.1	26	19.1	13	9.6	39	28.7	27	19.9	20	14.7	11	8.0
17. Atheist; Agnostic	16	0.1	2	12.5	0	0.0	0	0.0	1	6.3	4	25.0	9	56.2

500,000. The Jewish group is almost invisible on the farm, and reaches 76.7 per cent of the Jewish total in the largest cities.

Interesting features of Table V are these: the Baptists exceed their quota in cities of 100,000 to 500,000; the Episcopalians exceed theirs in every category except the farm; the undesignated Protestants do likewise from the 2,500 population level upward; the Congregationalists are ahead of their quota in every category

TABLE V

Religious Distribution by Political Preference

| | | | Voted Dewey 1944 | | Voted Roosevelt 1944 | | Didn't vote 1944 | |
	Cases	Per cent	Cases	Per cent of group	Cases	Per cent of group	Cases	Per cent of group
National sample	12,371	100.0	3,941	31.8	5,240	42.4	2,476	20.0
1. Roman Catholic	2,437	19.7	491	20.2	1,312	53.8	485	19.9
2. Methodist	2,179	17.6	824	37.8	810	37.2	421	19.3
3. Baptist	1,431	11.6	344	24.0	600	42.0	398	27.8
4. Presbyterian	980	7.9	470	48.0	312	31.8	155	15.8
5. Protestant, smaller bodies	904	7.3	267	29.5	359	39.7	223	24.7
6. Lutheran	766	6.2	320	41.8	266	34.7	134	17.5
7. Episcopal	599	4.8	265	44.2	213	35.6	93	15.5
8. Jewish	545	4.4	35	6.4	406	74.5	75	13.8
9. No preference	479	3.9	115	24.0	207	43.2	115	24.0
10. Protestant, undesignated .	476	3.9	163	34.2	184	38.7	96	20.2
11. Christian	395	3.2	129	32.7	171	43.3	77	19.5
12. Congregational	387	3.1	218	56.3	100	25.8	52	13.4
13. No answer or "Don't know"	322	2.6	84	26.1	137	42.5	81	25.2
14. Latter Day Saints (Mormon)	179	1.5	71	39.7	74	41.3	27	15.1
15. Christian Scientist	140	1.1	71	50.7	43	30.7	19	13.6
16. Reformed	136	1.1	70	51.5	37	27.2	23	16.9
17. Atheist; Agnostic	16	0.1	4	25.0	9	56.3	2	12.5

but the two highest, very far ahead in cities of 10,000 to 100,000, and far under in cities over 100,000; and the Christian Scientists have an impressive concentration in the large cities.

Political Preference. Because in the United States voting behavior is so very stereotyped that about 90 per cent of the people who exercise the franchise vote Republican consistently or vote Democratic consistently in election after election, it has been found best to represent "political preference" in terms of past

TABLE VI

Religious Distribution by Union Membership

	Cases	NO		YES (Not Specified)		YES, CIO		YES, A F of L		YES, OTHER	
		Cases	%	Cases	%	Cases	%	Cases	%	Cases	%
National Sample	12,167	9,865	81.1	176	1.4	739	6.1	1,131	9.3	256	2.1
1. Roman Catholic	2,400	1,727	72.0	44	1.8	228	9.5	337	14.0	64	2.7
2. Methodist	2,157	1,846	85.6	22	1.0	83	3.8	161	7.5	45	2.1
3. Baptist	1,405	1,175	83.6	31	2.2	81	5.8	92	6.5	26	1.9
4. Presbyterian	964	843	87.4	14	1.5	33	3.4	56	5.8	18	1.9
5. Protestant, smaller bodies	889	741	83.3	6	0.7	53	6.0	71	8.0	18	2.0
6. Lutheran	754	607	80.5	13	1.7	42	5.6	83	11.0	9	1.2
7. Episcopal	589	510	86.6	3	0.5	27	4.6	36	6.1	13	2.2
8. Jewish	537	415	77.3	7	1.3	51	9.5	53	9.9	11	2.0
9. No preference	469	348	74.2	7	1.5	44	9.4	62	13.2	8	1.7
10. Protestant, undesignated	469	351	74.8	12	2.6	39	8.3	54	11.5	13	2.8
11. Christian	390	335	86.0	2	0.5	10	2.6	36	9.2	7	1.7
12. Congregational	378	334	88.4	4	1.1	11	2.9	22	5.8	7	1.8
13. No answer or "Don't know"	302	242	80.1	3	1.1	17	5.6	30	9.9	10	3.3
14. Latter Day Saints (Mormon)	178	148	83.1	6	3.4	6	3.4	16	9.0	2	1.1
15. Christian Scientist	137	114	83.2	0	0.0	5	3.6	16	11.7	2	1.5
16. Reformed	133	118	88.7	2	1.5	6	4.5	5	3.8	2	1.5
17. Atheist; Agnostic	16	11	68.8	0	0.0	3	18.8	1	6.2	1	6.2

voting behavior. This is done in Table V. The categories are self-explanatory, except that the percentages across the page do not total 100. This is because those who were too young to vote in 1944, those who voted for another candidate (negligible in a sample of this size), and the "Don't remembers" are omitted.

The table speaks for itself. The twelve Protestant categories combined classify as follows: Dewey, 37.5 per cent; Roosevelt, 37.0; Didn't vote, 20.0. This, it will be noted by reference to the table, diverges sharply from the national distribution and much more sharply from the Catholic, except that the non-voting proportions are almost identical.

Union Membership. Great interest has been expressed in Protestant circles in the relation of the Protestant constituency to the labor movement. The basic factor is union membership. The questions to which the Union Membership categories indicate responses are as follows: "Are you (or is your husband) a member of a labor union?" If the answer was Yes, respondent was asked "Which one?" The first category, "Yes (not specified)," is used for those persons who said they were union members but did not reveal the union to which they belonged. "No" means that the person is not a union member. "Other" means the person is a member of a union other than a C.I.O. or A.F. of L. organization. The results are shown in Table VI.

It will be seen that all the religious groups are more largely represented in A.F. of L. than in C.I.O. unions, except the Reformed, and there the number is so small as not to be significant. The Catholic and Jewish groups are at the top in C.I.O. membership, and the Catholics exceed all the others in A.F. of L. membership — assuming, in both instances, that if the Not Specified category could be broken down it would not change the picture.

The twelve Protestant categories combined show the following percentage distribution: No, 84.4; Yes, 1.4; C.I.O., 4.7; A.F.L., 7.6; Other, 1.9. Obviously, union affiliation is substantially lower among Protestants than in the population as a whole, while among Catholics it is very much higher.

Economic Security Versus Individualism. The respondents were asked:

TABLE VII

Religious Distribution of Opinions on Guaranteed Economic Security

	Cases	Per cent	Individual "On his Own"		Guaranteed Economic Security		No Opinion		Qualified	
			Cases	Per cent of group	Cases	Per cent of group	Cases	Per cent of group	Cases	Per cent of group
National sample	5,932	100.0	3,107	52.4	2,617	44.1	196	3.3	12	0.2
1. Roman Catholic	1,084	18.3	430	39.7	625	57.7	27	2.5	2	0.1
2. Methodist	1,141	19.2	657	57.6	432	37.9	48	4.2	4	0.3
3. Baptist	964	16.3	432	44.8	493	51.1	38	4.0	1	0.1
4. Presbyterian	418	7.0	273	65.3	130	31.1	15	3.6	0	0.0
5. Protestant, smaller bodies	445	7.5	230	51.7	195	43.8	20	4.5	0	0.0
6. Lutheran	362	6.1	202	55.8	146	40.3	13	3.6	1	0.3
7. Episcopal	248	4.2	161	64.9	82	33.1	4	1.6	1	0.4
8. Jewish	197	3.3	85	43.2	110	55.8	2	1.0	0	0.0
9. No preference	182	3.0	78	42.9	98	53.8	6	3.3	0	0.0
10. Protestant, undesignated	245	4.1	134	54.7	105	42.9	6	2.4	0	0.0
11. Christian	185	3.1	125	67.6	55	29.7	5	2.7	0	0.0
12. Congregational	155	2.6	111	71.6	40	25.8	2	1.3	2	1.3
13. No answer or "Don't know"	128	2.2	70	54.7	50	39.1	8	6.2	0	0.0
14. Latter Day Saints (Mormon)	98	1.8	66	67.4	31	31.6	1	1.0	0	0.0
15. Christian Scientist	39	0.7	30	76.9	9	23.1	0	0.0	0	0.0
16. Reformed	25	0.4	14	56.0	11	44.0	0	0.0	0	0.0
17. Atheist; Agnostic	8	0.1	4	50.0	3	37.5	1	12.5	0	0.0
18. Other Non-Christian	8	0.1	5	62.5	2	25.0	0	0.0	1	12.5

Which of these statements do you most agree with? (Respondent was handed card with statements printed on it.)

1. The most important job for the government is to make
   certain that there are good opportunities for each person to
   get ahead on his own.

2. The most important job for the government is to guarantee
   every person a decent and steady job and standard of living.

The results are shown in Table VII. This table contains a surprise
or two. The Congregational group tops all the others except the
Christian Scientists in the Individual "On His Own" column.
The large Protestant bodies, except the Baptist, are all above their
quotas in this column, despite the fact that some of them have
carried on vigorous programs in support of the cause of economic
security for the masses. The Jewish group presents a contrast in
this respect.

It should be noted that the use of the word "guaranteed" in
the second column may have weighted the responses, since to
many minds it connotes a degree of control over the economy
that is feared.

INDEX